D1383213

HAUNTED

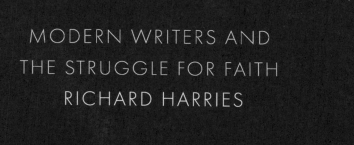

MODERN WRITERS AND
THE STRUGGLE FOR FAITH
RICHARD HARRIES

BY CHRIST

spck

Originally published in hardback in Great Britain in 2018

Society for Promoting Christian Knowledge
36 Causton Street
London SW1P 4ST
www.spck.org.uk

Paperback edition published 2019

British Library Cataloguing-in-Publication Data
A catalogue record for this book is available from the British Library

ISBN 978-0-281-07934-6
eBook ISBN 978-0-281-07935-3

1 3 5 7 9 10 8 6 4 2

Typeset by Fakenham Prepress Solutions, Fakenham, Norfolk NR21 8NN
Printed in Great Britain by Jellyfish Print Solutions

eBook by Fakenham Prepress Solutions, Fakenham, Norfolk NR21 8NN

Produced on paper from sustainable forests

Richard Harries is a Fellow of the Royal Society of Literature and an Honorary Fellow of the Academy of Medical Sciences. After 19 years as Bishop of Oxford, he was made a life peer (Lord Harries of Pentregarth) and he remains active in the House of Lords on human rights issues. He is the author of 28 books and his voice is well known to many through his regular contributions to BBC Radio 4's *Today* programme.

For Piers and Poh Sim Plowright,
with deep gratitude for their friendship
and in memory of Stewart Sutherland,
friend and former colleague who would,
I believe, have enjoyed this book

Contents

Introduction

Like many people, especially of my generation, books have always meant a great deal to me, and from a young age I could quickly get absorbed in what I was reading. The great magic about stories, novels and plays is that they take us into worlds different from the one with which we are familiar, but in such a way that our day-by-day world is illuminated. We enter into the lives of imaginary characters and find that the way we see and experience our usual life is subtly altered. Books affect us deeply and can change us in significant ways.

All books are written from a particular point of view. If the author tries to press that point of view too hard in a plot or characters the work will almost certainly fail as literature. The characters will seem one-dimensional and the plot artificial. The result will be propaganda. Some writing written from a Christian point of view makes this mistake. In any good writing, imaginative sympathy is at work and this enables the writer to enter into the minds of people with fundamentally opposed views or characters. This is indeed one of the marks that distinguishes literature from propaganda. It is one of the reasons why we find it so difficult to place someone like Shakespeare as being a believer or non-believer, a Catholic or a Protestant.

David Mamet's play *Oleanna* is about a university teacher who is accused by one of his female students of sexual harassment. I saw the play with my daughter. When we came out we realized my daughter had experienced the play through the student who believed she had been harassed; I had done so through the lecturer who believed the girl had manipulated him. When the play was shown in the USA, it sharply divided audiences in a similar way. That was a mark of its status as a genuine work of art.

One aspect of this capacity to be multifaceted means that reading a good novel, or seeing a great play, we are conscious again of the complexity of human life, the ambiguity of so much behaviour, the mixture of qualities and motives in all of us. All this is a very healthy and important antidote to moralism. There is a human tendency to divide the world up into goodies and baddies. This can be so if religion is brought into it, though moralism certainly isn't the preserve of religion. One of the great themes of Jesus in the Gospels is the way he tries to shake us out of all easy moralizing. We are directed to look at ourselves, at the great plank in our own eye before we call attention to the speck of dust in our neighbour's eye. So literature, in bringing home to us the complexity, ambiguity and thoroughly mixed nature of human behaviour spells out and reinforces one of the central elements in the New Testament.

However, and this point cannot be emphasized too strongly, we should not assume from this that good writing is without a point of view. It cannot be, because nothing in this life is value free or neutral. It comes out of the life experience of a particular writer who will have a distinctive feel for life whether or not he or she is able to articulate it. According to Philip Pullman, this is not only inevitable but necessary and good. Literature should, in his words, 'pack a moral punch'.[1] It is entirely natural and inevitable that some works should be written from an atheist point of view, and others from a Christian one. If the perspective is Christian this does not make it more or less worthy of consideration as literature. This needs stressing in our society today. At the same time, because good literature depends on empathetic imaginative power, a novel written from a Christian standpoint will at the same time feel the full force of atheism, and one from an atheist perspective will know something of the enchantment of the Christian faith.

It is possible to view literature as just one form of enjoyment or form of escape like football or chess. But in our own time its importance is far more crucial than that. In our own time especially, we look to novels, plays and poetry to understand better what it is to be alive, what it means to be human, living with other human beings. No less we look there to see what it means in practice, as a 'form of life' to use a phrase of Wittgenstein, to believe or not believe life has a meaning beyond any which we may choose to attribute to it.

These words apply to all forms of literature, but they also highlight the importance of literature that is written by Christian writers or on Christian themes. At a time when so much religious language has become either unbelievable or alien to many people it is in works of literature that we can begin to discover what the Christian faith is about and what is at stake. If, for example we want to explore the challenge to Christian belief posed by human suffering and the attempt to understand suffering theologically in the texture of life, we will read Albert Camus or Fyodor Dostoevsky. If we want to explore what faithfulness and martyrdom might involve in a brutal world, we might read Shusaku Endo's *Silence*.

Poetry, like novels, can express what it is to have faith but with two additional features that are particularly relevant today. So much of the language we use is recycled cliché, the linguistic sludge of a lazy culture. This is especially true of religious language, which has for many become tired, stale and lifeless. Poetry, in the words of T. S. Eliot can 'purify the dialect of the tribe'.[2] It can bring freshness and sharpness because poetry is as much a matter of sound as it is of image; it can hint, like music, of what is beyond words, the ultimately elusive mystery of the divine. As the Australian poet Les Murray put it, God is 'in the world as poetry is in the poem'.[3]

He goes on to say this is 'A law against closure'[4] To believe is to be open to a horizon beyond our present horizon, to refuse to clamp down in a settled outlook with stereotyped phrases, whether of a religious or anti-religious kind. Poetry keeps that horizon open.

This book considers 20 novelists or poets, in 15 chapters, who have meant a great deal to me over the years. They are not the only ones, but they are the ones for whom the pull of religion has been fundamental and in whose work we can best see what it is to believe or to protest against belief.

Historians write about the early modern period, meaning the late fifteenth century to the end of the eighteenth century. Modernism in music, literature and the visual arts is usually dated from around 1913. For the purposes of this book 'modern' means beginning with Fyodor Dostoevsky (1821–81). This is in part because he wrote the first psychological novels, exploring the complexity of human motives and the way unconscious forces so often drive our behaviour. But more significantly because the radical religious questions over which he agonized and which are reflected in his novels set the agenda for the possibility of religious faith in our time. Dostoevsky entered deeply into the atheism of his era, calling himself 'A child of his age' and, as has been written:

> This was an age in which a radical intelligentsia which had finally rejected religion was energetically propounding various forms of scientific atheism; an age like our own, in which Christianity, at least among the educated classes, was liable to go by default . . . in reading Dostoevskii we are in the presence of a genius wrestling with the problems of rethinking Christianity in the modern age.[5]

Many of the great Victorian agnostics who turned away from the Christian faith did not do so because of the rise of biblical criticism or the theory of evolution, but because what Christians called on them to believe struck them as morally inferior to their own ethical beliefs and standards.[6] The same is true today. Too often it is not the alleged unreasonableness of faith that turns people away but something about it that has put them off, which strikes them as morally or aesthetically unattractive.[7] In the person of Ivan

Karamazov, Dostoevsky gives voice more strongly than any other figure in literature to the moral objections to God. This is so powerfully stated that some modern figures, such as Camus, thought that this was indeed Dostoevsky's own view.

Emily Dickinson (1830–86) is another figure who powerfully represents our present conflicted attitude to religion. Again, there are two reasons why she belongs to our world almost more than her own. First, because of the innovative style of her poetry. She eschews conventional punctuation and uses a great number of dashes. She has her own system of capitalization, and a minimalist approach to language in which a single word comes to focus a whole sentence or verse. She broke with what was regarded as proper for poetry at the time and anticipated the radical developments of modernism. Second, and more pertinently, although deeply versed in the Calvinist milieu of the society in which she lived, she distanced herself from it and developed an intense inner life of her own. She might be described in terms of the modern cliché as being spiritual, not religious, except that this does not capture the passion and intensity of that spiritual life.

Gerard Manley Hopkins (1844–89) in one way did belong very much to his own time, in the sense that he was part of the talented group of people influenced by the Oxford Movement who first became Anglo-Catholics and then followed John Henry Newman in becoming Roman Catholics. Yet Hopkins became a major influence in the twentieth century and this continues into our own time. His poetry was not published until 1918, when it came as a shock to most. As the poet Elizabeth Jennings wrote, 'Hopkins has had a strong influence on every twentieth century poet from Auden downwards.'[8] For many today he is their favourite religious poet.

This poetry, with its extraordinary intensity, reflects both Hopkins's love of the beauty of the world, and the agony of his personal suffering, especially his later verses, 'the sonnets of desolation', which are the subject of the chapter on him in this book.

Edward Thomas (1878–1917) was not an obviously religious person, and, in contrast to war poets like Wilfred Owen, he did not reflect Christian themes or images in his work. But there is in his poetry a haunting quality which has been recognized by every reader, and which I term 'the elusive call'. In the chapter on Thomas, this quality is identified in the poetry and questions raised about it. Did it represent a haunting disappearance of faith, a faith which had been lost by so many of the *fin de siècle* generation? And if so was this loss permanent? It is because the poetry of Thomas raises this crucial question that I have included him in this book.

T. S. Eliot (1888–1965) wrote *The Waste Land* in 1922, arguably the most famous poem of the twentieth century, in which he seemed to speak for a disillusioned generation, shattered by the First World War and at sea without any traditional religious or moral landmarks in sight. Then in 1927 he was baptized as a Christian and shortly after announced to a startled world that he now identified as an Anglo-Catholic. In the chapter on Eliot, the reasons for that conversion are discussed together with a consideration of the difference it made to his life. Eliot's conversion was received with disbelief and scorn by most of the intelligentsia of the day. But Eliot's faith did not mean that he stopped being highly aware of all the arguments against his position. On the contrary, he said that a mature faith was inseparable from doubt.

Stevie Smith (1902–71) shared T. S. Eliot's love of Anglo-Catholicism and churchgoing was for her, at least in her younger days, a very happy experience. However, even then she began to have doubts, not about the veracity of the faith but about the morality of some of its teaching. In particular, she reacted against the idea of hell, and so strong did this aversion become over the years that she rejected Christianity while at the same time being strongly attracted to it. For her it was a mixture of sweetness and cruelty, and although she continued to be enchanted by it, she felt it had to be rejected on moral grounds.

Samuel Beckett (1906–89) will be thought of as an unusual person to include in this book. The reason for his inclusion is contained in a remark of the distinguished scholar, poet and dramatist Francis Warner. As a young man Dr Warner produced Beckett plays and as a result got to know Samuel Beckett. He once told me that Beckett was 'A Christ haunted man' and 'secular mystic'. It is that remark about Beckett which is contained in my title. Beckett's plays and novels seem to purvey a very bleak view of the world, though often one with much humour in it. But that sombre view, which might be thought of as a world without God, is one which has to be taken into account by believer and non-believer alike. Serious believers will feel the force of it as an alternative to their faith and similarly serious non-believers will feel the pull of a religious perspective on their lack of faith. Beckett was able to depict such a moving view of the human predicament without God just because he knew so deeply what it was that was absent.

W. H. Auden (1907–73) wrote that he left the Christian faith in which he had been brought up as a teenager in order to pursue the pleasures of the flesh. He rediscovered this faith again and made it his own in about 1940, after which it was a quiet, subterranean influence in all his writing.

He believed we had a choice between shouting in anger and despair at life or blessing what there is for being. He chose the latter course and made praise and gratitude for the ordinary things of life one of the main themes of his poetry. At the same time he thought that a serious faith necessarily involved a certain reticence.

William Golding (1911–93) in his novels reflects what is for many a classically Christian understanding of existence. First there is a strong sense of human sin, which can wreak havoc in any social group, and second there is the possibility of some kind of redemption, even if it is only in an increased self-awareness. Golding's own views are much more conflicted and more difficult to identify. In his acceptance speech for the Nobel Prize in Literature, he described himself as a universal pessimist and a cosmic optimist but it is not clear on what that cosmic optimism rested.

R. S. Thomas (1913–2000), more than any other poet in the second half of the twentieth century, reflected the feelings of those who experience God only as an absence. As well as writing vivid, moving poetry about the hard life of the hill farmers to whom he ministered as a priest in the Church in Wales, he explored all the inner contradictions he felt about the faith he preached.

Edwin Muir (1887–1959) and George Mackay Brown (1921–96) both came from the Orkneys and both knew much personal anguish in their lives. Edwin Muir, brought up in a Scottish Calvinist environment, was devastated by an experience in which he saw human beings simply as animals destined for the slaughter house. Gradually over the years he gained a sense of the human soul and in the end he was much drawn to the religion of the Incarnation. George Mackay Brown converted from indifference to Roman Catholicism.

Elizabeth Jennings (1926–2001) was a devout Roman Catholic who knew much personal travail in her life because of periods of mental instability. Her poetry reflects a personal journey in which she faces her inner fears and works through them, like Auden, to a sense of gratitude for existence and an ability to see grace in the people around her.

Graham Greene (1904–91), Flannery O'Connor (1925–64), Shusaku Endo (1923–96) and Evelyn Waugh (1903–66) were all novelists for whom Roman Catholicism was fundamental to some of their best-known novels. Another theme which unites them is a sense of grace in human failure. They deal with different kinds of failure but in all of them some element of grace can be seen glimmering, however dimly.

C. S. Lewis (1898–1963) and Philip Pullman (1946–) are both brilliant storytellers for young people. C. S. Lewis was converted from atheism to become the twentieth century's best-known Christian apologist. Some might cavil at Pullman's appearance in a book with the title *Haunted by Christ*. However, he is deeply antagonistic to the Christian view of the world as put forward by Lewis, and he is haunted in the sense that this has got far enough under his skin to cause him to write a major trilogy in fierce opposition to it. He has also written a book more directly attacking the Christian faith *The Good Man Jesus and the Scoundrel Christ*.

In the His Dark Materials trilogy, Pullman sets out an alternative vision to that of Lewis, in which people have to learn to stand on their own feet, take responsibility for lives and learn to love the earth in all its finitude. The strengths and weaknesses of both fictional worlds are identified.

Marilynne Robinson (1943–) has written a trilogy, *Gilead*, *Home* and *Lila* in which a Christian view of life is explored through three generations of Protestant pastors in Iowa. Theirs is a hard life and there is for them no easy resolution of the dilemmas of faith. What comes through is a sense of astonishment and wonder at existence with hope for the future.

Each chapter is headed by a short introductory paragraph setting out a few basic facts about the author discussed. The only exception is 'Grace in Failure' in which the basic facts about the four novelists appear in the main text on each author. The order of the chapters is based on the date of birth of the author discussed. The only exception to this is that, for reasons of the structure of the book, Marilynne Robinson is considered last in the book even though she was born three years before Philip Pullman, the subject of the previous chapter.

There is a tendency today for some people to subsume religious views under psychology, sociology or some other discipline but for all the writers considered here faith, or its lack, was fundamental to their being and outlook on life. The poet Gerard Manley Hopkins once wrote a rather pained letter to his friend Robert Bridges to say, in relation to his Catholic faith:

> It is a long time since such things had any significance for you. But what is strange and unpleasant is that you sometimes speak as if they had in reality none for me and you were only waiting for a certain disgust till I too should be disgusted with myself enough to throw off the mask . . . Yet I can hardly think you do not think I am in earnest. And let me say, to take no higher ground, that without earnestness there is nothing sound or beautiful in character and that a cynical vein much indulged coarsens everything in us.[9]

In short, these authors have to be taken on their own terms, with the reader taking seriously what they took seriously. There is a short story by Leo Tolstoy, 'What Men Live By', which was used as a chapter title in Alexander Solzhenitsyn's novel *Cancer Ward*. These chapters explore this crucially important question in relation to some of our finest writers. For me this has been a fascinating and enjoyable exercise. At school my house-master used to come round at night to check what people were up to and almost invariably he found me in bed reading a novel. Always he would remark, 'My boy, why aren't you working?' This book is, for me, the happy fruit of not working.

Richard Harries
King's College
London

1

Fyodor Dostoevsky
Through a furnace of doubt

Introduction

Dostoevsky (1821–81) left school at the age of 16 to train and practise as a military engineer. Beginning to write, he found success with his first novel *Poor Folk* (1846) and became part of a literary circle that was critical of tsarist Russia. The members were arrested and sentenced to death, a sentence which was commuted at the very last moment. Dostoevsky then spent four years in prison in Siberia and four more in military service in exile. On his release, he worked as a journalist and writer and travelled in Europe. Although he had success with his first novel, critical opinion turned against him and, afflicted with a severe addiction to gambling, he often had to beg for money. He was a passionately religious man, an Orthodox Christian, but beset with radical doubts. He wrote that his faith had come 'through a furnace of doubt'[1] and was focused on a deep attraction to the person of Jesus Christ. His best-known novels are *Notes from Underground* (1864), *Crime and Punishment* (1866), *The Idiot* (1869), *The Devils* (1872) and *The Brothers Karamazov* (1880).

Regarded as one of the greatest novelists of all time and a precursor of so much in the modern world, he has been translated into more than 170 languages.

A traumatic life

Dostoevsky was brought up in a devout home. His father came from a line of priests and had also trained in a seminary. Dostoevsky's mother was no less serious in her religion and he remembers happy times of prayer in their home on a Saturday night before the Liturgy on the Sunday. The memory of this happy, devout time was important to him later in life. His mother died when Dostoevsky was 16 and about that time he and his brother were sent to train as military engineers. He had been brought up with a rich literature of story and fable and had started reading widely when young, but he had no particular interest in, or talent for, military engineering. He had even less for a military way of life, being totally unsoldierly both in his gait and attitudes. He disliked the coarse lifestyle and quickly revealed the seriousness of his Christian faith in his compassion for the poor. When his regiment were stationed among people in a wretched state of poverty, he was shocked and organized a collection for them. Not surprisingly he was regarded as eccentric.

Poor Folk reflected his social concern and was the first novel in Russia to bring the poor to people's attention in fictional form. It was a critical triumph and Dostoevsky left the army to work as a freelance writer. Unfortunately some influential critics, like Ivan Turgenev, then turned against him and he felt totally humiliated. At the same time his early success led to his being invited into a literary circle with reforming ideas critical of tsarist Russia. He was arrested and imprisoned in a fortress for six months before being brought to trial.

We think our own times are ones of unprecedented change, social unrest and violence but the period in which Dostoevsky lived was arguably one of even greater disturbance. The French Revolution and its bloody aftermath were well within living memory. Even in relatively stable and partly democratic Britain there were bloody riots, when the Bishop of Bristol's palace for example was stormed and his effigy burnt. Terrorist acts by anarchic groups were a regular feature in a number of countries, while new ideas from Germany were threatening many established positions, including belief in God. In Russia itself, the underlying tension was greater than anywhere else because of autocratic tsarist rule, serfdom and the consequent agitation against the cruelty of such a system. All this is reflected in Dostoevsky's novels, and it was against this background that he was arrested, tried and sentenced to death.

Dostoevsky gives a detailed description of how he and his fellow accused were led out to the parade ground, blindfolded and received last words from the chaplain. Then at the last moment a message arrived from the tsar commuting the sentence to four years' imprisonment in Siberia followed by six years' military service there in internal exile, of which he served four years. The conditions in prison were indescribable owing to the cold, dirt, hunger and brutality. Dostoevsky also suffered from health problems, haemorrhoids and emphysema among them. There was a particular humiliation for Dostoevsky because though he felt deep compassion for his fellow inmates and saw himself as a voice for them, they turned on him on the grounds that he came from a noble family, even though he was sharing their lives to the full. Yet, despite all, his spirit did not fail, and he could write that his faith had been strengthened and his compassion deepened. He was allowed a New Testament and he studied it carefully. A few prisoners, including one particularly brutal one who attached himself to Dostoevsky, did begin to see something remarkable about him. A turning point was when, filled with utter loathing for his fellow prisoners, he remembered an incident in his childhood when he was frightened and a peasant had made the sign of the cross on him, comforting him greatly. This gave him a deep feeling of empathy for the Russian people and the Christ who kept them going through so much suffering.[2] It transformed his attitude to his fellow prisoners. At the same time it brought about a renewal of his Christian faith.

When Dostoevsky was eventually released, he tried to earn his living as a writer again, but often suffered from dire poverty, having to beg for money to survive. This was accentuated by his serious gambling addiction. However, when his first wife, after a very unhappy marriage, died, he married a stenographer, Anna, and with her travelled for four years in Europe, where eventually she managed to cure him of his addiction. We have a vivid account of this time from Anna herself, who says that the hardship they endured, especially the terrible grief when their first child died, brought them closer together and strengthened their faith. As someone who knew him at the time wrote, 'His manner changed, acquired greater mildness, sometimes verging on utter gentleness. Even his features bore traces of that frame of mind, and a tender smile would appear on his lips.'[3]

It was during this time abroad that he wrote *Crime and Punishment*. Not only were the times in which Dostoevsky lived extreme; his own personality was one which sought to test everything to the limit. In his last great novel, *The Brothers Karamazov*, Ivan seems to suggest that if God does not exist then everything is permitted.[4] It was this line which was taken up by Jean-Paul Sartre at the end of the Second World War as the founding principle of existentialism. It is an idea which is embodied in Raskolnikov, the central character of *Crime and Punishment*.

Crime and Punishment

Raskolnikov, a much troubled former student, murders Alyona, an elderly, corrupt pawnbroker. He offers a number of reasons for this but above all because he wants to see himself as a Napoleon figure, above good and evil, an idea which recurs at the end of the novel. This is a notion which

Raskolnikov at once wants to embrace and also sees as a temptation of the devil. Lizaveta, Alyona's half-sister stumbles upon the scene of the murder and Raskolnikov murders her as well. Raskolnikov is tormented by what he has done and acts in odd ways as though wanting to reveal the truth; in particular he is drawn to the policeman Porfiry, who suspects the truth. Raskolnikov is befriended by Sonia, a pure woman who has been forced into prostitution in order to save her family from starvation. The turning point in the book is when she reads to Raskolnikov the story of the raising of Lazarus from the dead. She is at once reluctant and fearful of reading it to him and yet desperate to do so, as though something great is at stake. At the same time Raskolnikov senses the intensity of her passion that he should hear the Gospel and hear it now. This emotional scene of the reading carries on for three pages.

> Here she stopped again, anticipating with a feeling of shame that her voice would once more tremble and snap.
>
> 'Jesus saith unto her, Thy brother shall rise again. Martha saith unto him, I know that he shall rise again in the resurrection of the last day. Jesus saith unto her '*I am the resurrection and the life*, he that believeth in me, though he were dead, yet shall he live: and whosoever liveth and believeth in me, though he were dead, yet shall he live: and whosoever liveth and believeth in me, shall never die. Believe thou this? She saith unto him' (and as though drawing her breath painfully, Sonia read slowly and distinctly to the end, as though she were herself making a public confession of her faith). 'Yea, Lord, I believe that thou art the Christ, the Son of God, which should come into the world.'[5]

Sonia continues with the same intensity to the end, longing for Raskolnikov's eyes to be opened like the eyes of those who saw Lazarus rise. At the end they sit in silence for five minutes; then Raskolnikov makes an abrupt dismissive remark.

Raskolnikov is locked up in his mental prison. He does not really hear or see others as people at all, thinking of Alyona, for example as 'a louse'. So this moment when he needs to hear a word, a word that will break into his self-enclosed torment and deliver him from it is key. He does not hear the liberating word at this point, but he does later through Sonia. For it is to Sonia that he eventually confesses his crime. She urges that he confess this in public and give himself up for arrest and punishment. Noticing that he is not wearing a cross, she gives him hers. Orthodox Christians not only wear a cross; they will sometimes exchange crosses as a sign of friendship. She gives him her cross as a sign that she will share his suffering, which she already in fact feels deeply. 'We'll suffer together, so let us bear our cross together.'[6] Raskolnikov does not accept the cross at this point; but says he will later, which he does.

This wearing of the cross is significant not only as a sign of shared suffering but of shared responsibility for the murder. For the cross which Sonia gives him is likely to be the one which the murdered Lizaveta had given her. Before this, Lizaveta had shared crosses with Alyona; so the cross was really Alyona's, given to Raskolnikov via Sonia.[7] So Sonia acts as a link of shared responsibility.

The idea of accepting responsibility for other people in their totality, which as we shall see is a major theme in Dostoevsky's novels, emerges here for the first time. But this sharing is not just a matter of helping them to bear the burden of what they have done; it is to help them take responsibility for it. Raskolnikov has refused to accept that he is an ordinary criminal; instead he plays around in his mind with fantasies of himself as a superman. He has to accept that he is like everyone else, a flawed human being, no different from Alyona, the corrupt pawnbroker he murdered. Through Sonia he does eventually gain this self-knowledge. She continues to keep close to Raskolnikov, making it clear she will follow him to Siberia. Eventually he does ask for her cross and prays, which leads him to announce in the street that he is a murderer and then give himself up.[8]

Sonia is clearly a Christ figure, or at least what Rowan Williams calls a *platzhalter* for Christ, 'someone who takes the place that belongs to the saviour within the human transaction of the narrative'.[9] It is a mistake however to think of Sonia as a passive person whose role is simply to suffer. She is strong in many ways, not least in the way she stands up to Raskolnikov and will not move away from him until he has accepted full responsibility for his life and actions as an ordinary sinful human being. When he first confesses to her, he asks what he should do:

'What are you to do?' she cried, suddenly jumping to her feet and her eyes, which till then had been full of tears, flashed fire. 'Get up'. She seized him by the shoulder, and he raised himself, looking at her almost in astonishment. 'Go at once, this very minute, and stand at the crossroads, bow down, first kiss the earth which you have defiled, and then bow down to all the four corners of the world – and say to all men aloud, I am a murderer! Then God will send you life again. Will you go? Will you?' She asked him trembling all over, seizing his hands and clasping them tightly in hers and looking at him with burning eyes.[10]

This is what he eventually did, when he had finally accepted her cross and prayed, even though people in the street took him for a crazy drunkard.[11]

In the theology of the Orthodox Church, the resurrection of Christ plays a much more central role than it does in the Western Churches, both Catholic and Protestant. In the West, the emphasis has been on the fall of humanity and the centrality of the cross in bringing about our reconciliation to God. Of course the resurrection is as crucial in the West as in the East, but the liturgy, prayers and preaching of the churches do not give that impression. For the Orthodox, while the fall has a place, it is more of a stumble, the effects are not so drastic, and the purpose of the Incarnation is to raise us into the life of Christ that we may share in the very life of God himself through a process of *theosis.* The resurrection of Christ is central to this deification. Furthermore Christ's resurrection is not seen in isolation from that of the faithful. Whereas in the West Christ is shown rising from the tomb in a very physical way, in Orthodoxy the main icon of the resurrection is symbolic, showing Christ plunging his cross into hell, overcoming evil and death, and pulling Adam, Eve and others free. It is a resurrection of humanity in Christ. This emphasis on the resurrection permeates the liturgy of the Orthodox Church and is not just confined to Easter. Furthermore, the Sunday before Lent is designated 'Lazarus Sunday', with the story of the raising of Lazarus being the Gospel reading of the day, making the point that even Lent has to be seen through the faith of Easter.

The reading of the Lazarus story to Raskolnikov and the wearing of the cross bear fruit as the novel proceeds. Raskolnikov is sent to prison in Siberia and, as mentioned, Sonia follows him there. At first he ignores her. But then he finds a New Testament under his pillow, the very one from which Sonia had read to him, which did in fact originally belong to Lizaveta. One thought flashes through his mind about Sonia, 'Is it possible that her convictions can be mine, too, now? Her feelings, her yearning, at least . . .'. The book ends with the suggestion that there is another story to be written, 'the story of the gradual rebirth of a man, the story of his gradual regeneration, of his gradual passing from one world to another, of his acquaintance with a new and hitherto unknown reality'.[12] That story is not yet written: it is to come, so there is a deliberate openness at the end in which it is made clear that Raskolnikov will have to pay a great price as he emerges out of his self-created hell. But it is a resurrection that is pointed to. The divine words addressed to Lazarus – 'Come forth' – have been heard and Raskolnikov will in due course stumble out of the death of his mental tomb.

The Idiot

At one point in *Crime and Punishment* Raskolnikov refers to Lizaveta and Sonia as 'holy fools, both of them'. This image of the holy fool comes into prominence in *The Idiot*. In the New Testament, St Paul refers to himself and Christians as 'fools for Christ's sake', meaning people who seem and act foolishly in the eyes of the world but who are driven by a higher purpose, Christ himself (1 Cor. 4.10). A tradition of 'holy fools' grew up, particularly in Eastern Christianity, and it was especially strong in tsarist Russia.[13] These holy fools acted strangely, appearing simple, but were often attributed with special spiritual insight and prophetic powers. Numbered among the saints in the Russian Orthodox Church are 35 holy fools. Early in *The Idiot* Rogozhin asks Prince Myshkin whether he is fond of the ladies. He replies that he has been ill since childhood and has no knowledge of them, to which Rogozhin responds, 'then you are a regular holy fool, prince, and such as you, God loves'.[14]

Dostoevsky wrote this novel during the four years that he travelled in Europe to escape his debtors in Russia. He and Anna, his new wife, moved from city to city, always penurious, living on borrowed money. The main cause of the poverty was Dostoevsky's addiction to gambling. As soon as they had begged and borrowed money he gambled it away. In addition, he had repeated attacks of epilepsy and suffered from emphysema. In this desperate situation, he realized that their only salvation was for him to write a new major novel, which would come out in serial form. The intention of this novel was clear: to depict a life that was perfect and beautiful.[15] Bringing this about however gave him great difficulty. He wrote and discarded eight drafts. Furthermore, ideas stated in his notebooks tended to change in the creative process of writing.

Prince Myshkin, from a noble Russian family, arrives in Russia having lived until then in a Swiss sanatorium. There he had felt most at home with children, with whom he spent most of his time. His physical appearance is that of Christ as depicted in an Orthodox icon.[16] Arriving in a noble house he immediately starts talking to a servant as though to an equal, and throughout the novel he is shown as humble and self-effacing. He has an innate goodness which leads him to be open and trusting of others, even when they are untrustworthy or disdainful of him. This is so even when he has insight into their character.[17] He gives people total attention, taking them seriously even when they are not serious themselves.[18] He wants to see good in them and this disarms them, so they warm to him.[19] He is always willing to suffer himself rather than say or do anything harsh to other people. This includes asking for their forgiveness.[20] Although people recognize that he is suffering, he says, 'I'm unworthy of my suffering.'[21] Indeed acceptance of humiliation and suffering is fundamental to his approach.[22] All this is very much in line with the Russian Orthodox concept of holiness, which of course has its roots in the teaching and example of Jesus in the Gospels.[23] The other ideal that surfaces from time to time, is that of Don Quixote, the gentle chivalrous knight. Myshkin is accused of trying to be such a figure.[24]

While people are drawn to Myshkin and he breaks down barriers so they feel they can open their hearts to him, his simplicity can also annoy them. They can get angry with him,[25] and as the plot unfolds it is clear that good hearted as he is, he is the cause of much confusion and pain, and in the end is partly responsible for a tragedy. The main plot revolves around Myshkin's love for a rich man's discarded mistress, Natasya Filippovna, in whose beautiful face he sees much suffering. At the same time he is loved by Aglaya, a general's daughter, who outwardly laughs at and is rude to him. One of the issues on the mind of all of them is whether Myshkin really loves Natasya or is willing to marry her only out of pity.[26] Another question is whether he loves Aglaya, or perhaps in his innocence and idealism is incapable of loving any human being in all his or her particularity.[27] He becomes aware that his extreme trust of others can be followed by an equally extreme suspiciousness, but there is no attempt to grow towards a realistic appraisal of actual people.[28] At one point he longs to escape and not be drawn into the real world with all its flaws,[29] and in the end he has a breakdown and returns to the sanatorium.

The main problem, according to Rowan Williams, is that Myshkin, having spent all his earlier life in the sanatorium has neither history nor memory. He has not been through a process of forming a mature self through actual choices. He has no hinterland.[30] This means he suddenly appears on the scene, and people react to his presence, and events happen around him, but he himself remains arrested as a person. He does not really grow through making difficult, adult choices. To this lack of history and memory needs to be added the point that he seems to lack any overall purpose in his life. In contrast to the historical Jesus, who emerged with a definite mission to teach and enact the kingdom of God in human affairs, who was driven by a mission to deeply disturb the way of the world, Myshkin seems to drift. He gets caught up in events rather than attempting to shape them in any way.[31] So it is that in his willingness to suffer and his capacity for pity people rightly sense, as well as the attractiveness of this, something lacking. Does he really relate to them as the person they are and is he truly affected by them. Early in the novel Aglaya accuses Myshkin of being a quietist, unaffected by events however terrible, and still able to be happy: 'to live like that is easy', she says.[32] Later she gets furious with him for his humility: 'Why are you so twisted up inside? Why have you no pride?'[33] Natasya writes to him to say, 'You are innocent and in your innocence lies all your perfection.' But innocence is an untried, untested goodness.[34] In their different ways, both women find Myshkin wanting and to both he causes great pain. So in the end we have to conclude that though Dostoevsky has indeed depicted some beautiful, Christlike qualities in Myshkin, he has for these reasons failed to convey a fully Christlike figure. His genius as a novelist has meant that as the plot unfolds, the figure he originally had in mind fails in the world of real people and actual events.

The theme of exchange of crosses in *Crime and Punishment* has already been noted. It is also present in *The Idiot*. Myshkin has a rival for the love of Natasya, Rogozhin, who eventually both marries and murders her.[35] The initiative for this sign of brotherhood is Rogozhin's but Myshkin goes along with it and accepts its implications, implications which will be drawn out more fully in considering *The Brothers Karamazov*.

The Brothers Karamazov

The Brothers Karamazov was the last novel Dostoevsky wrote, published not long before his death at a time when he was hugely revered and popular in Russia. It brings together many of his themes, three of which will be considered here. First is the concept of freedom as stated in the famous Grand Inquisitor scene. Christ returns to earth and confronts the Inquisitor but he, far from being sorry for the actions of the church accuses Christ of treating human beings as free, when in fact they find freedom a great burden which they want someone else to take away from them:

> We corrected your deed and based it on *miracle, mystery* and *authority*. And mankind rejoiced that they were once more led like sheep, and that at last such a terrible gift, which had brought them so much suffering, had been taken from their hearts.

The Inquisitor goes on to argue that in doing this the church loved humanity more than Christ and that it does not want his love. All the while Alyosha listens to this story, which has been told by his brother Ivan, in great agitation: 'But . . . that's absurd!' he cried, blushing. 'Your poem praises Jesus, it does not revile him . . . as you meant it to. And who will believe you about freedom?'

Ivan then finishes the story:

> When the inquisitor fell silent, he waited some time for his prisoner to reply. His silence weighed on him . . . The old man would have liked him to have said something, even something bitter, terrible. But suddenly he approaches the old man in silence and gently kisses him on his bloodless, ninety-year old lips. That is the whole answer![36]

This passage cannot just be seen as an attack on institutional Christianity, even though Dostoevsky's attitude to Roman Catholicism was notably intemperate, a hostility which goes very deep in Russian culture. For though in his very early manhood he was not always very observant in his practice, his Orthodox identity became fundamental to his person and his faith. Rather, it reflects his deep attachment to the Christ who respects our freedom, even when worldly considerations weigh heavily against him. This is made clear in the support D. H. Lawrence gave to the point of view of the Inquisitor. Lawrence wrote that in the story

> I hear the final and unanswerable criticism of Christ. And it is a deadly, devastating summing up, unanswerable because borne out by long experience of humanity. It is reality versus illusion, and the illusion was Jesus', while time itself retorts with the reality.[37]

It is in response to that understanding of the truth that we are to understand the words of Dostoevsky 'If someone were to prove to me that Christ was outside the truth, and it was really the case that the truth lay outside Christ, then I should choose to stay with Christ rather than with the truth.'[38]

He is not thinking of intellectual truth here, as though he would follow what he knew was false in order to be with Christ; rather it is the 'realist's' view of how the world works and the alleged necessity of going along with this. This is 'the truth' the Christ of the story rejects. And this is what we see incarnated in the Christ-bearers in his novels, Sonia, Myshkin and Father Zossima – their willingness to forgo any verbal, emotional or spiritual coercion.

In the letter of 1854 from which these words of Dostoevsky come, written shortly after his release from prison but when he was still living in internal exile, he describes himself as a 'child of unbelief and doubt' and says he expects to remain so until his death. At the same time he acknowledges his great thirst for faith and the suffering this has caused him. In his notebooks, later he wrote:

Even in Europe, there is not, nor ever was, such power of atheistic expression. It is not as a child that I believe in Christ and profess his teaching; my hosanna has burst through a purging flame of doubts.[39]

It is above all in *The Brothers Karamazov* that this faith and this scepticism come head to head, and it is important to note that both are given a strong voice. Stewart Sutherland, who has written well on Dostoevsky, used to give lectures at King's College, London, under the title 'Will the Real Mr Dostoevsky Stand Up?' This brings out one of the most fundamental features of the novels, especially *The Brothers Karamazov* – the multiple voices and perspectives, the polyphonic nature of the work.[40] Dostoevsky is able to do this so brilliantly because of his capacity to enter fully into such perspectives and give them a voice, and he is able to do this with such emotional power because they are all part of him. The voice of Ivan was part of him right up to the end. Are they given an equal place or does one prevail? If, as I would argue, it is the faith of people like Alyosha Karamazov and Alyosha's mentor Father Zossima which is finally persuasive in the novel, there is an openness at the end which still leaves the matter unresolved. There is no final resolution, and in terms of the novel there cannot be because, if there is such a final reconciliation and harmony, it lies beyond our sight in the future. Only then will we be able to see clearly for the first time a face of wisdom, power and love behind the universe; the face of the One who was justified in creating it in the first place.

Dostoevsky was not interested in abstract philosophical arguments about whether or not God exists. For him religion was primarily a matter of deep feeling expressed in acts of gratitude and love.[41] What did concern him was whether God was justified in creating a universe of such pain and universal suffering. Again, it was not theoretical issues of theodicy that concerned him but whether life should be lived with gratitude or in revolt. Even as a child Dostoevsky had been interested in Job's challenge to God, a book he read again later, and the issue comes to a head in a famous dialogue between Ivan and Alyosha. It is a moral challenge. Ivan tells some horrifying stories of children being hunted to death and says:

If the sufferings of children go to make up the sum of sufferings which is necessary for the purchase of truth, then I say beforehand that the entire truth is not worth such a price . . . we cannot afford to pay so much for admission. It is not God I don't accept, Alyosha, I merely most respectfully return him the ticket.[42]

Ivan was not prepared to live life under those conditions. When all that can be said has been said, here is the heart of the challenge. God was not justified in creating a world if an inevitable result was to produce situations when children die in agony from disease or human cruelty. Ivan then goes on to argue that even if we believe in a life after death, a heaven in which everything is reconciled, this still does not justify a world in which children are treated so cruelly:

> I do not want a mother to embrace the torturer who had her child torn to pieces by his dogs! She has no right to forgive him! If she likes she can forgive him for herself, she can forgive the torturer for the immeasurable suffering he has inflicted on her as a mother; but she has no right to forgive him for the sufferings of her tortured child. She has no right to forgive the torturer for that, even if her child were to forgive him! If that is so, if they have no right to forgive him, what becomes of the harmony? Is there in the whole world a being who could or would have the right to forgive? I don't want harmony. I don't want it out of the love I bear mankind. I want to remain with my suffering unavenged and my indignation unappeased, even if I were wrong.[43]

This is not the place to deal with the substance of this argument, which I have addressed elsewhere.[44] The point to note is simply that if Ivan is wrong, he can only be shown to be wrong in the future, in that final state which he rejects, and that state has still to come about. It lies in the realm of events, not thoughts, even if the event is as remote to our understanding as the coming of Christ in glory. The future lies open. Christians may hope that it will be a reality, will put their trust in the God who inspires such hope, and will seek to root their lives in the love which comes from such a God. But of its nature this cannot be a certainty for anyone who takes the reality of human choice seriously. This matter of human choice, of how we are to live in a world of crime, violence, passion and inner torment provides the substance of the novel. The three brothers, Dmitri (known as Mitya), Ivan and Alyosha are sons of a brutal, drunken father, who has been murdered. The plot revolves around the question of who committed the crime.

The first focus of the Christian position is on Father Zossima, a monk and *staretz*, an elder of the monastery, of deep holiness and penetrating spiritual insight, to whom others turn for wisdom and advice. He exhibits many of the most attractive features of Orthodox holiness: love of the earth, love of animals, above all the teaching that we are to forgive one another and accept our own guilt and responsibility for others. Zossima, who is greatly revered, but also the subject of jealousy, dies. His spiritual son is Alyosha, a novice monk, but surprisingly Zossima tells Alyosha that he must leave the monastery and live out his vocation in the world. This he does, and, as we have seen in the clash with Ivan, is called to be a Christ-bearer in the brutal world of the Karamazov family and its associates, with all its violence and wild passions. The novel ends, however, in a surprising way. In a subplot, a young boy, Ilyusha, has been killed. Alyosha gathers all the boy's friends and tells them to remember Ilyusha and their love for him and to continue to love one another. In short, the question of whether there can be any final resolution still lies in the future, in a new generation impelled by the mutual forgiveness taught by Zossima.

For most people it is Alyosha who is the significant Christian figure of the novel. However, Rowan Williams points out that early in the novel Zossima bowed to Mitya, despite the fact that Mitya lived a reprobate life. The significance of this is that Mitya is wrongfully accused and sentenced for the murder of his father, but is willing to accept the suffering. Ivan wanted to murder his father, but had not in fact done so. It is as though Mitya accepts responsibility for the crime by suffering for the whole dysfunctional family. In the end, Alyosha persuades him to escape going to prison, not to escape suffering but to live with a different kind of suffering.

There is no conclusive answer to Ivan's rejection of a final reconciliation and harmony, and whether, if there were such, it would justify the anguish brought about by God's creating the world in the first place. All is open. But the novel suggests that we are called to go on not only offering forgiveness to others but being responsible for them and asking forgiveness from them. The theme comes not only from the exchange of crosses which occurs in *Crime and Punishment* and *The Idiot* but from some words of Father Zossima's elder brother Markel, as remembered and recounted by Alyosha. Markel says, 'Truly each of us is guilty before everyone and for everyone, only people do not know it, and if they knew it the world would at once become paradise.'[45] This theme of responsibility which is so crucial to the novels does not mean taking responsibility away from others in a way that means they do not have to take responsibility for themselves. On the contrary, it is so to enter into others' burdens that they are released to take responsibility for themselves. Dostoevsky, through his imaginative sympathy, gives voice to perspectives not his own, and this is closely linked to the call to take responsibility for them. As Rowan Williams puts it:

> I become responsible when I can indeed 'answer' for what is not myself, when I can voice the needs and hopes of someone without collapsing them into my own. And to become responsible 'for all' must then mean that I set no limits in advance to those for whom I am obliged to speak: this is why taking responsibility is assimilated in Dostoevsky to the acknowledging of the dignity of every other.[46]

In the dialogue between Alyosha and Ivan on whether God was justified in creating a world of such suffering, especially the suffering of children, a picture is painted of the victim rising up to re-embrace the torturer, of all being reconciled. This seems at once both a moral possibility and a moral impossibility. It is a moral impossibility because the refusal of victims to forgive can have a moral dimension. There is a proper moral protest about forgiveness being talked of too easily. At the same time there are some wonderful examples of Christian victims offering forgiveness and of such reconciliation happening. What we can say is that if a final reconciliation and harmony were to come about it could only be on the basis of a universal sense of solidarity, of each being responsible to everyone for everyone.

In later life, Dostoevsky became a strong Slavophile, with its unfortunate nationalistic overtones, but this is not reflected in the novels. In the novels, it is the image of Christ which is set against the power of atheism. This was not just Christ as a beautiful example, but as the incarnate word:

> It is not Christ's moral teaching, nor Christ's doctrine, that will save the world but faith that the word has become flesh . . . only in this faith can we achieve divinisation, that ecstasy that binds us most closely to him and has the power of preventing us from straying from the true path.[47]

Dostoevsky entered deeply into the atheism of his time, which found a passionate voice in his novels because it was so much a part of him. In the censored chapter of *The Devils*, Bishop Tikhon declares that a complete atheist stands on the next to top rung of the ladder of perfect faith.[48] At the same time this pull of atheism made his thirst for faith even stronger and drove him to that word made flesh:

> I am a child of my age, a child of unbelief and doubt up to this very moment and (I am certain of it) to the grave. What terrible torments this thirst to believe has taught me and continues to cost me, burning more strongly in my soul the more contrary arguments there are. Nevertheless, God sometimes sends me moments of complete tranquillity. In such moments, I love and find myself loved by others and in such moments I have nurtured in myself a symbol of truth, in which everything is clear and holy for me. The symbol is very simple: it is the belief that there is nothing finer, profounder, more attractive, more reasonable, more courageous and more perfect than Christ.[49]

2

Emily Dickinson
A smouldering volcano

Introduction

Emily Dickinson (1830–86) was born into a prominent, but not wealthy, family. Her grandfather had founded Amherst College and her father, a lawyer, was for a time a representative for Massachusetts in Congress. She lived in Amherst, about 100 miles West of Boston, all her life, for most of it in the house built by her grandfather. Only 11 of her poems were published in her lifetime, and these anonymously. When she died, some 1,800 were found by her sister Lavinia, but disputes about their publication and alterations of some of her most original and distinguishing features meant that the first scholarly text did not appear until 1955. Ever since first publication, however, she was recognized as a remarkable voice and is now widely regarded as the USA's greatest poet.[1] Some 1,000 of her letters also survive, about one-tenth of those she wrote.[2] The 2016 film *A Quiet Passion*, directed by Terence Davies, brought the mystery of her life to a new audience but left that mystery unsolved.[3]

A withdrawn life

The first word that comes to mind when people think of Emily Dickinson is 'recluse'. After her father's death, she lived the last 12 years of her life entirely within the bounds of her house and garden, seeing only a few chosen intimates. Sometimes she refused actually to see them but spoke to them behind a door or via a note and little gifts. She dressed in a simple white dress. Even before this, from her early thirties, she went out only rarely. There has been much speculation about this behaviour, with explanations such as agoraphobia or a disappointed love affair. The general effect has been to think of her, in old-fashioned terminology, as 'batty' or fey or both, but this is entirely to miss the point of what was central to her life and what it is that makes her so distinctive. The reason she is of such lasting interest, not least for those concerned with questions of religious faith, is bound up with understanding the nature of her withdrawal from society as such, and why she sat light to some of the social norms of her own time.

Dickinson's father was a strong believer in women's education and she went first to Amherst Academy and then to Mount Holyoke Seminary for women. Amherst at that time was experiencing a series of religious revivals and the principal of Mount Holyoke, Miss Lyon, was a strong woman who wanted her pupils to share her own ardent evangelical faith. The story is told that before Christmas one year she asked those in her class who would be willing to fast and pray over Christmas to stand up. The 13-year-old Emily remained sitting. Miss Lyon then asked those who wished to be Christian to remain sitting. Emily stood up. This independence of spirit was fundamental to her character. She was her own person at every point in her life. She liked to describe herself variously as gypsy, rogue, infidel and pagan. Perhaps there was an element of sheer contrariness about some of her attitudes, about which we are not in a position to judge, but it is this desire to be true to her own deepest convictions and not to be pressured by other people's expectations that is the bedrock of her life. She writes about her soul that it was 'Sovereign of itself'.[4]

Amherst witnessed a series of revivals when Dickinson was a girl and young woman. She herself experienced a conversion, which meant much to her at the time, but then she turned away from the faith. A modern biographer, Alfred Habegger, put it well:

> This brief period of perfect joy, peace and communion with God had divided results. It established an absolute scale by which to measure all later experience, in that way confirming the child's exalted expectations. But it also made her wary of all solicitations to surrender and of her own quick responsiveness.[5]

She was never indifferent to the Christian faith, far from it, but in response to repeated calls to convert she wrote, 'I could not find my "yes".'[6] Such calls did not touch the deepest level of her being.

Dickinson had a period of illness as a child and either because of this or the religious pressure at the seminary her parents withdrew her from Mount Holyoke. Thereafter she lived at home but continued to read widely. Her letters as a child and young woman reveal her to be witty and sharp. They show her to be mischievous, playful and jaunty. She could be ironic and paradoxical. All these features she carried into later life and her poetry. She had a very close relationship with her elder brother, Austin, and they enjoyed joking and laughing together about the goings on around them, not least at what happened in church. She had a number of suitors and proposals of marriage but turned them down. She was a keen, indeed expert, horticulturalist with a very large garden and it was for this that she was best known locally, together with her prowess at baking. She made a few short visits to other cities and a more extended one to Cambridge for medical treatment when she feared she was going blind. Otherwise she remained at home looking after the household, later in life caring for her bed-ridden mother.

Until 1855 Dickinson had not strayed far from Amherst. That spring, accompanied by her mother and sister, she took one of her longest and farthest trips away from home. First, they spent three weeks in Washington. Then they went to Philadelphia for two weeks to visit family. In Philadelphia, she met Charles Wadsworth, a famous minister of the Arch Street Presbyterian Church, with whom she forged a strong friendship which lasted until his death in 1882. Despite seeing him only twice after 1855, she variously referred to him as 'my Philadelphia', 'my Clergyman', 'my dearest earthly friend' and 'my Shepherd from 'Little Girl'hood'.

In the late 1850s, the Dickinsons befriended Samuel Bowles, the owner and editor-in-chief of the *Springfield Republican*, and his wife, Mary. They visited the Dickinsons regularly for years to come. During this time Emily sent him over three dozen letters and nearly 50 poems. Their friendship brought out some of her most intense writing and Bowles published a few of her poems in his journal. It was from 1858 to 1861 that Dickinson is believed to have written a trio of letters that have been called 'The Master Letters'. These three letters, drafted to an unknown man simply referred to as 'Master', continue to be the subject of speculation. My own view is that they were probably written with Charles Wadsworth in mind but were never sent. A number of poems suggest that divine love cannot compare with the thrill of human love, and no wonder God is a jealous God.[7] It seems that at this time she went through an acute personal crisis. But out of it, in the early 1860s, came her most productive period. It was also her time of greatest pain.[8] In April 1862, Thomas Wentworth Higginson, a literary critic, radical abolitionist and ex-minister, wrote a lead piece for the *Atlantic Monthly*. Dickinson sent him some of her poems and a letter which asked, 'Are you too deeply occupied to say if my Verse is alive?'[9] It was not until he came to Amherst in 1870 that they met. Later he referred to her in the most detailed account of her that we have. He felt that he never was 'with any one who drained my nerve power so much. Without touching her, she drew from me. I am glad not to live near her.'[10] The correspondence with Higginson was crucial for her, and later she wrote to say that he saved her life.[11]

Outwardly a quiet, uneventful life. Inwardly, however, she was a smouldering volcano, as Higginson sensed. I believe that the main reason she later kept apart from the usual social intercourse was because of the intensity of that inner life. You cannot read her poems without sensing the fierce emotion with which they are charged, whether they are written in response to some aspect of nature, or come from wrestling with a private thought. The same is true of the letters. They are warm, passionate, frank to the point of exposing her vulnerability, with many an arresting phrase of the sort that we associate with the poetry. Her letters were very important to her.[12] She was capable of a range of very close relationships, such as those with her sister-in-law, Susan, her cousins and also with older men. When she could not see them, she maintained a relationship with them through letters. It was the usual superficial social visiting she seems to have eschewed. At the heart of this intensity was the sense of being alive, the sheer wonder and astonishment of existing as herself. Several of her poems suggest that this world is so wonderful that heaven cannot compare. Existence in itself was enough without further function.[13]

She thought that life itself was so amazing, nothing else could surpass it. So when Higginson pays her a much longed for but surprise visit she writes, 'The incredible never surprises us because it is the incredible.'[14] Life itself was incredible for her. Again, 'I find ecstasy in living – the mere sense of living is joy enough.'[15]

This inner life was so rich and intense it made most social intercourse pale into insignificance. 'To live is so startling, it leaves but little room for other occupations though friends are if possible an event more fair.'[16] Except for her family and chosen intimates, with whom she had warm and close relationships, ordinary social intercourse could come only as an unwelcome interruption to this heightened awareness. She wrote that if the soul had a divine guest at home it obliterated the need to go abroad.[17]

One poem that begins with the speaker in a chamber conscious of a 'shapeless friend' ends by suggesting that instinct esteems this friend to be 'Immortality'.[18] But this raises a crucial question, and is an appropriate point to offer a warning. The question is 'To whom are these poems addressed?' They are very personal. The word 'I' recurs many, many more times than any other. The question is most pressing in those poems which could either be addressed to God or to a human lover. Dickinson clearly fell in love at least twice, and there is also the exceptionally close relationship she had with her brother's wife, Susan, the recipient of so many of her letters.

The people who love God, are expecting to go to meeting don't *you* go Susie, not to *their* meeting, but come with me this morning to the church within our hearts, where the bells are always ringing, and the preacher whose name is love – shall intercede there for us.[19]

Some poems can be read as to a beloved person. But equally they can be read as to some ultimate reality. The warning is one which Dickinson herself gives, when she first sends a few of her poems for consideration. She explicitly says that the subject of a poem is not to be identified with the poet herself. 'When I state myself, as the Representative of the Verse – it does not mean – me – but a supposed person.'[20] This needs to be heeded, for she had such a rich and vivid imagination that she could identify with a range of perspectives on the world and adopt many a persona. On the other hand, she would not have been able to write these poems unless they came out of her; in other words there is something of herself in them, however much she might want to distance herself in theory from such an identification. So, with that warning in mind, to whom are the poems addressed? Some of course are to particular people, with their needs in mind, especially at times of bereavement. Others may indeed be to a human lover. Some are to Christ or the Christian God. At least one is to beauty. But the most mysterious and hard to grasp are not to any of these. I believe they are ruminations with her deepest self, her soul's soul. These poems are really in the form of an inner dialogue, as though her conscious self is addressing the self she is in the process of becoming. In what seems to be the record of a powerful mystical experience, she writes of a might detecting her and setting her 'kernel in'.[21] This does not rule out a belief in God or Christ but it means these other addressees will come into view in and through this dialogue of self with self. In a poem reflecting on consciousness, she suggests that the relationship of 'itself unto itself' is beyond anything we can discover. While another version of the same poem talks of being attended by 'a single hound', this is not the hound of heaven of Francis Thompson but 'its own identity'.[22]

In another poem, she writes about exploring herself and finding the 'Undiscovered Continent'.[23] In a letter, she writes about God's building a heart within her which outgrew her.[24] All in all, as Higginson reported her saying, 'There is always one thing to be grateful for – that one is oneself and not somebody else.'[25]

This inner dialogue, linked as it is with the fierce desire to be true to her deepest convictions, is also integrally united with her sense of herself as a poet. Some early poems, mostly valentines, survive, but her emergence as a poet begins after her initial correspondence with Higginson mentioned above. He wrote back encouragingly but advised against immediate publication. She never pressed for publication and despite others urging her to do so, especially Helen Hunt Jackson, a well-known writer at the time, who did so in the strongest terms, she refused.[26] At the same time she was highly aware of fame. It is a natural desire of any writer to have his or her work recognized and appreciated. Dickinson was no exception and the word 'fame' occurs a number of times in her poems. However, she clearly made a decision not to seek earthly fame, but fame of another kind, not just as a poet but as a person. She writes about renunciation and the pain this involves in two poems.[27] She also wrote that to publish is to auction the mind and this could be justified only on the grounds of poverty.[28]

She cared very deeply about her poetry. She made fair copies of some 300 of her poems and stitched them into fascicles in order to preserve them. They were essential to her very being; yet even more important to her was her being itself and its integrity:

> Fame of Myself, to justify,
> All other plaudits be
> Superfluous – An Incense
> Beyond Necessity –
>
> Fame of Myself to lack – Although
> My Name be else Supreme –
> This were an Honor honorless –
> A futile Diadem –[29]

Although so far as I know she does not use the word in explicitly Christian terms she had an overwhelming sense of 'vocation', a strong sense of purpose and direction to her life. This was to write her poetry, but this itself was part of the wider purpose of her life as a whole, which included bringing comfort to others, especially the bereaved, through what she wrote. She wrote that every life had a goal, and converged to some centre. That goal may not be gained in one life but eternity enabled the endeavour to continue.[30] In another poem, she uses the Calvinist idea of election, but with a twist, to think of herself electing herself, her own unique soul.[31]

It should be clear from all this that any idea of Emily Dickinson as some shy, fragile, fey soul is a total travesty. She was charged with an extraordinary strength; indeed she would need to be in order to follow the path she did, so different from what would have been expected of a woman in her position. In one poem, she likens her life to 'a loaded gun'.[32] In another, she looks down into the depths of herself and sees there 'an assassin'.[33] It is a startling image, but it was perhaps only the fact that she had a killer instinct, a ruthlessness that enabled her to make the renunciation that she writes about: the renunciation of a conventional life, the renunciation of people's expectations of her, and the renunciation of publication that might have led to human fame in her lifetime. The most telling image, however, one that occurs a number of times, is of her life as a smouldering volcano. She uses this in one of her so-called Master letters.[34] Outwardly calm, but with the capacity for a major eruption only just contained. It is the central image in six of her poems. In one of them, what is hidden but about to explode is her loneliness. In another, it is her secret of immortality. In another, the stillness hides within an 'appalling Ordnance' of pain and anguish:

> If the stillness is Volcanic
> In the human face
> When upon a pain Titanic
> Features keep their place –
>
> If at length the smouldering anguish
> Will not overcome –
> And the palpitating vineyard
> In the dust be thrown?[35]

Ambivalence to the Christian faith

How does what has been written so far relate to traditional Christian belief? Special care is needed at this point because Emily Dickinson's poems reflect so many different moods that it is all too easy to create a Dickinson in one's own image as hostile to the church, a believer who distanced herself from the institution or an agnostic. One thing is certain. Her education, early churchgoing and the culture in which she lived made her very familiar with traditional Christian images and beliefs. For nearly all her childhood she sat at the feet of a very good preacher, whose powerful use of language influenced her. At the same time she was capable of great hilarity and derision at what went on in church.[36] Although herself having an overwhelming consciousness of immortality, she could be sharp if people seemed too assured about it in the face of death: 'Dying is a wild night and a new road.'[37]

Dickinson uses the word 'Jesus' 20 times in her poems and letters, Christ ten times and Jesus Christ once. These came naturally to her. But sometimes she uses them to distance herself from them, sometimes in a jokey, light-hearted manner and sometimes in a challenging way. For example she can refer to 'our old neighbour God', which is not hostile but is hardly the sentiment of a passionate believer in the God who was preached to her. Sometimes she admits to just not knowing, or to being at sea without any guidance as to where she is going. She raises the familiar questions about unanswered prayer, about God being indifferent to us and being like adamant or flint. They reflect all her boldness and independence of spirit she showed as a child. Sometimes they are at once serious and light hearted.[38] She delights in paradox.

The references to Christ and Christian themes are never straightforward. She can make a bold claim and then give it her own twist, or she can begin opaquely and slip in a Christian sentiment. She thinks of Christ in a way similar to the epistle to the Hebrews, as the 'tender pioneer' whose 'sure foot proceeding' we can follow. But in an earlier verse she makes it clear that what she follows is the example of Christ's trusting no one, only himself, which she suggests endorses her own similar approach.[39]

She calls paradise 'the uncertain certainty', but says we infer its existence from 'Its Bisecting/Messenger', this being Christ who holds together earth and heaven, God and humanity.[40]

Some poems clearly indicate an identification with a gospel attitude. This is particularly true of the penitent thief crucified beside Jesus.[41] Particularly arresting is this poem with its chivalric imagery:

Recollect the Face of me
When in thy Felicity
Due in Paradise today
Guest of mine assuredly –

Other Courtesies have been –
Other Courtesy may be –
We commend ourselves to thee
Paragon of Chivalry.[42]

She is clearly moved by Philippians 2.1–10 in its depiction of divine humility. For she writes that Christ 'stooped until he touched the grave'.[43] The theme of judgement also appears in more than one poem.

She can express an exemplary Christian sense of unworthiness for the divine indwelling, 'I – the undivine abode', together with a Calvinist understanding of election, 'his elect content', and a Catholic feel for church and sacrament, but it is her soul which is the church.[44] Again, there is a sense of unworthiness, together with a rather intimate, slightly humorous touch in a poem in which she asks the saviour to carry her 'imperial heart'.[45]

Crucifixion is a theme in some of her poems, but the image does not just refer to Christ's death. Crucifixion happens multiple times in multiple lives.[46] She knows that she herself will suffer and deems to call herself 'Queen of Calvary' and 'Empress of Calvary'.[47] She identifies with Christ's cry of dereliction even though faith still 'bleats' to understand.[48] She gets some comfort from the fact that Christ has undergone crucifixion but with a characteristic Dickinson surprise writes:

> Jesus! thy Crucifix
> Enable thee to guess
> The smaller size –
>
> Jesus! Thy *second* face
> Mind thee – in Paradise
> Of Ours![49]

The use of three exclamation marks in four lines vividly evokes the boldness with which she is calling on Christ. The theme is an orthodox one, that Christ's suffering enables him to enter into ours, but the tone is not one that would be used by the average worshipper and the second verse has a deliberate cheekiness about it.[50]

Death is a theme in so many of her poems; nevertheless it is the conviction of immortality that is the strongest note. She writes that she stands alive to witness to 'the certainty of immortality'.[51] This includes both an intense sense of living now and what is all encompassing at death. She writes in connection with a baby who has died young, '"Seven weeks" is a long life – if it is all lived –'.[52] She claims not to have been able to tell the time until she was 15.

In trying to understand Emily Dickinson's religious perspective, it is crucial to bear in mind that what she does not say is as important as what she does say. The poetry is highly distilled and compressed with every extraneous word cut away. The result is that each word she does use is heavily freighted. This is brought home by her innovative punctuation, in particular by her frequent use of the dash, which gives a moment's pause, a sliver of silence for a word to linger, the mind to ponder and the spirit to be aware of what may be unsaid, because words cannot convey it. More specifically there are a number of poems which indicate the limits of language and the importance of silence.[53] In one poem about growth in nature and humans, she writes that each must achieve itself through 'the solitary prowess' of 'a silent life'.[54] This is in part because the deepest truths can only be hinted at, not conveyed fully. They point to a silence beyond which nothing can be said. Even more is this the case in what are claimed to be revealed truths. As she puts it in one well-known poem, we are to tell all the truth but we are to 'tell it slant'.[55] Dickinson had a deep sense of gratitude but she wrote that 'mute appreciation, deeper than we reach – all our Lord demands'.[56] She loved the silence of the night.[57]

It was the failure of so many Christians to recognize this which I think was one of the reasons that led Dickinson to distance herself from churchgoing. For in church there is a great deal of confident talk about God and his ways, particularly in Dickinson's time about conversion and predestination. Dickinson found this doubly distasteful. First because of that confidence, which she thought was unwarranted, and second because of the too easy, familiar way such language was thrown about. She knew in herself that the divine mystery was such as to reduce her to silence, or at least to tiptoe around it in her poems.

The same view emerges in her attitude to human beings. One poem says that she fears someone of 'frugal speech', someone who is silent. She goes on to say she can cope with those who harangue or babble, but of someone who carefully weighs words she is wary: 'I fear that He is Grand –'.[58]

In relation to the divine, she puts it succinctly:

> Embarrassment of one another
> And God
> Is Revelation's limit,
> Aloud is nothing that is chief,
> But still
> Divinity dwells under seal.[59]

This is a poem of faith, for there is a divinity, but also of the limitation of words in talking about that awareness. She makes the same point in a letter to Higginson.[60] In one poem, she says that she has found the words to every thought she ever had, except 'One', that ultimate mystery with whom she engaged in a lifelong struggle.[61] In another, she writes of silence being 'the perfectest communion', one that is heard only within. It ends with a specific Christian reference to the apostle who said 'Behold!' without having seen,[62] which is probably a reference to John 20.29. So many of Dickinson's poems are in fact ways of saying 'Behold!': look – be aware of the overwhelming reality or beauty or mystery; be silent. People of prayer tell us that beyond meditation in words, even beyond the focus on a single word, there is sheer silence, simple contemplation. In her poem on her period of prayer, Dickinson writes that in the silence creation stopped for her. Then, tellingly, she says that in awe she 'worshipped' but did not pray.[63] Many will recognize in this the deepest kind of prayer. The 'One' that Dickinson could not name is the glory that met her in nature and in the deepest place of her own soul; that divine mystery which was her passion but which she always knew would finally elude any words she wanted to use about it.

Death and immortality

As mentioned earlier, awareness of death was a fundamental feature of Dickinson's life and poetry. Scores of poems deal with the subject, as do her letters. She stresses that death can come at any moment and that we have to prepare for it. She imagined herself dying. She lived at a time of high mortality, as well as through the Civil War, when many new cemeteries were being built, and the room she had at home for many years overlooked a graveyard. When a child, she was badly shaken by the death of a young cousin and later by the deaths of the usually older men she had become close to, beginning with the young principal of Amherst Academy which she had attended. At the end of her life she was particularly devastated by the death of a much-loved nephew, Gilbert, the son of Austin and Sue, and her letters refer to many other sad deaths about which she felt deeply. At one stage she even collapsed unconscious after a series of grievous losses. In one poem where she imagines death coming suddenly, she writes:

> The possibility – to pass
> Without a Moment's Bell –
> Into Conjecturer's presence –
> Is like a Face of Steel –
> That suddenly looks into ours
> With a metallic grin –
> The Cordiality of Death –
> Who drills his Welcome – in – [64]

The images in this poem are grim but her frequent reflections on death were far from morbid. First of all they intensified the strength of feeling for her friends. As she wrote to Higginson when he was serving in the Union cause, 'Perhaps death – gave me awe for my friends – striking sharp and early, for I held them since – in a brittle love, more alarm than peace.'[65] The nearness and universality of death also made her even more acutely conscious of the miracle of being alive herself. The heightened awareness of death, for all the sadness and grief it brought, heightened her awareness of life, of her own life in its immediacy and possibilities. Regarding the sorrow of war with its many deaths, she wrote that like Robert Browning she 'sang off charnel steps. Every day life feels mightier, and what we have the power to be, more stupendous.'[66] More than that, this awareness was so intense, and of such quality, that it was, for her, immortality. She believed in a life after death as she made clear in many letters, but when she uses the word 'immortality' she is not thinking of a state we have to await until death to enter, but rather a state of awareness now. In this respect, it is comparable to the use of the phrase 'eternal life' in St John's Gospel. It is real life, true life, life which death cannot diminish, that we can receive now. So the twin poles of her poetry are death and immortality, the one enhancing the sense of the other.

This awareness of immortality was not confined to occasions of death, however. It came to her all the time in every possible way:

> The Only News I know
> Is Bulletins all Day
> From Immortality
>
> The Only Shows I see –
> Tomorrow and Today –
> Perchance Eternity –
>
> The Only One I meet
> Is God – the Only Street –
> Existence – This traversed
>
> If Other News there be –
> Or admirable Show –
> I'll tell it You –[67]

A great many of these bulletins of immortality came to her through nature. Her poems come as responses to sunrises and sunsets, thunderstorms, birds and flowers. Robins were particular favourites, and they are mentioned 40 times in poems and 50 in letters, sometimes being termed 'Gabriel'. She likes to think of herself as diminutive as a robin. Another favourite bird was the bobolink, or American blackbird,[68] who receives ten mentions in the poems. She was sensitive to all the changing seasons. 'These Behaviours of the Year hurt almost like Music – shifting when it ease us most.'[69]

As much as Hopkins she sees the world charged with the glory of God, and understands the world in sacramental terms. In one poem on birds returning in June, she writes about 'the Sacrament of summer days', of 'Last Communion', of 'consecrated bread' and 'immortal wine'.[70] Like William Blake and Francis Thompson, to mention just two people, she thought that our failure to see the glory of the world was because we do not open our eyes properly. It is our 'unfurnished eyes'[71] that miss the many-splendoured thing.

Although for her it is a sense of immortality now that matters, she makes it abundantly clear in her many letters of comfort to the newly bereaved that the person they loved still has some kind of continuing existence. As she put it in a letter to her cousins Louisa and Frances Norcross in 1882, 'I believe we shall be in some manner cherished by our Maker – that the one who gave us this remarkable earth has the power still further to surprise that which he caused. Beyond that all is silence.'72

This is an admirably Christian sentence, focusing as it does not on some alleged part of us which will outlive death but upon God the giver and cherisher. The same is true in her poem suggesting that at the resurrection it is love that scoops up the dust and chants, 'Live!'73 Again, she refers to those she admires who are dead as 'certificate for Immortality'.74 That said, the predominant theme of so many poems is of the glory of immortality experienced now. She takes exception to a clergyman who told her father and sister that 'this corruptible shall put on Incorruption' because she thought that people experienced immortality now.

Glory may come through nature but there is also something tantalizing about such experiences of glory. As with many other writers on nature and beauty, there is, with Dickinson, that which at once lures and eludes us; so there is both ecstasy and pain. She can be left with 'A Discontent' that was too difficult to put into speech.75 Ecstasy is another important word for her. It is not one most people use in a serious sense and very few would lay claim to experiences of it but she writes about the soul being at 'white heat'.76

Towards the end of her life she suffered a number of grievous bereavements. Her father died in 1874, her mother in 1882 and her eight-year-old nephew in 1883. Of her circle of friends Samuel Bowles died in 1878, Josiah Holland in 1881, Charles Wadsworth in 1882, Otis Lord in 1884 and Helen Hunt Jackson in 1885. She also felt bereaved by deaths of favourite authors. At this time of great sadness she wrote:

> Take all away from me, but leave me Ecstasy,
> And I am richer then
> Than all my fellow men –
> Ill it becometh me, to dwell so wealthily,
> when at my very Door are those possessing more,
> In abject poverty?77

This is interesting for its first sentiment, indicating however much she grieved over the loss of friends the most fundamental fact about her own being was her ecstasy. But it is no less interesting for the last two lines, which express a vocation to share this ecstasy with those who did not have it, who as a result are in abject poverty. This made her want to share her words, expressed in poems and letters, especially with those who were grieving.[78] Dickinson stopped going to church and ceased to pray in any conventional sense. Instead, she felt called to sing through her poetry. She wrote to the Norcross cousins that she sang because she could not pray.[79] Again, she wrote to Emily Holland, 'My business is to sing.'[80] This was the way she chose to respond to death. Awareness of death heightened her awareness of life and this led her to sing in poems. She was in fact musical and could sometimes be heard at night composing her own music but she knew that the music of her poetry had to come from within her.[81] It was above all in the poetry that she sang, even through the times of darkness that she experienced.[82] She also believed that her experience would lead her to bring 'a fuller tone' than the birds who arrived early in the day.[83] At one point she hears such music in herself that it surpasses anything she has heard before and it seems a faint rehearsal for the music round the throne.[84]

It should be stressed that this singing through poetry was not just the cheerful song of a sunny nature for whom life seemed good. Not only was Dickinson highly conscious of death, deeply grieving the loss of those she loved; she knew an even deeper darkness. She never makes explicit what this is, but she refers variously to 'the gift of Screws',[85] 'A woe so monstrous' that it tore her all day,[86] and a loneliness whose depths she could not sound.[87] She denies that 'time assuages'.[88] She says that neither speech nor tears convey the greatest anguish. The heart with the heaviest freight on it does not move.[89] Some of this anguish may reflect actual situations in her own life, especially the crisis she went through at the end of the 1850s, but deeper than that her anguish may be the other pole to her capacity for ecstasy. Without in any way suggesting that she was bipolar, which I do not think she was, the increased awareness which raised her to such heights could also make her acutely conscious of the horror of her human consciousness lodged in a fragile body, part of a tale of sound and fury which sometimes seemed to signify nothing. Whether or not this is so she saw this anguish as an essential feature of her life, in the end inseparable from her capacity for joy. Her Calvinist background comes out again when she writes about our pre-appointed pain, but it has a characteristic twist when she writes that this pain is one we are compelled to choose for ourselves.[90]

Dickinson's preoccupation with her inner dialogue might give the impression that she was solipsistic or self-centred in a narrow way. The opposite is true. She believed that love was the greatest reality, and sought to live her life in that light: 'Love lasts – all there is.'[91] She cared deeply about her family and friends, revering her father and nursing her sick mother for many years. Perhaps the clearest indication of her care are the many letters she wrote to friends and stranger alike seeking to offer them some comfort in their bereavement. She took as much trouble over these letters as she did over her poems. She also saw her poems as gifts for others, songs to help them through the difficulties of life. She saw this as a real ministry. What she understood herself as bringing others was not just sympathy but her joy, her sense of immortality, her ecstasy, all of which were inseparable from her capacity for anguish. She brought this to those who thirsted, as was indicated in the poem on ecstasy quoted above. Again, one poem begins with the thought of bringing unaccustomed wine to parched lips. Wine is a biblical symbol of joy, but it also comes as the Gethsemane cup of suffering.[92]

All this love she saw as a filament of divine love, a love revealed in the beauty of the world:

> The Love a Life can show Below
> Is but a filament, I know,
> Of that diviner thing
> That faints upon the face at noon –
> And smites the tinder in the Sun –
> And hinders Gabriel's Wing –
>
> 'Tis this – in Music – hints and sways –
> And far abroad on Summer days –
> Distils uncertain pain –
> 'Tis this that enamors in the East –
> And tints the Transit in the West
> With harrowing Iodine –
>
> 'Tis this – invites – appals – endows –
> Flits – glimmers – proves – dissolves –
> Returns – suggests – convicts – enchants –
> Then – flings in Paradise –[93]

Dickinson's struggle with faith, a dimension in nearly all those 1,800 poems and many of those 1,000 letters is too complex to sum up in any neat formula. On my reading, she had such a rich and intense inner life it led her to distance herself from some of the social conventions of the day, such as regular visits to others. It also led her to distance herself from conventional churchgoing which could appear only thin or banal in the light of her own profound experience. She pursued an inner dialogue with her deepest self, which was at the same time a dialogue with the divine mystery. In the light of this, she felt a special calling to be true to and develop that self, a calling in which writing poetry was fundamental. She renounced worldly fame, as she did much conventional life, in pursuit of this. This was not a selfish life, but one lived as a filament of divine love, expressed both in the care she gave her family and friends in deed and words. It is not surprising that in a poem about the wonder of the mountains around her she should term herself a 'wayward nun', whose service is 'to You'.[94] To anyone who appreciates the religious life, perhaps even the Trappist vocation of silence, her vocation should not seem strange. She was wayward, in pursuing it without any institutional reference, but at the same time heroic.

It is one of her most well-known poems that perhaps best summarizes Emily Dickinson's struggle with faith:

> This World is not Conclusion.
> A Species stands beyond –
> Invisible as Music –
> But Positive, as Sound –
> It beckons, and it baffles –
> Philosophy, don't know –
> And through a riddle, at the last –
> Sagacity, must go –
> To guess it, puzzles scholars –
> To gain it, Men have borne
> Contempt of Generations
> And crucifixion shown –
> Faith slips – and laughs, and rallies –
> Blushes, if any see –
> Plucks at a twig of Evidence –
> And asks a Vane, the way –
> Much Gesture, from the Pulpit –
> Strong Hallelujahs roll –
> Narcotics cannot still the Tooth
> That nibbles at the soul –[95]

The poem begins with a bold affirmation but then goes on to stress the lack of certainty and elusiveness of the claim. There is her characteristic humour in 'Much Gesture, from the Pulpit – / Strong Hallelujahs roll', lines which vividly conveys her looking on at what is going on in the church service amused and unimpressed. There is reticence, for faith blushes if it is seen, but finally it is a claim that will not let her go.

Dickinson was, understandably, a great admirer of George Eliot. When a biography of Eliot was published that revealed Eliot's lack of piety,

Dickinson defended her, arguing that we could not judge her and saying, 'The gift of belief which her greatness denied her, I trust she receives in the childhood of the kingdom of heaven.'[96]

We might say the same about Emily Dickinson, except that, as we have seen, her belief, though idiosyncratic, was much stronger than that of George Eliot and certainly more intense and serious than that of most conventional churchgoers.

3

Gerard Manley Hopkins
'Away grief's gasping'

Introduction

Gerard Manley Hopkins (1844–89) showed academic and artistic talent
from an early age. At Oxford he was influenced by the Oxford Movement
and became an Anglo-Catholic. After the example of John Henry
Newman, he was received into the Roman Catholic Church in 1866.
Resolving to become a Jesuit he symbolically burnt his poems, though
not before sending a few to Robert Bridges. He had various academic
and pastoral appointments before going to Dublin as Professor of Greek
and Latin at University College. He had started to write poetry again,
but his 'The Wreck of the Deutschland' was regarded as too difficult
to publish. His poetry was eventually published in 1918 by his friend
Robert Bridges, some 20 years after Hopkins's death. After some bewil-
derment, this poetry came to be hugely admired as breaking remarkable
new ground. Hopkins had learnt Welsh when he was at St Beuno's and
was influenced by the Welsh *cynghanedd* form of poetry. This together
with a desire to stand in the tradition of Anglo-Saxon rather than
Anglo-Norman English led him to the use of innovative sprung rhythm
which uses stress on the first syllable of a foot, which may have a varying
number of syllables, rather than a steady rhythm with a set number of
syllables per foot and the stress following a pattern. He combines this
with assonance or internal rhyming and vivid imagery to set a new
direction for English poetry after the rather flat late Victorian period.
T. S. Eliot wrote of him, 'The originality and beauty of his verse, and
often the greatness of the poetry, are incontestable.'[1] Hopkins was not a
depressive, but the circumstances of his life towards the end were such
as to bring him close to despair. Like Job he brings his anguish, and
complaint, before God.

Written in blood

Recent writing on Hopkins has been marked by stress on the unhappiness of his life. This is so, for example, in Robert Martin's biography,[2] which emphasizes the loneliness of Hopkins and the roots of this in his repressed homosexuality. In no way do I wish to belittle or underestimate the anguish which Hopkins often felt. For someone who is suffering there is nothing worse than an attitude of 'It's not nearly as bad as you think,' and we do the dead a disservice to take up that attitude towards them. It is clear to even the most untutored reader that the sonnets he wrote in Dublin were indeed, as he said, 'written in blood'.[3] The pain in them can be felt. Nevertheless, this mental suffering needs to be put into perspective, not least the perspective of his own consciously accepted Christian discipline in its Ignatian form.

My concern is with the final Dublin years of Hopkins, from 1884 until his death five years later in 1889. More specifically I am concerned with the poetry of that period. Hopkins went regularly to confession and spiritual direction. If he had brought those last poems to his director, and that director was a sensitive and wise soul friend, also schooled in Ignatian spirituality, what might he say to Hopkins? In setting up this perspective, I am not, I believe, being presumptuous because as a devout priest and Jesuit this was the one, above all others, that Hopkins accepted.

The suffering was real and had a number of causes. First, Dublin at that time was an unattractive city: shabby, crowded and poverty stricken.[4] Hopkins wrote to Bridges to say that it was as smoky as London and covered in soot. His sister said Hopkins 'was made miserable by the untidiness, disorder and dirt of Irish ways, the ugliness of it all'.[5] Hopkins was acutely sensitive to surroundings, to the environment, and the squalor seeped into his soul. There was inadequate public drainage, resulting in numerous diseases and this was clearly a cause of the typhoid which killed him. The college in which he lived was poor, uncomfortable and had no decent sanitation.

Second, there was the burden of a vast, inhuman amount of marking to do. Every year he had to set papers and then mark between 1,300 and 1,800 scripts. Even for someone who flicked through exam papers this would be a gigantic task. But Hopkins was not only intellectually finely tuned, he was hyper-conscientious. People told of seeing him in the middle of the night with a towel around his head. His letters are full of the numbers loaded on him. But it wasn't just the numbers. It was that, as a highly creative mind, he saw no value in this kind of learning. Someone once defined a lecture as that which passes from the notes of the lecturer to the notes of the student without passing through the mind of either. That was not Hopkins's method of lecturing and his students derided him because it wasn't, but it was what the system expected and threw up in exam papers. It was, wrote Hopkins, 'great, very great drudgery'.[6]

Not surprisingly, Hopkins was not a successful teacher. His classes erupted in uproar. His fellow Jesuits found him eccentric. Not surprisingly, the surroundings, the burden of work and the lack of satisfaction in his teaching brought about a succession of minor illnesses which aggravated his general debilitated condition. He had trouble with his eyes and also had numerous other physical complaints. Yet, as will be considered, none of this gets to the heart of his unhappiness. This oppressive scene, however, needs to be balanced. It was not the whole picture.

Hopkins may have seemed odd but was treated kindly by his Jesuit brethren. Beginning with Robert Bridges there has been an attempt to blame the Jesuits for Hopkins's troubles. In fact, as Martin writes, 'The society seems to have done all it could to take care of him, short of giving him permanent sick leave, which would obviously have been of little help'.[7] Among the Jesuits in Dublin was a particular friend, Robert Curtis, about whom Hopkins wrote, 'He is my comfort beyond what I can say and a kind of Godsend I never expected to have'.[8] Hopkins went on delightful holidays, sometimes in the company of this Robert Curtis. They shared a passion for walking and swimming and like Hopkins Curtis was clever and well read.

Then, although his brethren had not the remotest understanding of the calibre of Hopkins's mind and spirit, and on occasion laughed at him, they were not entirely unappreciative. When R. W. Dixon went to Dublin four years after Hopkins's death, he found that one of the priests who had known him well 'had a great opinion of Gerard, without, I think, knowing of his genius. He spoke of him as a most delightful companion, and as excellent in his calling, and so on . . .'[9] In one of the Sonnets of Desolation, Hopkins emphasizes that he is a stranger, cut off from his family by religion, from England by its lack of appreciation of his creative thought and from Ireland by both his Englishness and his political views: 'Now I am at a third remove,' he writes. But we need to give full force to the line that continued, 'Not but in all removed I can / kind love both give and get'.[10]

In his letters, he does from time to time unburden himself and give us a glimpse of the inner strain. But this is in part what letters to friends are for. And those same letters show the most intense interest in life, in all its aspects. They are full of discussions of poetry and poets, painting, etymology and science. There are cheerful letters to his family. In particular, there is a growing enthusiasm for the details of musical composition. Not long before he died he said, almost in passing, in a letter to Bridges, 'I am ill today, but no matter for that as my spirits are good.'[11] When Hopkins's father went to Dublin after his death, he found 'golden opinions on all sides and devoted friends',[12] as he wrote in a letter to one of Gerard's school friends. The fond wish of a father of course, but still to be taken into account.

It is against this background that the sonnets need to be considered.

On 17 May 1885, Hopkins wrote to Bridges, 'I have after a long silence written two sonnets, which I am touching: if ever anything was written in blood one of these was.'[13] On 1 September 1885, he wrote to Bridges, 'I shall shortly have some sonnets to send you, five or more. Four of these came like inspirations unbidden and against my will.'[14]

'Carrion Comfort' has been taken as evidence that Hopkins contemplated suicide. Perhaps he did. What is quite clear, however, is that he firmly rejected this course, as well as the despair which gave rise to the thought:

> Not, I'll not, carrion comfort, Despair, not feast on thee;
> Not untwist – slack they may be – these last strands of man
> In me ór, most weary, cry *I can no more.* I can;
> Can something, hope, wish day come, not choose not to be.[15]

Hopkins asserts that however oppressed he feels by melancholy he can still 'not choose not to be'. By use of the double negative he indicates both the extent of the depression and the firmly disciplined, affirmative will to choose life. It brings to mind Paul Tillich's *The Courage to Be*, where he writes that 'even in the despair about meaning being affirms itself through us. The act of accepting meaninglessness is in itself a meaningful act. It is an act of faith.'[16] Hopkins is more positive and less paradoxical but what he and Tillich have in common is the discovery of meaning in the depths of depression. Some of the contemporaries of Hopkins made a different decision. On 24 April 1885, Hopkins wrote to a friend of his, Alexander Baillie, mentioning Oxford friends who had recently committed suicide:

> Three of my intimate friends at Oxford have just drowned themselves, a good many more of my acquaintances and contemporaries have died by their own hands in other ways. It must be, and the fact brings it home to me, a dreadful feature of our days.[17]

It is against this background that we can see the strength and force of Hopkins's deliberate 'not choose not to be'.

He goes on in 'Carrion Comfort' to write of the apparent terror of God, his lion-like limbs and his tempest. Hopkins wonders why God should be like this to him. The obvious answer is that it is a kind of winnowing: 'That my chaff might fly; my grain lie, sheer and clear.' Rather surprisingly, the poem goes on beyond that answer. It is that in all his turmoil and travail his heart 'lapped strength, stole joy, would laugh, chéer'. There seems an echo here of Psalm 84.5–7, which in the Book of Common Prayer version reads:

> Blessed is the man whose strength is in thee: in whose
>   heart are thy ways.
> Who going through the vale of misery use it for a well:
>   and the pools are filled with water.
> They will go from strength to strength.

Yet again, however, Hopkins moves on in a surprising way. Whom should we cheer? God, who flung him down, or Hopkins himself, who fought God? There is no pious resignation here. This is an extraordinarily modern note, with its sense of dignity of the human struggle, even in its rebellion against fate and God. This willingness to argue with God recurs later in

> Thou are indeed just, Lord, if I contend
> With thee; but, sir, so what I plead is just.[18]

Such boldness to have it out with God is there in the Hebrew Scriptures in Abraham, in Job and in the developed Jewish tradition. It has come to be a commonplace of Christian spirituality in the past two decades. But it is freshly modern in Hopkins. 'Carrion Comfort' ends, 'Of now done darkness I wretch lay wrestling with (my God!) my God.' The image is derived from Jacob's wrestling all night with God, recorded in Genesis. The 'my God!' in parentheses is particularly fine. It expresses astonishment that it is God with whom he is wrestling, and also religious acknowledgement, as in Thomas's 'My Lord and my God' (John 20.28).

'Carrion Comfort' contains a reference to 'that year of now done darkness'. It refers to a darkness in the past and could, therefore, as some have argued, be placed after the other poems. The next poem, however, takes us to the heart of the whirlwind:

> No worst, there is none. Pitched past pitch of grief,
> More pangs will, schooled at forepangs, wilder wring
> Comforter, where, where is your comforting?[19]

It contains the famous lines:

> O the mind, mind has mountains; cliffs of fall
> Frightful, sheer, no-man-fathomed. Hold them cheap
> May who ne'er hung there.

The first line, 'No worst, there is none', could have come straight from Samuel Beckett. We feel the pain of Hopkins in almost every line. Robert Martin writes that the poem 'advances the argument until he has to acknowledge that only the destruction of the individual can save him from self-torment'.[20] But this is not the full truth of the last two lines. Hopkins writes:

> Here! Creep,
> Wretch, under a comfort serves in a whirlwind: all
> Life does end and each day dies with sleep.

Hopkins, like Lear, to whom scholars have found a number of references in this poem, stands in a great storm. But the poem is less about self-destruction than it is about survival. Mountaineers in bad weather put up a tent or creep under a rock. Hopkins sees sleep, the foretaste of a greater sleep, as a way of surviving the storm of self-torment and destruction. It is true that sleep in such circumstances is a blessed relief. But it is also a way of hanging on, of surviving until another day when things may be better. It is the technique of people who know what they can and what they cannot manage – 'Nor does long our small / Durance deal with that steep or deep' – and who choose the only possible way of surviving.

The next poem begins:

> To seem the stranger lies my lot, my life
> Among strangers.[21]

In short, Hopkins feels removed from his parents by religion, from England, because they have not appreciated his creative thought, and from Ireland, where he is an Englishman whose views do not chime with either side. Hopkins refers to England as the wife of his creating thought. On this, Martin comments, 'Hopkins has drawn his metaphors from his deep absorption with his own loneliness when those nearest to him were otherwise engaged.'[22]

The charge that Hopkins is absorbed in his own loneliness will be considered later. The reader does of course notice the reference to 'wife', but the suggestion that the force of the poem lies in the experience of loneliness hardly does justice to its climax. Although Hopkins is cut off from other people in so many ways, he can in all situations 'kind love both give and get'. The conclusion reads:

> Only what word
>> Wisest my heart breeds dark heaven's baffling ban
> Bars or hells spell thwarts. This to hoard unheard,
> Heard unheeded, leaves me a lonely began.

This suggests that his deepest source of frustration and anguish is his failure to be published and the lack of recognition of his creative writing. Hopkins had tried, but failed to get his great poem 'The Wreck of the Deutschland' published. His most discriminating friends, Robert Bridges and R. W. Dixon, could not understand some of the poetry that meant most to him. Even the scholarly articles he wrote as Professor of Greek could not find an outlet. His political views were unheeded.

Although Hopkins renounced the writing of poetry when he became a Jesuit and started writing again almost by accident, it is clear that after his religious faith the creative side of his nature, expressed especially in his poetry, meant more to him than anything else in his life. His letters are full of discussions of poetry and music, with perceptive judgements about other poets. As a Jesuit he had renounced worldly fame for himself, as the famous prayer of St Ignatius puts it, 'Teach us, good Lord, to labour and not to ask for any reward, save that of knowing that we do thy will.' Nevertheless, he recognized the need for others to have public recognition. He wrote to Robert Bridges in surprisingly forthright terms:

> By the bye, I say it deliberately and before God, I would have you and Canon Dixon and all true poets remember that fame, the being known, though in itself one of the most dangerous things to man, is nevertheless the true and appointed heir, element, and setting of genius and its works.[23]

He goes on to say that although art and fame might not matter spiritually in the ordinary way of events, Christ's words about virtue apply to the work of artists of all kinds: 'Let your light shine before men that they may see your good works (say, of art) and glorify your Father in heaven.' (That is, acknowledge that they have an absolute excellence in them and are steps in the scale of infinite and inexhaustive excellence.)[24]

That is a high doctrine of art and its recognition. One he had renounced for himself but which he saw as, if not absolutely necessary, nevertheless the true medium for poets. As a Jesuit Hopkins followed the path of self-denial, even to the point of refusing to write poetry for much of his time as a religious; but it is clear that is where his emotions were still invested. His wisest words were hoarded 'unheard' of; if they were heard they were 'unheeded'. This above all was his anguish.

The poem beginning 'I wake and feel the fell of dark, not day' is the most terrible of the Terrible Sonnets. There is no glimmer of light:

> I am gall, I am heartburn. God's most deep decree
> Bitter would have me taste: my taste was me;
> Bones built in me, flesh filled, blood brimmed the curse.
>
> Selfyeast of spirit a dull dough sours. I see
> The lost are like this, and their scourge to be
> As I am mine, their sweating selves; but worse.[25]

There is here a sense of self-disgust: 'their sweating selves'. But the particular poignancy and anguish of this for Hopkins is that he, more than anyone, valued the self and his sense of self. As a result of the influence of Duns Scotus at Oxford he had come to exult in the individual and the particular, especially the individual, self. Everything in nature does its own thing, as people used to say, and this includes us:

> Each mortal thing does one thing and the same:
> Deals out that being indoors each one dwells;
> Selves-goes itself; *myself* it speaks and spells,
> Crying *what I do is me: for that I came.*[26]

What he writes in this poem is in the same spirit as his meditation on the *Spiritual Exercise* of St Ignatius Loyola. Here he follows through the argument from creation to Creator but in a highly distinctive way. He is less concerned with creation in its generality than with the individual. It is because each individual is so uniquely unique that we look for that which is even more uniquely unique, God, as the only possible source and cause. Hopkins writes:

> When I consider my selfbeing, my consciousness and feeling of myself, that taste of myself, of I and *me* above and in all things, which is more distinctive than the taste of ale or alum, more distinctive than the smell of walnutleaf or camphor . . . nothing else in nature comes near this unspeakable stress of pitch, distinctiveness and selving, this selfbeing of my own.[27]

It is against the background of this intense sense of self, not in a selfish or self-absorbed way but as a heightened awareness of what it is to be a unique me, that we must see the horror of this poem. Hopkins, so conscious of the distinctiveness of his self, tastes only bitterness, sourness, sweating anguish. This is indeed hell. 'The lost are like this'.

'Patience, hard thing!'[28] begins the next poem. The word 'patience' is related to the Latin root *patior*, meaning to suffer. Therefore to pray for patience is to pray for war and wounds. Patience is also the name of a dock leaf which roots in a particularly harsh soil: deprivation and setbacks. Here also ivy grows:

> Natural heart's ivy, Patience masks
> Our ruins of wrecked past purpose. There she basks
> Purple eyes and seas of liquid leaves all day.

This image has been much admired. The ivy basking in the sun forms a kind of ocean through which we can see the wreck. Some commentators have concentrated on the fact that ivy is poisonous. But ivy is a traditional Christian symbol of everlasting life. Furthermore, although the beauty of ivy can have a certain menace about it, the purple berries and leaves shining in the sun have a rich and strong beauty about them, as Edvard Munch depicted so well in one of his paintings.

Beneath the ocean we can hear the timbers of the wreck: 'Our hearts grate on themselves'. Nevertheless, although we rebel against this, that same rebellious will bids God to bend us to him even so. No one can fail to discern the pain and the sternness in these images.

> And where he is who more and more distils
> Delicious kindness? – He is patient. Patience fills
> His crisp combs, and that comes those ways we know.

The reference is to honeycombs and distilling; that is, pressing the honey out. Psalm 19 would have been well known to Hopkins. It refers to the stat-utes of the Lord as 'More to be desired are they than gold, yea, than much find gold: sweeter also than honey and the honeycomb' (v. 10). Out of this hard-won patience comes delicious kindness. For God himself is patient and he it is who fills these honeycombs with his peace and presence. Hopkins knew this from the lives of the saints and in his own experience: 'that comes those ways we know'. St Ignatius in his *Spiritual Exercises* had written, 'Let him who is in desolation strive to remain in patience, a virtue contrary to the troubles which harass him; and let him think that he will shortly be consoled.'[29] There may not be much sign in the poem that Hopkins himself had yet experienced the consolations of patience. Nevertheless, as Norman MacKenzie has rightly pointed out, this poem represents an advance upon the blackest of the other dark sonnets because instead of concentrating on the blackness of the way, it focuses forward on the route along which in God's good time the ability to surmount frustrations will come.

In July 1886, Hopkins had written to Richard Dixon to console him for not being elected to the Chair of Poetry in Oxford. He points out, 'that life is short and we are lucky to get even a short spell. The lives of the great conquerors were cut short. Above all, Christ our Lord: his career was cut short.'[30] Robert Martin comments on this letter that Hopkins 'was beginning to console himself with that most dangerous of comforts, that it is better to fail than to win, and for his example he chose Christ'.[31] This may be the most dangerous of doctrines. Nevertheless it is worth considering the paragraph in full. What Hopkins wrote was:

> Above all Christ our Lord: his career was cut short and, whereas he would have wished to succeed by success – for it is insane to lay yourself out to failure, prudence is the first of the cardinal virtues, and he was the most prudent of men – nevertheless, he was doomed to succeed by failure; his plans were baffled, his hopes dashed, and his work was done by being broken off undone. However much he understood all this he found it an intolerable grief to submit to it. He left the example: it is very strengthening. But except in that sense it is not consoling.[32]

It is crystal clear from this paragraph that Hopkins was fully aware of the dangers of invoking failure and that it should not be sought for its own sake. The sanity and balance of this paragraph stands in startling contrast to the judgements of some recent commentators on Hopkins with their continual harping on his disappointment and sadness. Hopkins felt all the anguish of his wrecked past purposes. But as a Christian and a Jesuit he persevered in the way of patience, knowing God is patient and experiencing at least something of the consolation that comes from the way of obedience.

The next poem traces, however gradually, the emergence from darkest dark. It adopts the tone of a kindly confessor and counsellor:

> My own heart let me have more pity on: let
> me live to my sad self hereafter kind.[33]

Hopkins had once described a friend as a 'self-tormentor'. It was this to which he himself was prone. He brought into his Roman Catholicism all the self-scrutinizing rectitude of high Victorian Anglo-Catholicism. This self-tormenting left him like a blind man in a dark dungeon or all thirst in a world of wet: desperate, longing and helpless. It is not only the tone of this poem, full of pity, that is striking. It is the movement from addressing the heart in the third person in the first verse, 'My own heart let me have more pity on', to the identification with the suffering in the second verse, 'I cast for comfort I can no more get', on to the third verse in which he addresses the soul directly:

> Soul, self; come, poor Jackself, I do advise
> You, jaded, let be; call off thoughts awhile
> Elsewhere; leave comfort root-room.

The message he gives his sad self is one basic to life, let alone the Christian life. If we strive too hard for a particular experience we are likely to lose it. If we let go and trust the unexpected then surprisingly blessing can come. Only God knows the time and the size of this joy. But it is like the smile of the sky that we see between mountains sometimes which 'lights a lovely mile' as Hopkins put it.

Hopkins wrote a few more poems before he died in 1889: 'Tom's Garland', in which he enters into the despair and rage of the unemployed: 'Harry Ploughman'; 'Epithalamion', which is full of sensuous delight in nature and male bathing but which fails to finish its stated theme of seeing this as an image of married love; a rather bitter one in which he gets his moods in perspective by seeing the distorted reflection of his face in a spoon; a poem of apology and explanation to Robert Bridges; and three others now to be considered.

First the poem he was asked to write in honour of St Alphonsus Rodriguez, a labourer of the Society of Jesus in Majorca. Over the years Christian theologians have discussed whether Christian martyrdom or the inner spiritual struggle is more valiant. Alphonsus Rodriguez underwent the latter. A lay brother who lived from 1533 to 1617 in Majorca and who for 40 years was the hall porter of the Jesuit College in Palma, he yet underwent fearsome spiritual travail. Outwardly his life seemed so serene on this beautiful and temperate island. But his spiritual writings, which would have been known to Hopkins, relate fierce struggles. In 1888, Alphonsus Rodriguez was canonized and for the celebration of his first feast day on 30 October Jesuits in other provinces were asked to send tributes. It was this that evoked the poem by Hopkins. It begins by recognizing the honour that is 'flashed off exploit', whether of soldiers in battle or of martyrs. But the inner struggle is no less heroic. For God's struggle with creation, though hidden, ends triumphant. The 40 years that Alphonsus Rodriguez spent as a door-keeper were not wasted:

> But be the war within, the brand we wield
> Unseen, the heroic breast not outward-steeled,
> Earth hears no hurtle then from fiercest fray.
> Yet God (that hews mountain and continent)
> Earth, all, out: who, with trickling increment,
> Veins violets and tall trees makes more and more)

> Could crowd career with conquest while there went
> Those years and years by of world without event
> That in Majorca Alfonso watched the door.[34]

It is a poem which reflects Hopkins himself fully committed to the path of inner discipleship, and to a scale of Christian values in which this hidden interior discipline is seen as triumphant. The poem, like Edward Thomas's 'Adlestrop', leaves the hearer or reader at once focused and lingering: sharply particular, and yet opening up to the eternal:

> Those years and years by of world without event
> That in Majorca Alfonso watched the door.

The complaint that good people suffer while the wicked prosper is one often heard in the Bible, particularly in the psalms. In a poem on this theme, Hopkins takes words from Jeremiah 12.1 to protest against God's ways:

> Thou art indeed just, Lord, if I contend
> With thee; but sir, so what I please is just.
> Why do sinners' ways prosper? And why must
> Disappointment all I endeavour end?[35]

He goes on to contrast nature blossoming all around him with his own barren state:

> birds build – but not I build; no, but strain,
> Time's eunuch, and not breed one work that wakes.
> Mine, O thou Lord of life, send my roots rain.

The sense that from a creative point of view he was producing nothing worthwhile expressed in the image of being a eunuch is one which recurs in Hopkins. Modern critics have made much of it. He first used it as an undergraduate, lamenting the unfruitfulness of his life without Digby Dolben, a young friend for whom Hopkins had developed a deep attachment and who drowned at the age of 19. On 1 September 1885, Hopkins wrote to Robert Bridges that it wasn't so much the thought that none of his work would see the light of day that really depressed him but the failure of his creative spirit: 'If I could but produce work I should not mind its being buried, silenced, and going no further; but it kills me to be time's eunuch and never to beget.'[36] Again, 'All impulse fails me: I can give myself no sufficient reason for going on. Nothing comes: I am a eunuch – but it is for the Kingdom of Heaven's sake.' Robert Martin emphasizes the use of sexual metaphor to describe the barren state of his soul.[37] But sexual metaphor, we might remark, is used throughout the Bible. What is more remarkable than the image is the fact that though Hopkins felt totally uncreative he was in fact producing some of his finest work. It is ironic that one of his most enduring poems would be based on the conviction that no work of his would ever endure. In contrast to some previous criticism of Hopkins which stressed his misery, more recent studies take a different view. Martin Dubois draws a distinction between the lyric 'I' and the autobiographical 'I', suggesting that the Terrible Sonnets should be seen as 'dramatic fictions . . . pictures of the way a man might pray' in the manner of George Herbert, whilst Desmond Egan describes the same poems as 'sonnets of hope'.[38]

Immortal diamond

This brings us to the heart of the paradox, the divine irony, of Hopkins. For in 1918, nearly 30 years after his death, Robert Bridges published a collection of Hopkins's verse. Poets were impressed and began to be influenced. Critics soon held him as one of the greatest of modern poets, quickly given his place in the great tradition. The source of his deepest frustration and unhappiness is the sphere of his lasting fame. Earlier he had complained of heaven's baffling ban which had kept his creative words bursting inside him: 'This to hoard unheard, heard unheeded, leaves me a lonely began.' But for the past hundred years, his words have been both heard and heeded.

Hopkins, many years before, had written so lightly:

Shape nothing, lips; be lovely-dumb:
It is the shut, the curfew sent
From there where all surrenders come
Which only makes you eloquent.[39]

He had lived out that life of surrender, that lack of publication, that lack of recognition, that lack of understanding. But from that surrender there came an eloquence that has enthralled the world. It would not, perhaps, have surprised Hopkins totally. For he wanted recognition and at the heart of his faith was a hope that a life of obedience, a life surrendered trustingly to God, would, in God's good time, in time or out of time, bring forth fruit.

The final poem to be considered is 'That Nature is a Heraclitean Fire and of the Comfort of the Resurrection'. The first part is taken up with a wonderful evocation of the movement and vitality of nature, the clouds moving in the sky, the light filtering through the trees, the wind blowing everything about and drying up the mud. This sense of the aliveness of nature has the feel of Van Gogh's landscapes. But this continuous movement is not merely a description. It is also an image of nature as a great bonfire. Ancient philosophers speculated about the composition of the basic elements of nature. Heraclitus, one of the pre-Socratic philosophers thought that the substrate or underlying matter of the universe was fire. Everything was fire in a constant state of change. He alluded to a constant change of state occurring in the elements, a downward movement causing fire to transmute into sea, which in turn condenses into earth; and an upward return movement, which the earth rarefies into water and that again separates out into clouds of moisture, and the fire of which even the sun and the stars are made. Hopkins depicts the upward cycle in nature. Sun, fire and the wind are drying the storm-flooded ground. In contrast to this upward movement, however, stands man, a spark in this bonfire destined for a tiny glow before going out. 'Man, how fast his firedint, his mark on mind, is gone!' Then Hopkins brings Paul's view of the resurrection into the picture: 'Behold, I show you a mystery: we shall not all sleep, but we shall all be changed, in a moment, in a twinkling of an eye . . . For this corruptible must put on incorruption and this mortal must put on immortality!' (1 Cor. 15.51–53):

> Man, how fast his firedint, his mark on mind, is gone!
> Both are in an unfathomable, all is in an enormous dark
> Drowned. O pity and indignation! Manshape, that shone
> Sheer off, disseveral, a star, death blots black out; nor mark
>   Is any of him at all so stark
> But vastness blurs and time beats level. Enough! The Resurrection,
> A heart's-clarion! Away grief's gasping, joyless days, dejection
>   Across my foundering deck shone
> A beacon, an eternal beam. Flesh fade, and mortal trash
> Fall to the residuary worm; world's wildfire, leave but ash:
>   In a flash, at a trumpet crash,
> I am all at once what Christ is, since he was what I am, and
> This Jack, joke, poor potsherd, patch, matchwood, immortal diamond,
>   Is immortal diamond.[40]

Human beings can be described from different points of view. We are a jack of all trades, a bad joke, a piece of broken pottery, an ill-matched piece of cloth (or in Elizabethan parlance a fool), a jagged fragment of splintered wood. Yet we also have or are divine soul, immortal diamond, which is revealed after the fire in all its glorious beauty.

'Jack' is a word that Hopkins used a number of times to describe human beings. He had no illusions or pretensions about what, considered from many angles, we are. But he was also conscious of his unique individuality, known to himself and known to God. He once wrote a lovely hymn:

> Thee, God, I come from, to Thee go,
> All day long I like fountain flow
> From thy hand out, swayed about
> Mote-like in thy mighty glow.[41]

The poem on the resurrection, written in Dublin in 1888, shows no diminution in Hopkins's powers as a poet. His sense of nature, his capacity to intertwine fresh imagery with profound reflection is at its height. His faith is full blooded and expectant. Nor does this poem lend itself to the criticism of a Freud or a Marx that it is looking for an illusionary compensation in another world. It is this world that is celebrated, human beings here and now that are affirmed, but human beings properly understood as unique selves or souls with the capacity to become like Christ. One cannot help noticing that Robert Martin's biography with its emphasis on Hopkins's loneliness, repressed homosexuality and unhappiness does not even refer to this poem. Yet the consensus of critical judgement is that it is one of his finest creations.

As Hopkins died he was heard to say two or three times, 'I am so happy, I am so happy. I loved my life.'[42] Despite this I do not in any way underestimate the periods of anguish in the last years of Hopkins. My point is that we need to see this in the perspective of his consciously accepted discipline as a Christian and as a Jesuit. From this point of view, the sonnets, though terrible indeed, betray a mind that is totally sane and faithful. When biographers and critics ignore this dimension, they are inclined continuously to misinterpret, to get him wrong, as Eric Griffiths showed in his review of Martin's biography.[43] Griffiths argues that Hopkins was not being evasive, as though he had something shameful to hide. On the contrary, he was conscious that his life was hid with Christ in God, as Paul put it. 'Away grief's gasping, joyless days, dejection'. We might wish that Hopkins had experienced more human happiness: but that he knew Christian joy I have no doubt; a foretaste of that revealing of the immortal diamond, which was his own unique, suffering, struggling, amazingly creative self.

4

Edward Thomas
The elusive call

Introduction

Edward Thomas (1878–1917) was a freelance writer who wrote particularly well about the natural world. He married young, but the marriage became unhappy. We have a moving account of it from Helen, his wife. In 1913, he met the American poet Robert Frost, who saw the potential for poetry in Thomas's prose writing.[1] In 1915, he joined the army and was killed at Arras in 1917. Nearly all his poetry was published posthumously. Like Frost's it uses the easy diction of everyday speech. Thomas is both admired by literary critics and has wide popular appeal, his poem 'Adlestrop' being voted the nation's favourite poem. While other poets focused on war in the trenches, Thomas showed the effect of the war at home, as in 'As the team's head brass.'

Thomas had no formal religious belief but he is considered here because he marks an important link between the high seriousness of Victorians about religion and a modern world apparently at ease with secularism.

A haunting note in the poetry

All commentators recognize that one of the distinctive features of the poetry of Edward Thomas is what I term 'the elusive call'.

Not surprisingly this characteristic is described in a number of different ways by those who know and love the poetry of Edward Thomas, which itself highlights the elusive nature of what is being referred to. John Powell Ward does in fact use the word 'elusive'. He writes that Thomas's writing was 'often curiously elusive. This doesn't at all mean obscure, for we get his small, natural scenes clearly and at once. But something of the trees, weeds, or garden fences was just out of reach.'[2] He goes on to note that Thomas occasionally ties this elusive sense not only to place but to time. Dannie Abse writes about 'his yearning for something lost which cannot be quite named or entirely recovered'.[3] David Constantine notes how this is reflected in the language itself by quoting Thomas's feeling the 'shape of his sentences and altering continually with some unseen end in view'.[4] Kevin Crossley-Holland gives it an explicitly spiritual meaning when he writes about the poems 'so often leading from the actual to the numinous'.[5] Helen Farish writes of 'a world which hovers somewhere on the periphery of the poet's vision, a glimpsed timelessness or wholeness'.[6] Grevel Lindop refers to the subtle plainness of language that 'expresses some mystery, impermanence and longing which casts an irresistible spell'.[7] James Nash writes about some sense 'of being lost in something much larger than oneself'.[8] These are just some of the great variety of ways in which people have tried to describe that elusive sense.

First of all I will seek to identify some of the elements which go towards giving his poetry this elusive quality. The poem in which this appears in its most unambiguous form is 'The Glory'.[9] Here 'The glory of the beauty of the morning' tempts him 'to something sweeter than love'. At the same time it leaves him scorning all he can ever do or be beside the loveliness and happiness he imagines dwells in 'beauty's presence'. The poem ends with a sense of discontent and a series of unanswered questions about what the cause of this might be with its strong final image 'I cannot bite the day to the core'. The image is one of eating, consuming, taking a beautiful and nutritious apple into oneself. This is not just a reference to his inability to answer the questions. He wants to make the beauty that tempts him part of himself, but 'I cannot bite the day to the core'. This is an image to which I will return later.

In a great number of poems, over forty of them, birds play a significant role, often thrushes and blackbirds. Thomas had an intense love of nature in all its seasons and all its details. In all the seasons of nature, he could find something to celebrate, and he noticed and loved details which pass most of us by, like the dust on nettles in the corner of a farmyard, or the snail shells left by winter and still there in the spring. But clearly the singing of birds moved him more than any other aspect, and became the vehicle of the elusive call of my chapter title.[10] In 'The unknown bird',[11] he is haunted by the sound of a bird whose notes neither he nor naturalists can recognize. This is a bird he really hears, but also it is

> As if a cock crowed past the edge of the world,
> As if the bird or I were in a dream.

Now, years later when the poet remembers that sound, he becomes 'Light as that bird wandering beyond my shore'.[12]

In trying to understand Edward Thomas, it is vital that we see him against the background of his time, 1878–1917. Much of that period has been designated *fin de siècle*, with all that phrase implies. Edward and Helen did not share in the decadence associated with some of their contemporaries in that movement of feeling and sensibility. They lived rather respectable and hard-working lives. But they did see themselves as progressives, caught up in the latest intellectual developments. They had sloughed off conventional religion, and they found it natural to express their love sexually without waiting for marriage.

Sociologists of religion look to the 1960s as the time when the outward expression of the Christian religion dramatically declined in the UK. And most of us will probably work on the assumption that before that time people were much more conforming. That is partly true, for the Second World War led to something of a religious revival, as reflected for example in the number of people offering themselves for ordination after the war until the end of the 1950s. But if we go back before that, the picture is very different. Adrian Hastings has written of the period before 1920:

> The dominant political class was largely unbelieving. If one thinks of Asquith, Haldane, Balfour, Lloyd George, Churchill, H. A. L. Fisher, one cannot well speak of degrees of Christian orthodoxy, but only of degrees of scepticism. There was hardly a straightforward Christian believer in the front rank of politics in these years.[13]

That was the political class, who outwardly had to show some outward support of the Church of England for political reasons. But Edward and Helen had no such constraints. They simply saw themselves as progressive young things, belonging to the intellectual and artistic avant-garde.

Another feature of the period relevant to understanding Thomas is the aesthetic movement, with its intense desire for beauty for its own sake, associated for example with Walter Pater, whom Thomas read and admired. This often went with a morbid melancholy, even despair, which led to a desire for suicide, one which was sometimes all too real. As already noted in the chapter on Gerard Manley Hopkins, three of his intimate friends at Oxford had drowned themselves and many more of his acquaintances and contemporaries had committed suicide in other ways.[14]

We know from Helen how tormented Edward was at times. As she wrote:

> When these days came, with no apparent reason for their coming, bringing to him a deep spiritual unrest and discontent, he would be silent for hours,

and perhaps stride out of the house, angry and bitter and cruel, and walk and walk far into the night, and come home, worn out with deadly fatigue.[15]

In their first talks, she records that 'there was often hinted that deep spiritual unrest, which as yet we did not recognize, much less realise how it was to overshadow so much of his life and mine'.[16] It is noteworthy that she deliberately uses the term 'spiritual unrest'.

I do not intend to attempt a psychological analysis of Thomas, except to note the fact that he hated his father. More pertinent is that he had to do a huge amount of hackwork simply in order to survive financially. This was for him, as it would be for any creative person, a great burden and the source of some of his discontent. But it was allied to a strong sense that he did not know what his true path in life would or should be. 'The Signpost'[17] has the line 'Which way shall I go?', a question he anticipates will be with him at 60 as it was at 20. He will always be 'Wondering where he shall journey, O where?'

Not surprisingly this quest for his true path in life is closely connected with a quest for his true self; his hunt for 'The Other',[18] the title of the fine poem in which the other he pursues always slips away just ahead of him.

The poignant paradox is that in writing these poems in the last months of his life, Thomas did find his path, his vocation and himself, but he was not to know that or have it validated by the world until after his death.

Another source for the melancholy was his relationship to Helen. Her account of their early love, with its mixture of innocence and eroticism, the former heightening the latter, is still powerful.[19] But from her account, and his poems, it is clear he could not match the continuing physical intensity of her devotion to him, while at the same time still remembering their early passion. In 'No One So Much As You', he regrets that

> I have kept
>
> Only a fretting
>
> That I could not return
> All that you gave
> And could not ever burn
> With the love you have,
>
> Till sometimes it did seem
> Better it were
> Never to see you more
> Than linger here

With only gratitude
Instead of love –
A pine in solitude
Cradling a dove.[20]

This, together with the constraints of living with and trying to support a young family, often made him want to escape. As 'Wind and Mist' puts it:

But flint and clay and childbirth were too real
For this cloud-castle.[21]

Out for a walk with friends the words 'home' and 'homesick' come up playfully in the conversation but 'No more', writes Thomas in 'Home':

If I should ever more admit
Than the mere word I could not endure it
For a day longer: this captivity
Must somehow come to an end, else I should be
Another man, as often now I seem,
Or this life be only an evil dream.[22]

As so often with Thomas the different themes and images overlap one another. For home is not just that domestic captivity, itself an expression of the captivity of life, but in one of the two poems called 'Home' (this time without the inverted commas of reported speech), he says:

This is my grief. That land,
My home, I have never seen;
No traveller tells of it,
However far he has been.[23]

Another example of themes coming together is in 'And You, Helen' when he set out the gifts he would like to give her, and the final one is

And myself, too, if I could find
Where it lay hidden and it proved kind.[24]

It is not surprising that given this set of circumstances images of escape should be so strong in his poetry. First, there is the very fact that he needed to get out and spend many days walking in the English countryside. This is not of course to deny his genuine love of that countryside, but it is clear that it was not only an appreciative love, but a deep-seated need to be away from home and walking alone. This is reflected in the number of poems that have images of roads, paths and journeys. Even more vividly, it occurs in the number of poems that focus on people of the road, people who spend their time travelling apparently free from the constraints of ordinary life, such as gypsies or 'The Huxter',[25] very often with a song on their lips like

> I'm bound away for ever,
> Away somewhere, away for ever.[26]

The emphasis is on 'for ever', which sometimes means the character just disappearing.

These outward journeys reflect an inner flight that often expresses itself in strange images, as when looking up one day he imagines himself as a tench stuck in the mud which would float to the surface among the lily leaves and see nothing but sky.[27]

This leads naturally into his desire for death, which at times was clearly very serious indeed. Helen tells of one time when he spent the whole night walking, having taken the revolver with him, and the relief she felt when eventually he reappeared. At 20, one poem suggests, he wished he had never been born.[28] Some lines which describe being caught in a rain storm express his longing for death:

> Myriads of broken reeds all still and stiff,
> Like me who have no love which this wild rain
> Has not dissolved except the love of death,
> If love it be towards what is perfect and
> Cannot, the tempest tells me, disappoint.[29]

It is this which helps us to understand why, at the age of 37, Thomas enlisted in the army. It was not of course the only reason. There was a genuine love of the English soil, which he wanted to protect. Then, at a time of extreme difficulty when he was earning a living as a freelance writer during war time, the army meant a regular income of some sort for his young family. But joining up, as it has done for so many, solved the problem of direction, vocation and destiny. It is not that he hoped to be killed in the conflict, at least so far as we know, but he was relieved to be able to hand his life's future over to fate. Studies on patterns of suicide show that the familiar distinction between those determined to kill themselves and those who are simply uttering a cry for help is false. In some Pacific islands, for example, someone will take a canoe out to sea in shark-infested waters, leaving it to chance whether or not he or she survives. They do not have to make the decision: fate makes it for them. This well describes Thomas's approach to the war:

> 'No one cares less than I,
> Nobody knows but God,

Whether I am destined to lie
Under a foreign clod,'
Were the words I made to the bugle call in the morning.

But laughing, storming, scorning,
Only the bugles know
What the bugles say in the morning,
And they do not care, when they blow
The call that I heard and made words to early this morning.[30]

Perhaps the impulse towards death was even stronger than a carelessness about it. When he was a young journalist, Andrew McNeillie interviewed Carey Morris, who knew Thomas and recounted that he had that 'doomed look' that he deplored.[31] Lachlan Mackinnon writes about Thomas's going from the hillside where his memorial stands 'to seek the death / his poems ached for'.[32]

If Thomas was more than 'half in love with easeful death'[33] it was not just because it solved problems of his future, but because it gave him escape from his self-tormenting self.[34]

In 'Lights Out', he writes.

The tall forest towers;
Its cloudy foliage lowers
Ahead, shelf above shelf;
Its silence I hear and obey
That I may lose my way
And myself.[35]

D. H. Lawrence also writes about what he calls oblivion, but in one of his finest poems, 'Shadows',[36] it is because he hopes to come forth 'on a new morning, a new man'. For Thomas, death leads neither to a renewed existence on this earth nor a heavenly one, but to a poetic fantasy of freedom and bliss. The poem that begins 'I love roads' continues:

Now all roads lead to France
And heavy is the tread
Of the living; but the dead
Returning lightly dance.[37]

In another poem, he hears a bell on a buoy out at sea:

Sweeter I never heard, mother, no, not in all Wales.
I should like to be lying under that foam,
Dead, but able to hear the sound of the bell,
And certain that you would often come

> And rest, listening happily,
> I should be happy if that could be.[38]

Thomas is more interesting than this when he is more hauntingly lyrical, as in his lovely poem 'Out in the Dark',[39] or when exploring the puzzling ambiguity of his responses, as in 'Old Man', about a herb with a bitter scent which evokes an experience he cannot remember:

> I cannot like the scent,
> Yet I would rather give up others more sweet,
> With no meaning, than this bitter one.
>
> I have mislaid the key. I sniff the spray
> And think of nothing; I see and I hear nothing;
> Yet seem, too, to be listening, lying in wait
> For what I should, yet never can, remember:
> Only an avenue, dark, nameless, without end.[40]

Another aspect of the elusive call is what remained in Thomas of late Romanticism. In 1774, Wolfgang von Goethe had created the prototype of the Romantic hero in his semi-autobiographical novel *The Sorrows of Young Werther*, in which, among other things, the hero commits suicide. Thomas Carlyle, who persuaded a whole generation of Victorians to read him, described the novel as giving expression to a nameless unrest and longing that was widespread at the time. But Romanticism has also been well described as 'spilt religion',[41] as we see it for example in the paintings of Caspar David Friedrich. Thomas said that his favourite poet among the ancients was Percy Bysshe Shelley.[42] But what remained of late-Romanticism in Thomas was combined with a modernist tendency, a feature which was brought out so strongly in *Branch-lines*. So the Romanticism is at one and the same time a Romanticism subverted. As Edna Longley put it, 'his mingled desire and failure to recreate romantic unities'.[43]

Perhaps related to this in some way was both his Welshness and the Celtic revival. Although the phrase 'Celtic revival' is now associated mainly with the Irish literary movement, there was also a resurgent interest in things Welsh in the nineteenth century. In his book on Wales, it is difficult to get at Edward Thomas's true feelings about being Welsh,[44] as he writes about those who claim to be Celtic with a strong dose of irony. However, a later poet, R. S. Thomas who wrote about Edward believed that despite the fact that the term 'Celtic imagination' is a discredited one, this is a partial reason for the vein of melancholy and dissatisfaction which runs through Edward Thomas's verse. He writes, 'Yet one Welshman, at least, toys with the idea that the melancholy and wry whimsicality, the longing to make the glimpsed good place permanent, which appear in Thomas's verse, may have had a Welsh source.'[45]

R. S. Thomas thinks that a line from a Welsh poem 'At Abercauwg the cuckoos sing' fascinated Edward Thomas. As will be discussed, that line certainly fascinated R. S. himself and he refers to it in both a prose piece and a poem he wrote. But I have not myself yet been able to trace the reference to it in Edward Thomas.

At the opposite end from any sense of romantic yearning is the hard rock of the contingent: the fact that things simply happen; things are done which cannot be undone; things that irrevocably shape the future. It is difficult to think of a poet who conveys this more sharply than Thomas. Most famously of course it is there in what is for many his finest poem, 'As the Team's Head Brass',[46] but also for example in 'Up in the Wind',[47] and not surprisingly it is often linked to the war.[48] There is no meaning in these events, no meaning to be made out of them; they are simply, to be noted, intensely noted.

Sometimes this noting is associated with a silence and a stillness. Stillness against the background of sound as in 'Adlestrop', but often the stillness of an ancient painting as in 'The Manor Farm':

> The church and yew
> And farmhouse slept in a Sunday silentness.
> The air raised not a straw. The steep farm roof,
> With tiles duskily glowing, entertained
> The mid-day sun; and up and down the roof
> White pigeons nestled. There was no sound but one.
> Three cart-horses were looking over a gate
> Drowsily through their forelocks, swishing their tails
> Against a fly, a solitary fly.[49]

The use of both sound and movement to bring out this moment, which is at once intensely visual and sharply auditory comes out very well in 'Tears'.[50] The sound is the sound of hounds baying and the music of 'The British Grenadiers'; the scene is of hounds streaming by and soldiers changing guard. But these remembered sounds and sights are something that 'pierces the solitude and silence'.

This brings out the fact that the moments that Thomas remembers and evokes are nearly always against the background of movement: of roads and paths, of people on journeys. And all this is part of the great movement of time as past, present and future. It is not just a timeless moment on the one hand or a narrative on the other, but the one as part of the whole. Patrick McGuiness puts it well:

His poems don't try to escape time by launching themselves vertically as it were, up and out of it, cordoning off the lyric instant from Time's annihilating sweep the way lesser poems might. Rather, they are intent on inhabiting the moment across the full range of its tenses the *is*, the *was*, and the *will be*.[51]

So in 'As the Team's Head Brass' the short conversations are set against the background of the circling plough; and the whole is set against the background of before the war, during the war and after the war. It is not so much a timeless moment as the whole sweep of time, past, present and future taken up and held for our view. In 'The Mill-Water', the silence is against the background of the never still mill stream and this against the background that it was once a working mill. As often as not it is a conversation within a narrative, an encounter within a journey.

I have suggested that there is a whole range of factors that played into Thomas's sense of discontent and longing: his frustration with his work, his relationship with Helen, the *fin de siècle* mood of the times, including its playing with the idea of death, the late, subverted Romanticism especially that part of it that related to his Welshness, and the disbelief of the times. I want now to look at that last element a little more closely. The key quality of modernism, according to John Wain is 'this isolation of unbelief', a loneliness 'far more intense than the loneliness that arises from the mere absence of other human beings'.[52]

The elusive call and religion

As a child Edward Thomas was taken regularly to chapel but loathed it. He writes about it using strong language. The atmosphere he remembers is 'a mild poison steadily creeping into me on all sides'.[53] Chapel and Sunday school were to him 'cruel ceremonious punishments'.[54] His father had originally been something of a free thinker, and Thomas also remembers some jocular sceptical conversations with his father about the devil. Something of this scepticism may have got into Edward early, which was reinforced later when his father became a regular chapelgoer. This was further strengthened by the fact that he came to hate his father.

As an adult his letters and poems express an entirely negative attitude to religion. In his war diaries, note that when someone tackles him about God and claims that marvellous escapes are ordained, he replies, 'So are the marvellous escapes of certain telegraph poles, houses, etc.'[55] A friend who wrote to him is described as pointing out the 'security and sweetness of his refuge in the fat bosom of the church. I feel that my salvation depends on a person.'[56] In one poem reflecting on the war, he wrote:

> Men strike and bear the stroke
> Of war as ever, audacious or resigned,
> And God still sits aloft in the array
> That we have wrought for him, stone-deaf and stone-blind.[57]

This story of a conventional, often evangelical, upbringing and reaction against it is one of the familiar narratives in nineteenth- and early twentieth-century literature. But if many became agnostics or atheists, often combining this with some form of socialism, others took another path and became Roman Catholics or Anglo-Catholics. Ronald Knox, one of the best-known Roman Catholics of the day and one of the cleverest men of his generation was the son of an Evangelical bishop of Liverpool. In his autobiography, he said a man must have a religion and it must be different from that of his father. This is a profound psychological truth which fitted the pattern of many at that time, one which involved both continuity and discontinuity with a formative upbringing. Whether that path, rather than the other, was taken depended on many factors: the people encountered, the milieu inhabited and the experiences which life offered. All we can say is that none of these factors in the life of Edward Thomas were such as to take him on that path to a renewed understanding of religious faith, even though it was clearly a path that appealed to many people with a similar intellectual and aesthetic temperament.

I will look briefly at three such people, who are all considered later in this book, as one aspect of their experience is relevant here.

C. S. Lewis (1898–1963) also fought in the First World War and for the first part of his life was a militant atheist. In his autobiography, he writes about the touch of beauty, longing and loss in a way that resonates with Edward Thomas.[58] He argued that although we tend to locate the touch of glory in the past, sometimes in childhood, as in William Wordsworth and Thomas Traherne, it escapes us even there because it is in fact a touch from beyond, a touch of heavenly glory.[59] In a wonderful wartime essay, he writes about this glory in these words:

> We do not want merely to *see* beauty . . . we want something else that can hardly be put into words – to be united to the beauty we see, to pass into it, to receive it into ourselves, to bathe in it, to become part of it.

He suggests that this is what we see in the myths of gods and goddesses, and in the biblical picture of heaven:

> At present . . . we cannot mingle with the splendours we see. But all the leaves of the New Testament are rustling with the rumour that it will not

always be so . . . We are summoned to pass in through nature, beyond her, into that splendour which she fitfully reflects.[60]

We could say that Lewis shared something of the temperament of a late Romantic, but after his conversion to Christianity discovered that the tantalizing, elusive quality he had met in experiences of beauty found its fulfilment in a divine beauty. Thomas ended his poem on 'Glory' by saying, 'We cannot bite the day to the core'. For Lewis, this desire to pass into beauty and become part of it became focused on the glory of God. The remarkable Frenchwoman Simone Weil used a similar image in writing about beauty:

It is a sphinx, an enigma, a mystery which is painfully tantalising. We should like to feed upon it but it is merely something to look at, it appears only from a certain distance. The great trouble in human life is that looking and eating are two different operations. Only beyond the sky, in the country inhabited by God, are they one and the same operation.[61]

Another interesting comparison with Edward Thomas is T. S. Eliot (1888–1965), who was just ten years younger than Thomas. He was shaped not just by the *fin de siècle* and the impact of the world war but by the broken, crazy aftermath, which he reflected so effectively in his earlier poetry. Like Thomas he is concerned with time. But whereas for Thomas past, present and future are seen as a whole, in a unified narrative, in Eliot, the past and the future, in their different ways have their focus mainly in the present, and what matters is our awareness of this, the still point of the turning world, the timeless moment. It is most powerfully visualized in 'Little Gidding':

Here, the intersection of the timeless moment
Is England and nowhere. Never and always.[62]

Thomas in his poetry conveyed those still, silent moments. But with him we remain lingering with them as in 'Adlestrop'. For Eliot they have another dimension, for it is in these moments that we are aware of 'A condition of complete simplicity (costing not less than everything).' This is always a matter of 'Quick now, here, now, always'.[63]

The final point of comparison I want to make is with the later Thomas, R. S., born in 1913. R. S. Thomas was a very serious birdwatcher but birds in his poetry do not carry the resonance they do in Edward's. They are not a vehicle for a call beyond themselves. In one poem, the call of a bird reveals a farmer's loneliness. In another, the rareness of a rare bird is like the rareness of moments of grace in prayer; in another beautiful lyric to his wife after her death, he compares her to a delicate bird.

More central to R. S. Thomas is the theme of the absence of God, his elusiveness, his always going before. We never find him, but only the place where he has been. In short, there is not a yearning for something unformulated, but the exploration of a God who by definition cannot be with us in any obvious sense. As with Lewis and Eliot, feelings and attitudes that at another time and in another person might have taken a rather different form became focused and channelled by a religious vocabulary. In a later chapter on R. S. Thomas, I quote a poem[64] and a piece of prose[65] on the theme of Abercauwg, in which the poet suggests the essential elusiveness of God.

What was in Edward Thomas an unaccounted-for sense of dissatisfaction becomes in R. S. Thomas an elusiveness that is accepted and integrated, because it accords with his fundamental view of human existence and belief in a God whom we can never properly grasp.

Earlier I quoted the description of Romanticism as 'spilt religion'. That description perfectly fits the poem Edward wrote for his birthday, 'March the Third', in which he described birds singing and bells ringing:

> And when it falls on Sunday, bells
> Are a wild natural voice that dwells
> On hillsides; but the birds' songs have
> The holiness gone from the bells.[66]

I am not suggesting that Edward Thomas had a naturally religious temperament. We do not know. What we do know is that his experience of religion was unfortunate and he lived at a time when religious faith was not a serious option for the intellectual avant-garde. In addition, it appeared he never came into contact with the kinds of people or became part of a milieu where religion might have appeared an attractive and serious option to someone of his sensibility. It could be, of course, that he was a person of a naturally religious sensibility, but for both personal and cultural reasons a religious vocabulary was not open to him. Yet given the earlier quotations about his hatred of religion, there are two surprising remarks from the time just before and just after he went to Oxford. He wrote to his friend Harry Hooton:

> I am impatient to get to Lincoln College. One thing I hope to get there – religion. I find such a need of that, as an informing spirit in all I do and am. If I can be serious enough, I hope to find satisfaction in the Church of England: it will be my fault if I don't. I want, as Milton says in those pathetic closing lines of his Epic, 'a place of rest' . . .[67]

Then, in his notebook at the end of his time at Oxford, he wrote:

> One of my greatest regrets is that I did not attend chapel at Lincoln. The lack
> of it is a loss to my 'prospect and horizon'; it is comparable to the lack of a
> mother's sweetness in one's early education.[68]

Wilfred Owen, who once thought seriously of being ordained, uses religious vocabulary to very good effect in heightening our sense of the pity and waste of war. But Thomas said, 'I never understood quite what was meant by God.'[69]

What Edward Thomas experienced raises a question. The kind of yearning we see in him, that sense of an elusive call, does it belong exclusively to a particular period in history – that period of rapid change, industrialization, changing countryside and loss of faith? Or is it part of the human condition in every age? It is interesting that the large number of distinguished poets who love the poetry of Edward Thomas and have been influenced by it have not carried this sense into their own poetry. Of course it may be that in adolescence a good number of people feel what Thomas felt, and it is marked how many poets first responded to him at that time of their lives. But leaving adolescence aside, do we now live in a time where such feelings are no longer part of the emotional and spiritual climate?

There is a powerful, persistent strand in Christian devotion which says that such feelings belong to humanity as such. St Augustine prayed, 'Our hearts are restless until they rest in you.' George Herbert in his poem 'The Pulley' suggests that God deliberately makes us with a 'repining restlessness' so that we find a final satisfaction only in him. C. S. Lewis, in his self-examination after he had married and satisfied all his sexual desires, noted that he was still aware of another kind of need, another kind of want. For it is one of the basic themes of Christian teaching that we will continue to have unsatisfied longings until we focus them on God, when they become transmuted into another kind of longing. But I leave the mystery of our unsatisfied longings, and whether they can find their satisfaction only in God, as a question.

I leave the last word to Thomas, who in his poem 'Melancholy' does suggest that the elusive call does not come to him alone but is felt more widely:

> Yet naught did my despair
> But sweeten the strange sweetness, while through the wild air
> All day long I heard a distant cuckoo calling
> And soft as dulcimers, sounds of near water falling,
> And, softer, and remote as if in history,
> Rumours of what had touched my friends, my foes, or me.[70]

5

T. S. Eliot
Out of hell

Introduction

T. S. Eliot (1888–1965) was born in St Louis, Missouri; but his roots were in Boston, Massachusetts, where his family were leading Unitarians. He studied at Harvard, the Sorbonne and Oxford before joining Lloyds Bank in 1917. He founded *The Criterion* and placed it at the cutting edge of European literature. He published *The Waste Land* in 1922, which made a bigger impact than any other twentieth-century poem. It was seen as the voice of a disillusioned generation, but no less expressed the pain and distress of Eliot's first marriage. Eliot was also the most discerning critic of the time, the great arbiter of taste who shaped people's evaluation of poetry and poets for generations to come. This was further reinforced when he became a director of Faber & Faber. In 1927, he was baptized and adopted a disciplined life as an Anglo-Catholic Christian. This was reflected in his poetry and culminated in *Four Quartets* (1935–42), the major Christian poem of the century, rivalled only by the less well-known 'Horae Canonicae' of W. H. Auden. Eliot attempted to revive poetic drama and *Murder in the Cathedral* is still staged, but his West End plays suffered in comparison with the very different kind of play being performed after the Second World War. After the death of his first wife, he found happiness in a marriage to Valerie Fletcher, who guarded his legacy and meticulously edited his correspondence.

Eliot's early religious history

In his foreword to *For Lancelot Andrewes*, published in 1928, Eliot announced to a startled world that his general point of view could be described as 'classicist in literature, royalist in politics and Anglo-Catholic in religion'. The previous year, on 29 June 1927, he had been baptized behind locked doors in the church at Finstock near Oxford, later the church of Barbara Pym, and the following morning had been confirmed at Cuddesdon by the Bishop of Oxford, Thomas Strong. The restless, literary clergyman who baptized him, W. F. Stead, was sworn to secrecy. 'I *hate* spectacular "conversions"', wrote Eliot.[1]

I approach that conversion with three interlinked questions in mind. From what was he converted? Why did he convert? What was the immediate effect of that conversion? The seven volumes of Eliot's letters so far published are a helpful way into some answers. I will end by considering briefly how his new-found faith is reflected in some of the poems he wrote at the time.

Eliot was brought up in the heart of New England Unitarianism. His mother's father-in-law, Walter Greenleaf Eliot, a leading light in the movement, was a great hero and family role model, and the whole family held a prominent position in the church; indeed Eliot later described them as 'the Borgias of the Papacy',[2] though anything less like the Borgias in moral character would be hard to imagine. For this Unitarianism was characterized by a strong sense of moral duty, high-mindedness and the importance of education. From an early age, he had instilled into him the ideals of unselfishness and public service, not least through the Unitarian church the family attended on Sundays. This exacting demand pressed heavily on him throughout his life. But emotionally and spiritually this form of religion had no appeal to young Tom and when he went as a student to Harvard he was indifferent to the church.

Even as a young boy Eliot had read a life of the Buddha and at Harvard he read widely in Eastern philosophy and mysticism, and learnt Sanskrit and Pali. His latest biographer, Robert Crawford, sets out in some detail the extensive range of these courses.[3] Later, when he was doing further study at Oxford, this fascination with mysticism continued.[4] He responded very positively to Rabindranath Tagore and he read Evelyn Underhill.

This interest was not just theoretical. For, about the time of his graduation ceremony from Harvard, he had the first of a few experiences, the memories of which were to haunt him all his life. As Lyndall Gordon put it, 'While walking one day in Boston, he saw the streets suddenly shrink and divide. His every day preoccupations, his past, all the claims of the future fell away and he was enfolded in a great silence.'[5]

In June 1910, he wrote a poem called 'Silence', which is now in print as one of his previously uncollected poems. In this, he wrote of everything becoming still, but it was a terrifying peace.[6]

A little later, in Paris, he tells of a ring of silence which closed round him and sealed him off in a state of beatific security from the floods of life. Interestingly he did not immediately interpret these experiences in religious terms, even though as I have noted he was at the time deeply into

Eastern mysticism.[7] They are reflected in *The Waste Land*, where he wrote of 'Looking into the heart of light, the silence.'

Later, in the first part of the *Four Quartets*, Eliot's poetry reflects a visit he paid with Emily Hale to a Cotswold manor house, Burnt Norton, and in particular the moment when they stood by the empty swimming pool. An experience that previously he had interpreted in very general terms he there incorporated into a Christian framework:

> Dry the pool, dry concrete, brown edged,
> And the pool was filled with water out of sunlight,
> And the lotos rose, quietly, quietly,
> The surface glittered out of heart of light.

Another thread in the background to Eliot's conversion was the fact that he had had a Roman Catholic nanny to whom he was devoted. She used to take him on occasion to the colourful Church of the Immaculate Conception, which, he said, 'I liked very much.' Also, as he said later, he remembered a theological argument about God as first cause 'being put to me, at the age of six, by a devoutly Catholic Irish nursemaid'.[8]

This attraction towards Roman Catholicism re-emerged much later in intellectual form when he was reflecting on the nature of tradition. As is well known, Eliot came to think that you could be truly modern only if you were deeply steeped in a tradition; otherwise you were simply in danger of repeating the past by being swept up in the fads of the present. Indeed he said that anyone who wanted to continue as a poet beyond their thirtieth year had to write with the whole sweep of European literature, from Homer onwards, in their bones.

It is clear from volume 2 of Eliot's letters, covering the period 1923–5, that in his editing of *The Criterion* at the time he was looking for a clear moral and intellectual point of view to set against the ramshackle, hedonistic culture of the 1920s. He was also drawn to the work of Thomas Aquinas. He knew his Aristotle and appreciated the Aristotelian element in Aquinas but believed that Catholic philosophers like Jacques Maritain had been too emotional. He wanted to pick his way slowly and with great exactitude, aware of the problems posed by modern psychology, especially to what he called the problem of religious belief. As well as reading a number of other Roman Catholic theologians, he suggested, when reflecting on contemporary poetry in 1917, that people read a nineteenth-century papal encyclical on tradition. He was not a member of any church, and he mocked 'the true church' in his poem 'The Hippopotamus', but he used to visit Anglo-Catholic city churches during the lunch hour and he was conscious of Catholicism as 'The only church which can even pretend to maintain a philosophy of its own, a philosophy, as we are increasingly aware, which is succeeding in establishing a claim to be taken quite seriously.'[9]

There is another aspect of this emphasis on tradition. Delivering some extramural lecture on French literature in Ilkley, West Yorkshire, in order to earn some more money, he stressed the need for form and restraint in writing. In contrast to Romanticism, 'A classicist in art and literature will therefore be likely to adhere to a monarchical form of government, and to the Catholic Church.' This is because 'At the bottom of man's heart there is always the beast' and therefore 'man requires an askesis'; that is, strict spiritual self-discipline.[10]

Another element in the movement of his mind and heart was his reading of Lancelot Andrewes, John Donne and George Herbert from 1918 onwards as part of his consideration of the sermon as 'perhaps the most difficult form of art'.[11] Eliot was being drawn in the same way that C. S. Lewis found himself hugely attracted to Christian authors some time before he himself converted.

There is one further consideration about Eliot's pre-conversion outlook: his scepticism. Eliot always had a questioning, critical mind; it was one of the aspects of his character that fed into his great sense of mischievous humour, which he retained even in his darkest period. Then when he was studying at Oxford he became particularly interested in sceptical attitudes which called any dogmatic point of view into question. This corrosive scepticism went along with his developing interest in mysticism.[12] As he put it to a friend, 'I have had for several years a distrust of strong convictions in any theory or creed which can be formulated . . . One must have theories but one need not believe in them!'[13] His scepticism was not only directed towards the beliefs of others, but more relentlessly towards his own.[14]

This then was the background from which Eliot was converted.

First, from his Unitarian upbringing he retained a strong sense of duty but reacted against its dry, overoptimistic view of life. As he put it, 'Unitarianism is a bad preparation for brass tacks like birth, copulation, death, hell, heaven and insanity.'[15]

Second, there was his developing interest in Eastern religions and mysticism, together with some powerful experiences of heightened awareness, which at the time he did not interpret in religious terms.

Third, his reaction against individualism and Romanticism led him not just to see the importance of tradition in literature but the strength of

Catholic Christianity with its realistic understanding of the seed of evil in the human heart and the consequent need for self-discipline.

Fourth, there was a sceptical side to him by nature which was reinforced by his philosophical studies. As we shall see, this remained part of him even after his conversion.

Eliot announced his new belief in 1928 in a sudden peremptory manner. But of course the various elements just mentioned were fermenting and mixing along the way. In 1910, he wrote some blasphemous poems, which is noteworthy because he regarded blasphemy as stemming from the 'partial belief' of a mind in a peculiar and unusual state of spiritual sickness and it might even be 'A way of affirming belief.'[16] Then in 1914 he was to write some visionary lines which over the years developed into *The Waste Land*, finally finished in 1921. The poem was later dismissed by Eliot as a personal grouse against life, but was of course seen by others as the voice of a disillusioned generation. Though Sanskrit in some of its wording and Buddhist in some of its imagery, it is a poem that not only contains Christian themes but has a strong sense of the Christian imperative to lead an exemplary life pressing through it. Then in 1926 to the surprise of his brother and sister-in-law, who were with him on a visit to Rome, Eliot suddenly fell on his knees before Michelangelo's *Pietà*. About the same time, he was struck by the number of people kneeling in the city churches he visited. An aunt of his had written to a friend who had joined the Episcopal Church, 'Do you kneel down in church and call yourself a miserable sinner? Neither I nor my family will ever do that.' But that gesture of abasement and worship was increasingly what Eliot did want to do, and which he did the following year when he was baptized. This was followed some months later by his first confession. Eliot wrote to W. F. Stead, who had helped him on his way to baptism, that he had an extraordinary sense of surrender and gain as if he had crossed a very wide, deep river, never to return.'[17]

The reasons for his conversion

So we come to the second question: Why did Eliot convert? And the clue is given in the very stark and definite way in which he describes his new commitment as classicist, monarchist and Catholic. He wanted more than a vague mysticism and more than a self-sufficient moralism. He wanted something with a clear structure and discipline to it. Classicism might be defined in a number of ways, but one thing is certain is that it is opposed to what Eliot describes as the undisciplined squads of emotion which drive so many of our words. Again, royalism can be variously understood but at the least it indicates structure and degree, and, as Shakespeare put it in *Troilus and Cressida*:

Take but degree away, untune that string,
And, hark, what discord follows! each thing meets in mere oppugnancy.[18]

Barry Spurr's thoroughly researched book shows the influence of T. S. Eliot's very clear and definite Anglo-Catholic beliefs and practices on Eliot's poetry and other writing at the time. Spurr argues that it is impossible to engage with Eliot's poetry without a knowledge of the *very particular* religious *milieu* in which Eliot found his spiritual home, as it existed from the 1920s to about 1955, and Spurr describes it for those unfamiliar with it today. Indeed it is part of Spurr's thesis that this particular Anglo-Catholic world no longer exists and needs explanation as much as any other period of history.

The immediate background to Eliot's conversion and his urgent need for a definite structure and discipline was the fact that his life was a desperately unhappy mess. The anguished, hellish marriage of Tom and his first wife, Vivienne, together with his trying to do his job at the bank and later at Faber & Faber, his keeping up his serious literary work and earning enough money to pay for his wife's heavy medical expenses were taking an increasingly heavy toll on him. He was barely coping; indeed, was on the edge of a breakdown. He needed something to hold his own life together, and similarly it was the desire to find something more solid than the individualism, relativism and emotionalism which he thought were rotting Western civilization. He was looking for a secure political order that could be sustained by an objective moral realm. He was later to write:

The Christian scheme seemed the only possible scheme which found a place for values which I must maintain or perish (and belief comes first and practice second), the belief, for instance, in holy living and holy dying, in sanctity, chastity, humility, austerity.[19]

It was for this reason that he much regretted the intellectual breakup of Europe and the rise of Protestantism, and why he preferred the outlook of the thirteenth century to the seventeenth. All this helps us to understand why he was drawn to the French thinker Charles Maurras, now considered to be of dubious reputation, who though an atheist, was also looking for an ordered alternative to the chaos of Western culture as it then stood.

Another factor in his move to the Christian faith was the thinness of Bertrand Russell's arguments. He wrote to Russell, who was an old friend, about his pamphlet on Christianity to say that it was a piece of childish folly and that the arguments in it had been familiar to him at the age of six or eight. He took serious atheism very seriously and said that 'Atheism should always be encouraged for the sake of the Faith.'[20] But about Russell (and to Russell), he said, 'What I dislike is the smell of the corpse of Protestantism passing down the river.'[21]

Eliot had a very pessimistic view of human nature, his own and other people's. All human relationships, he thought, turned out to be a delusion and a cheat. However, 'the love of God takes the place of the cynicism which otherwise is inevitable to every rational person'. On the basis of this love of God, then, every human love is enhanced and can be celebrated. The reference to cynicism is from a very important letter to Geoffrey Faber, who had accused him of being too austere, in which Eliot beautifully sets out the right relationship between the love of God, and the most material of pleasures.[22]

Of particular interest in volume 6 of the collected letters is Eliot's correspondence with Stephen Spender in connection with his 1932 broadcasts in which Eliot discloses something of how his mind moved towards faith. As mentioned, he said he needed to hold to values without which he would perish, but values, in his view, depended on religion. Those values would be expressed in highly disciplined Christian living.[23] He had nothing but scorn for the average product of the English school system, which sought, he believed, to turn out gentlemen rather than Christians, the two being antithetical.[24] He also argues that the real choice to be made is between Christianity and communism, though he certainly did not want to be aligned with the usual anti-communists. He said he loathed both communism and the society in which he was then living. He reserved further scorn for the Conservative Party of the time, which he saw as nothing more than an unsavoury alliance of liberalism and laissez-faire economics. He looked for an alternative, Christian way of ordering society, an idea which took book form some seven years later. For now he needed a structure and a discipline to hold his own life together. The Anglo-Catholicism of the 1920s provided just that. The Puritan element from his New England upbringing could find an outlet in the rigours of self-examination and confession, his mystical yearning could find its true goal and fulfilment in adoration of the God who became incarnate, the defining difference for him between his new creed and his Unitarian background. In Anglo-Catholicism, this came in sacramental form with a sense of mystery and awe in which his desire to worship could find proper expression. His belief in the importance of tradition found its home in his sense of belonging to the one holy, catholic and apostolic Church.

There is of course the question as to why he became an Anglican rather than a Roman Catholic. It would have been very natural for him to become a Roman Catholic given what became his Thomistic philosophy of life and because of his wide knowledge of and deep sympathy with European culture. But he valued the greater freedom of thought allowed by the Church of England and the more moderate *via media* it provided to religious excesses. When he had first started to read sermons in 1918 for their literary form, he had been excited by Donne; later however it was the sober approach of Lancelot Andrewes with its settled resolute will to holiness that drew him.[25] Then, not least, he was conscious of his English family forebears and fitting naturally into his heritage as an English Christian and not just a European intellectual.

Eliot's new life

And this leads on to the third question: What was the immediate effect of Eliot's conversion? The answer again, is quite clear: a new discipline of life. As mentioned, he made his first confession and that discipline continued. Indeed he sought a new confessor, one who would be much more severe with him.[26] He became a nearly daily communicant and agreed to be churchwarden of St Stephen's, Gloucester Road, in London, a role he held for 25 years. There is a telling anecdote from Herbert Read, who was staying with Eliot in the spare bedroom when he said he was woken up in the morning by a slight noise. He saw a hand sliding through the door to reach first for an umbrella and then a bowler hat, before the door slipped shut again. It was Eliot going off to early morning communion. It was the first indication he had that Eliot had become a Christian. Some lines from *Four Quartets* succinctly sum up this approach to life. Eliot refers to those moments in life when we are taken out of ourselves, for example, by music; but, as he writes, these are only hints followed by guesses. What matters are the basic disciplines of the Christian life: prayer and observance, thought and action.

There is a revealing letter to Paul Elmer More in which Eliot refers to people who seem to have no need of religion:

They may be very good or very happy: they simply seem to miss nothing, to be unconscious of any void – the void I find in the middle of all human happiness and all human relations and which there is only one thing to fill. I am one whom this sense of void tends to drive towards asceticism or sensuality, and only Christianity helps to reconcile me to life, which is otherwise disgusting. But the people I have in mind – the good ones are much more puzzling than the bad – have an easy and innocent acceptance of life that I simply cannot understand. It is more bewildering than the 'problem of evil'.[27]

Some people when they convert become narrow and intolerant in defence of their new faith. Almost the opposite happened to Eliot. He became if anything even more intellectually open to a range of truth. He continued to select or commission articles for *The Criterion* on the same grounds as before. Nearly all the people he knew were shocked and outraged by the new turn in Eliot's life but he remained remarkably unfazed by their attacks on him, and he continued to have good relations even with people who had sharply, and for the wrong reasons, savaged his faith. He remained friends with people who had very different views of life to his own (nearly all the people he knew), and continued to offer objective literary judgements about the literary worth of their writing. There was no insecure defensiveness about him. This was because he had first faced in himself all the worst things that others might say. Conrad Aiken, for example, had criticized *For Lancelot Andrewes* as showing 'A thin and vinegarish hostility to the modern world . . . a complete abdication of intelligence', and so on, to which Eliot replied:

> You may be right. Most of these criticisms I had anticipated, or made myself. Thrice armed is he who knows what a humbug he is. My progress, if I ever make any, will be purging myself of a large number of impure motives.[28]

More widely, he welcomed the new hostile situation in which Christians now found themselves, for it released the Christian faith from what had burdened it since the eighteenth century; namely, being a badge of respectability for the English middle classes.

We get an idea of the kind of intellectual culture in which Eliot moved in a letter he wrote to Paul Elmer More, who had followed a somewhat similar route to Eliot himself. Eliot wrote, 'I might almost say that I never met any Christians until after I had made up my mind to become one.'[29] He knew that his conversion would expose him to 'ridicule' but this did not daunt him. As he said, 'anyone who has been moving in intellectual circles and comes to the Church may experience an odd, rather exhilarating feeling of isolation'.

His new faith was a definite one, in the sense that it fully adopted the creed and outlook of the Anglo-Catholicism of the day and was hostile to any liberalizing tendencies.[30] We find this at its most startling in his attitude to Paul Elmer More's views on hell. He liked and respected More but found his view of hell too liberal. 'Is your God Santa Claus?' he asked, and continued, 'to me, the phrase "to be damned for the glory of God" is sense not paradox'.[31]

Throughout the letters of the period there are the same strong, lucid opinions on a whole range of subjects, literary, political and religious; stern and uncompromising in tone, yet also self-mocking and caring towards the recipient. They indicate the kind of difference becoming a Christian, and in particular an Anglo-Catholic, made to his life. 'I know just enough – and no more – of "the peace of God" to know that it is an extraordinarily painful blessing.'[32] Again, 'faith is not a substitute for anything: it does not give the things life has refused, but something else; and in the ordinary sense it does not make one happier'.[33]

I mentioned Eliot's sceptical cast of mind. This did not change with his conversion. He continued to be highly critical of Western culture and religion, of course, but neither did he allow the fundamental questions about faith to go away: rather, he believed that in one sense they intensified. One of the reasons that Eliot was drawn to Blaise Pascal was that he 'faced unflinchingly the demon of doubt which is inseparable from the spirit of belief'.[34] Again:

> Every man who thinks and lives by thought must have his own scepticism, that which stops at the question, that which ends in denial or that which leads to faith and which is somehow integrated into the faith which transcends it.[35]

As he wrote, 'The more conscious becomes the belief, so the more conscious becomes unbelief: indifference, doubt and scepticism appear . . . A higher religion imposes a conflict, a division, torment and struggle within the individual.'[36]

As Eliot brought out in his letter to Geoffrey Faber, he relished the ordinary pleasures of life and indeed found them enhanced by his religion. Later on in life, with his second marriage, he was to discover an unexpected happiness in love. But for this period of his life what he discovered through his faith was something tougher:

> To me, religion has brought at least the perception of something above morals, and therefore extremely terrifying; it has brought me not happiness, but the sense of something above happiness and therefore more terrifying than ordinary pain and misery; the very dark night and the desert.[37]

In 1927, the year of his conversion, Eliot wrote 'The Journey of the Magi'. He wrote it quickly between church and lunch one Sunday morning with the aid of half a bottle of gin. The imagery, much of it based on Lancelot

Andrewes' Christmas sermon of 1662, describes a long hard journey to Bethlehem. Some of the imagery clearly draws on the New Testament, and some of it, though highly evocative, seems obscure. Eliot remarked that a scene might mean much to a person, but little to the poet, or vice versa, nothing to the person but much to the poet. Some of the imagery in this poem is of the latter kind.

The poem as a whole clearly reflects Eliot's own journey to faith and the long journey that lay ahead. As he put it to his friend Paul Elmer More:

> Most critics appear to think that my Catholicism is merely an escape, an evasion . . . it [is] rather trying to have supposed to have settled oneself in an easy chair, when one has just begun a long journey afoot.[38]

He already knows that this journey, though it involves the recognition of a birth, means for him a personal death: a displacement of the self, a prising away of the self's attachments from so much of what he had valued before. Afterwards the Magi leave the Christ child to return home but 'no longer at ease here, in the old dispensation'.

So as Eliot put it elsewhere, 'We are certainly a minority, even in what are called Christian countries; we find the minds of the people about us growing more and more alien, so that on vital matters we often find we have no common assumptions.'[39]

The next poem he wrote about this time, in 1928, was 'A Song for Simeon'. This describes a world being destroyed, in imagery taken from the words of Jesus, with the repeated liturgical refrain 'Grant us thy peace', taken from the Agnus Dei. It switches at the end to 'Grant me thy peace', with the words about Mary 'And a sword shall pierce thy heart also' added. It ends, as does the Nunc Dimittis, said every day at Evensong with 'Let they servant depart / Having seen thy salvation.' This reflects Eliot's own new-found salvation, but is full of premonition for the pain ahead and a desire to depart this life.

This poem is another expression of Eliot's long-standing conviction of the need to stand in a tradition, a conviction deeply reinforced by his becoming a Christian. For this brings, for the Catholic and Orthodox Christian, a sense of Christians in every age belonging together, the liturgy of the Church being the voice of the whole body of Christ.

In 1929, he wrote 'Animula'. The first bold words, 'Issues from the hand of God, the simple soul', come from Dante's *Purgatorio*. But as the poem goes on, the soul is revealed as far from simple. Eliot had previously criticized Wordsworth and others for indulging in the imagined radiance of childhood. The soul may be simple as it comes from God but very different when it emerges in a time when it is irresolute and selfish, unable to go forward or retreat.

In such a world, as Eliot found, the only peace is in preparing for death. As one line goes, 'Living first in the silence after the viaticum', the viaticum being the last rites people receive when they know they are dying.

Again, the poem ends in a prayer, the words of the Angelus, but with a difference: not 'Pray for us now and at the hour of our death' but 'at the hour of our birth' in this disordered and disfigured world.

The key poem for light it sheds on what his conversion meant to Eliot emotionally and spiritually is *Ash Wednesday*. Although published in its present form in 1930, the four sections were all completed by 1928, some of them published separately, and the themes had obviously been in his mind before the key date of 1927, when he announced his new faith to the world. He disliked it being called a religious, let alone a devotional, poem; rather he said it marked a stage in a person's life. To put it in very prosaic terms, it is a poem of renunciation, a resolve not to turn back to what the world values, a determination not to look back with longing, regrets or nostalgia. It is a poem in which all hope is given up because, in the words of St John of the Cross which he used later in 'Burnt Norton', 'hope would be hope for the wrong thing'. So *Ash Wednesday* begins with the hope that he will not have to turn again.

The key opening line comes from Guido Cavalcanti, the thirteenth-century Italian poet whom Eliot, like Pound, much admired: 'perch'io non spero di tornar già mai'. The line lodged itself in Eliot's mind and he could not rest until he had used it. The poem is full of other borrowing, borrowing, rather than allusion being Eliot's method, and borrowing from the psalms and other parts of Scripture, the liturgy and prayers of the Church. These references are often clear in themselves but people complained then and continue to do so about the poem's obscurity. Eliot believed a poem should be obscure. Like life or any living thing it needs to be appreciated for the mystery of itself, in itself. It is not a conundrum that has to be solved.[40] Some of the imagery, he admitted, like the yew tree and the veiled sister, even came from his recurrent dreams. They give the poem a hallucinatory, filmlike effect, and this, combined with its incantatory tone, endows it with a haunting quality.

That said, Eliot is quite clear on what the poem is fundamentally about, for he said it was a 'deliberate modern *Vita Nuova*' of Dante.[41] In that book, Dante's sight of Beatrice kindles his love and that love leads him to the Virgin Mary and onward up the mountain of purgatory. Eliot seems to have had his own Beatrice in Emily Hale, an American friend with whom he corresponded over the years. Once Eliot discussed with W. F. Stead how Dante's love for Beatrice had passed over into the love of God in the *Vita Nuova*. 'I have had that experience,' said Eliot eagerly and rather shyly and then lapsed into silence.[42] It was Emily Hale who went with Eliot to Burnt Norton in September 1934, a visit which inspired not only the title of the poem but a mystical moment by the empty pool described earlier. Before that moment in the poem had come the thought of paths not followed.

The persona of the poem is in the desert, Ezekiel's valley of dry bones; everywhere is desolation, disillusion; the air is dry and all is dead. But a lady appears who points to Mary, who leads him out of the desert. As Eliot wrote, 'I have found my own love for a woman enhanced, intensified and purified by meditation on the virgin.'[43]

But it was in the desert he had found the secret of peace, again from Dante, this time *Paradiso*, canto III: 'E'n la sua volontade è nostra pace', which Eliot translates as 'our peace in his will'. The poem ends:

> Blessed sister, holy mother, spirit of the fountain, spirit of the garden,
> Suffer us not to mock ourselves with falsehood
> Teach us to care and not to care
> Teach us to sit still
> Even among these rocks,
> Our peace in His will
> And even among these rocks
> Sister, mother
> And spirit of the river, spirit of the sea,
> Suffer me not to be separated
>
> And let my cry come unto thee.[44]

Then, finally, there is 'Marina' published in 1930. It is, I have to admit, a poem that had rather passed me by until Rowan Williams and I shared a day speaking on Eliot and he remarked that it so moved him, he was not able to read it aloud in public. It is also noteworthy that Eliot said it was his favourite poem. The dominant image is based on the recognition by Shakespeare's Pericles of his supposedly lost daughter, Marina. But there is an implied contrast with Seneca's *Hercules Furens* in which Hercules comes to and finds he has killed his children, for it is addressed to 'O my daughter'.[45] The boat on which the poet sets sail is an old one, much repaired, and the poem is full of the imagery of Maine, which meant so much to Eliot and which comes to full flower later in 'The Dry Salvages'. However, here the imagery is not of that coast itself, but of a reconnection with something in himself set off by Emily Hale, already mentioned in my discussion of *Ash Wednesday*. Emily Hale, his Beatrice, not only channelled his love towards God but acted as a muse in releasing his poetry. Hers is a face through which grace comes and that grace/face is 'dissolved in place'. On this voyage, he 'Made this unknowing, half conscious, unknown, my own', living in time beyond time with

> The awakened lips parted, the hope, the new ships.

> What seas what shores what granite islands towards my timbers
> And woodthrush calling through the fog
> My daughter.[46]

It is interesting that Eliot admitted that his desire for progeny had once been very acute.[47] So like *Pericles*, Shakespeare's play which Eliot much admired, the poem is about recognition. Eliot recognized that his pent-up desire to love could be channelled towards God by his newly awakened feeling for Emily, as symbolized in his childhood memories of the Maine coast. Maine was the scene of Eliot's most ambitious sailing ventures. As Lyndall Gordon puts it, 'It is there, in imagination, that his voyager is "awakened" as the longed-for call comes through the fog, and suppressed emotion for the long-lost yet familiar woman breaks out in a cry of recognition.'[48]

This was the intense new life that Eliot lived behind the carapace of successful publisher, man of letters and austere, celibate Christian.

6

Stevie Smith
A jaunty desperation

Introduction

Stevie Smith (1902–71) published *Novel on Yellow Paper* in 1936. This was very well received, as were three other novels written at the time. Later, however, she became unfashionable and found it difficult to get her work published. However, she emerged from this comparative obscurity with her collection of poems *Not Waving but Drowning* (1957), after which her reputation steadily grew. In the 1960s, she became a popular performer at public poetry readings, where she recited or chanted her own poems alongside much younger writers. She received the Cholmondeley Award in 1966, and in 1969 was awarded the Queen's Gold Medal for Poetry.

Since her death she has increasingly been recognized as an important voice. The publication of her *Collected Poems* in 1975 was a landmark in establishing her as a uniquely original poet, as did *Me Again*, the 1981 anthology of her previously uncollected writings. Hugh Whitemore's 1981 biographical play *Stevie* helped to popularize her. It was later made into a film starring Glenda Jackson and Mona Washbourne. Some of the poems featured in the film are set to haunting music composed by Patrick Gowers and played by the guitarist John Williams. The republication of her three novels as Virago Modern Classics in 1980 introduced them to new readers.

Rejecting the enchantment of religion

According to Henry Thoreau most people live lives of quiet desperation. Stevie Smith was not quiet in this sense: she made her desperation known in her poetry. But she did so in a way which was jaunty, or, in old-fashioned terms, chipper. In one of her poems, 'Away, Melancholy', with its theme of 'Away with it, let it go', she writes of everything in nature carrying on in its own way, including man with his 'hey ho melancholy'.[1]

She lived just such a life, a life of jaunty desperation, and all her poems have this unique, unforgettable tone. This tone is further reinforced by the line drawings she used to illustrate them, described by Janet Montefiore as reminiscent of Edward Lear and James Thurber. The mood is well caught in her best-known poem in which onlookers on a beach see an arm above the water cheerfully waving, a man enjoying himself as he splashes about. But he's drowning, and always has been too far out all his life 'not waving but drowning'.[2]

This drowning was very much a reality for Stevie Smith. She said she first thought of suicide early in life but paradoxically the thought empowered her: 'I actually thought of suicide for the first time when I was eight. The thought cheered me up wonderfully and quite saved my life. For if one can remove oneself at any time from the world, why particularly now?'[3]

At the age of three Stevie Smith moved with her mother and sister to Palmers Green, already a proud new outer London suburb. Her father had left home and in due course her mother's sister came to live with them. This aunt, nicknamed 'The Lion', was the major influence on Stevie's life. The Lion's independence of mind and sharp, quirky feminism became very much part of Stevie herself. They lived at 1 Avondale Road, which now has a plaque to Stevie, and it was here she lived all her life, 'a house of female habitation' occupied by brave women who did not let fear enter the door.[4]

Her poem 'Avondale' describes the birds swooping and calling and the children playing in the street, all of which she calls 'a very pleasant sight'. But there were a number of unpleasant features of this life. One was her being away ill with tuberculosis in a sanatorium for three years. Another were her thoughts of suicide, as mentioned, and then there was the death of her mother when Stevie was 16. Outwardly it was a very uneventful life. After school locally, Stevie Smith worked as a typist in a publishers for 30 years until she had a breakdown, made a suicide attempt and retired with a very modest pension. At the same time, however, her creative side was active, as expressed in the three novels she published in early life. She had tried to get some poems published in the 1930s but was not successful. However, as mentioned in the introduction, she found unexpected fame with her poetry in the 1960s.

The family at number 1 Avondale Road was a churchgoing one and Stevie loved it. As she wrote, 'I was brought up in a household where there was great love and a great faith in the Christian religion according to the tenets of the Church of England. I enjoyed my religion. I enjoyed the church services.'[5]

She was a devout High Anglican and the pull of what she experienced as a child and a young woman never left her, but haunted her all her life. Although she wrote a poem with the refrain about religion 'Blow it away, have done with it', she could never quite blow it away or have done with it.[6] Even as a child, however, she had worries about the doctrine of hell and whether it could be reconciled with a God of love.

Her thoughts about religion, particularly her negative thoughts, became fully articulate in the late 1950s. This was in one way rather surprising. It was a time in which churches benefited from the new mood of seriousness brought on by the Second World War. In Cambridge, for example, undergraduates in their hundreds came to dialogues in the University Church, where the eloquent Mervyn Stockwood, later Bishop of Southwark, was vicar. Furthermore there were a number of literary figures who were serious Anglicans; not only T. S. Eliot and W. H. Auden but Dorothy Sayers and Rose Macaulay among others. Some of them met regularly at St Anne's in Soho together with some literary-minded clergymen. Stevie might well have found herself at home as a member of that group. In fact, she rather reacted against this trend. She wrote scornfully of 'the hurrying back to religion' in the post-war world, and attributed religious conversion to 'a degeneracy of the nerves'.[7]

The first major outing of her thoughts on religion was in November 1957 to the Cambridge Humanists, in which she spoke of 'The Necessity of Not Believing'.[8] This lecture with various additions and changes was delivered elsewhere, including to the group of Anglican literary figures gathered round St Anne's, Soho, where it had the rather milder title of 'Some Impediments to Christian Commitment'.[9] She tried to get it broadcast but there was no success with the BBC for this or her other thoughts on Christianity. Perhaps it was thought they were not portentous enough for the Third Programme while being too serious for the Home Service.

The word 'Necessity' is important. For Stevie Smith it was not so much a question of finding certain tenets of the faith unbelievable as finding them immoral. It was a *moral* necessity to reject them. The Christian Church has never taken this kind of objection seriously enough, always assuming blandly that though it may be mistaken it occupied the high moral ground. Stevie Smith made it quite clear that it did not. Although people liked to think of her as whimsical, she was deeply serious on this subject with an integrity that made her quite fierce on occasions.

Her earliest objection remained her strongest one, the doctrine of hell. She would not be put off by any argument that this was simply a development of the later Church. She finds it located in the teaching of Jesus himself. And although she recognized that the Anglican Church no longer preached hellfire, she had fun finding teaching about hell in pamphlets produced by the Catholic Truth Society. Christian apologists at the time put forward various counter-arguments but she was not convinced.[10]

If hell is thought of in terms of God's sentencing people to everlasting torment, then of course it must be rejected on moral grounds. Stevie Smith faced up to the fact that, in the New Testament, Jesus taught the reality of hell but she still rejected it as immoral. But the fact is that we create our own hell, here or hereafter. To turn in on oneself in bitterness and resentment in an environment of unutterable love is to create hell in the midst of heaven. That hell will last as long as that self-enclosed carapace remains in place. What Christians can believe, in the words of William Golding's *Pincher Martin*, referred to in Chapter 9, is that there is a 'compassion that is timeless and without mercy', which plays on our defences and seeks to wear them away. A character in one of Beckett's plays refers to 'the other hell', for we know hell here too. As mentioned in the chapter on his conversion, T. S. Eliot much liked and admired the American scholar Paul Elmer More. But he was deeply shocked that More did not believe in hell. 'Is your God Santa Claus?' he asked, and continued, '"to be damned for the glory of God" is sense not paradox.'[11] As he put it:

The man who disbelieves in any future life whatever is also a believer in hell. For in this life one makes, now and then, important decisions or at least allows circumstances to decide, and some of these decisions are such as have consequences for the rest of our mortal life. Some people find themselves consequently in circumstances such that the whole of their mortal life *must* be a torment to them. And if there is no future life then Hell is, for such people, here and now. And I can see nothing worse in a Hell which endures to eternity and a Hell which endures until mere annihilation, the mere stretch of endless time, which is the only way in which we can ordinarily apprehend 'immortal life', seems to me to make no difference. People go to hell, I take it, because they choose to; they cannot get out because they cannot change themselves.[12]

This sophisticated answer, clearly coming out of Eliot's own hellish first marriage, may be compelling, but Stevie Smith's objections still have to be faced seriously. When a child hears stories from the Hebrew Scriptures about God's punishing people, and Jesus' teaching that sinners are to be subject to everlasting fire, it is, and ought to be, a shock to the moral sensitivity of anyone growing up in a modern liberal society. There are a number of things that can be said, and were said, to Stevie Smith by people who faced the question and did not lose their faith. This does not deny the importance of honestly addressing the question or recognizing the integrity of someone like Stevie Smith for whom hell proved a fatal stumbling block.

The other aspect of Christianity that played on the mind of Stevie Smith was the Inquisition and other cruelties perpetrated by the Catholic Church. This again has to be faced up to. We can ask whether such cruelty would not also have been there if the ruling ideology had been political rather than religious. But still the question presses, not least in the modern world, in which there are still some twisted forms of religion which are perversely cruel. The fact is that no religious institution is exempt from the sin which besets human life, and when religions get distorted the harm they inflict can be even more devastating than a political ideology that has gone wrong. In both cases, the key factor is power. That is why although in modern liberal democracies there are still some Christian churches that have close links with the state, they have wisely been stripped of any real power.

A third objection raised by Stevie Smith was what is termed a 'penal substitutionary' view of the atonement, in which, to put it crudely, human beings are thought of as deserving eternal punishment but God's son dies in our place to give us the gift of eternal life. Many Christians would argue that that is not how the New Testament understands the meaning of Christ's death, and we have only to instance the parable of the prodigal son in which forgiveness is offered without any mention of a death because of sin. It is also to stretch legitimate imagery, which is always metaphorical, beyond what it was meant to go. Nevertheless it remains true that a good number of Christian groups do preach and teach an oversimplified view of the death of Christ, which does not do justice to the deeper more nuanced understanding in the Bible, and which can strike others as morally intolerable. However, for many this view is the heart of the faith. So again, Stevie Smith was right to face up to it, even if she was not able to think her way through it.

These passionate moral objections, and people noted how passionately she held them, were held in her mind by an equally strong tug, as she called it, to the beauties of the faith. In one poem, she recognizes that she rages against the faith because of Jesus' words about people being sent into everlasting torment, while at the same time knowing that she was much drawn to his character and his teaching on love. In one poem, which likens God to someone frowning on us and sacrificing his son for us she writes that he does not want us to love him above everything else; he only wants us to 'hear him sing'.[13]

So to the end of her life Stevie Smith was riven in two. She continued to be 'enchanted', to use another of her favourite words, by the Christian faith in which she had been brought up, but saw the moral necessity of rejecting it. She said, 'How can one's heart *not* go out to the idea that a God of absolute love is in charge of the universe?'[14] She knew there was a wonderful richness and excitement in the faith, and without it there was a terrible loneliness and loss. But it had to be rejected. At once attracted and repelled, she wrote that Christianity was a 'mixture of sweetness and cruelty' but it was necessary to reject the sweetness because she wore 'a smoky dress out of hell fires'.[15]

Frances Spalding has written that, in spite of her unbelief, 'Stevie is a religious poet, not only because she deals with the kind of doubt that is part of religious experience but also because religious themes and images recur.'[16]

More strongly than that, I would suggest she is a religious poet first of all because she feels the enormous attraction of the Christian faith as much as any orthodox believer. She knows its pull, its draw, its enchantment. She is a modern religious poet because she brings moral arguments to bear on its teaching and finds some of it wanting. As such she stands in the tradition of Dostoevsky, albeit with a somewhat different moral critique. Whereas his objection was to the whole idea of a Creator who could bring into being a world of so much cruelty, her objections focus on what she judged to be cruel aspects of the teaching of the Church.

When Stevie Smith gave up her office job, she eked out her pension with reviewing. Then, when her poetry gained her a reputation, she reviewed many books on religious subjects, which gave her an opportunity to make her views on a range of religious themes more widely known. She was also a good letter writer, and all her writing is distinguished by firm views at once sharp and witty. Like her Aunt Lion she was no respecter of persons. She appeared on The Brains Trust on several occasions and said of her well-known fellow panellists, such as A. J. Ayer and Marghanita Laski, 'How [they] *do go on*.' She was asked to write a piece on Eliot's *Murder in the Cathedral*, and while she much admired his writing she found the strong Christian theme 'abominable'.

She was on good terms with a number of clergy and she particularly valued her visits to the Benedictines at Buckfast. These friendships took lovely form in a poem she wrote with two parts to it, one from an agnostic to his religious friend and the other from a religious man to his agnostic friend. Both end with the identical refrain

> And yet he is more gracious than I,
> He has such a gracious personality.[17]

Sadly, such an approach in argument, this willingness to eschew the moral high ground, particularly religious argument, is all too rare. If it was more prevalent, while fierce differences would remain they would be drained of their bitterness. Not surprisingly a number of religious figures were drawn to Stevie, recognizing in her a conflict within themselves. Stevie Smith's friend Father Gerard Irvine likened her to Jacob, 'who would not let God go for the whole long night of life'.[18] And Thomas Merton, the American Trappist monk, one of the most perceptive and best-known writers on religion at the time, admitted he was crazy about Stevie Smith's poems and found in them 'a lot of true religion'.[19]

One of Stevie Smith's worries was how people would develop moral virtues if they were not shaped by the kind of Christian upbringing she herself had experienced. *The Guardian* commissioned her to write a poem for Whitsun, the feast of the Holy Spirit. It aroused a great deal of interest, with many letters in response of both praise and disagreement. It was a long poem called 'How Do You See?', in which she rehearses all her moral objections to the Christian faith as well as her frustration that the Church gives no satisfactory answer to so many questions. It ends on a real note of anguish that if we do not teach children to be good, without the enchantment of fairy stories pretending to be true (by which she meant Christianity), 'we shall kill everybody'.[20]

That challenge remains: how to teach people to be good without enchantment. Earlier she had ended a review in which she castigated the penal substitutionary view of the atonement with the words 'Will people always hanker after religion, must they always have it, will they never for conscience's sake, put it away, be good for goodness' sake, not God's?'[21]

Stevie Smith's poems, for all their artful cheeriness, are seriously felt, but one poem in particular seems to come from an especially deep and mysterious place. She begins:

> Poor human race that must
> Feed on pain, or choose another dish
> And hunger worse.

She goes on to say that we have to drink the cup of pain or go thirsty for ever and we have to eat all the dish we have been given:

> I am thy friend. I wish
> You to sup full of the dish
> I gave you and the drink,
> And so to fatness come more than you think
> In health of opened heart and know peace.

Grief spake these words to me in a dream. I thought
He spoke no more than grace allowed
And no less than truth.[22]

All Stevie Smith's poems are personal, but this seems especially revealing, for it clearly comes out of the long pain of her life. The pain of doing a humdrum job as secretary when her talents fitted her for something more exacting. The pain of working in an office run by men whom she did not think much of; indeed of living in a world, before women's rights were recognized, which was dominated by men; the pain of trying to get her work noticed in what she thought of as the ramshackle self-interested world of publishing. Working for a time for a publisher she wrote to a friend:

> Generally they are awfully nice . . . all the same these middle-brows, with their regrettable-deplorable-bounce and energy are England's bane, the walking illustration of that blood-curdling truth – that the Better is the Enemy of the Good.[23]

In the poem this pain brings to her mind the scene of Christ in the Garden of Gethsemane when he prays that the cup of suffering be taken from him. A friend comes to her in a dream and tells her she has to take the cup and drink it all up. But this will lead to the fatness of a heart enlarged by sympathy. She ends by admitting the truth of this message.

It is a poem in which we feel she has worked something through at a very deep level. It was that opened heart which spoke to so many, a heart at once attracted and repelled by religion, enchanted by its beauty but appalled by some of its teaching. It is a poem which deserves to be better known.

Stevie Smith's importance as a religious poet lies in her unshaded attitude of ambivalence towards religion. For her it was both a strong yes and an equally strong no. People who have faith feel with her the strong sense of attraction towards it and are puzzled that so many fail to experience this pull. They want to say, 'All right, Christianity may be untrue and there are indeed some telling moral objections to some aspects of it, but at least recognize that this is the most wonderful story in the world, and if it was true it would transform the way you see life.' As she put it, 'How can one's heart *not* go out to the idea that a God of absolute love is in charge of the universe, and that in the end All will be well?'[24] Those without faith often share the objections but are clearly not held by this enchantment, as Stevie was.

7

Samuel Beckett
Secular mystic

Introduction

Samuel Beckett (1906–89) was brought up in the Dublin suburb of
Foxrock and studied French, Italian and English at Trinity College Dublin.
He went to teach at the École Normale Supérieure and while in Paris met
James Joyce, who had a powerful impact on him. He assisted Joyce with
the novel he was working on. After a short period of lecturing at Trinity
College Dublin, he returned to Paris and during the Second World War
joined the French Resistance, nearly being caught by the Gestapo on a
number of occasions. He was decorated for these endeavours but never
talked about them. Up to this point he had written novels and poetry in
a modernist style and though some were published he was not successful
commercially. After 1947, he wrote most of his work in French, translating
it later into English. His life changed dramatically with the first perform-
ances of *Waiting for Godot* in 1955, which eventually became a huge
critical and popular success. He continued to write plays but in an increasingly minimalist manner. Regarded as one of the last of the modernists
and a founder of the 'theatre of the absurd' he received the Nobel Prize for
Literature in 1969, characteristically giving away all the prize money. He
was an intensely private man of fierce artistic integrity.

Nothing but pain

Beckett's mother was a devout Protestant churchwoman, and he was
brought up in her faith. He went to church on Sundays and was taught to
say his prayers.[1] She was a strong woman with whom he had a conflicted
relationship of love, resistance and guilt and this is a significant factor in
his attitude to religion. It was when he was a teenager that Beckett lost
his faith. This was partly because of the terrible suffering he saw in parts
of Dublin and partly because of an unsatisfactory theodicy he heard
from a local clergyman. This rejection of God on the grounds of human

anguish was further reinforced when his brother, a devout Christian, died after much suffering. Acute sensitivity to the agony of life was to be the predominant feature of all his writing. 'PAIN PAIN PAIN' he wrote on a poster at the time, which he pinned to a wall.[2]

Although Beckett could not accept that there was a God of love behind the universe, his writing is steeped in Christian imagery, and God makes his presence felt by not being there. There is an emptiness, an absence which would not have been the case if God had existed. This means that Beckett deals with some of the themes usually addressed by religion but in a way which subverts a Christian understanding of them. An obvious one is the brevity of life.

At a burial, when the body is ready at the graveside, a priest using the 1662 Prayer Book says, 'Man that is born of woman has but a short time to live, and is full of misery.' This view of life underlies every line Beckett writes. One of his plays is called *Breath*.[3] These are the stage directions:

CURTAIN
1. Faint light on stage littered with miscellaneous rubbish. Hold about five seconds.
2. Faint brief cry and immediately inspiration and slow increase of light together reaching maximum together in about ten seconds. Silence and hold about five seconds.
3. Expiration and slow decrease of light together reaching minimum together (light as in 1) in about ten seconds and immediately cry as before. Silence and hold about five seconds.

This play, which lasts 35 seconds, and which Beckett has described as 'a farce in five acts', hardly needs a commentary. But, as Ruby Cohn has written, it contains Beckett's staples: 'symmetry, repetition, inversion, the wresting of sound from silence, a flicker of light against the dark, dying, but no definable death.'[4]

A sense of the brevity of life, which receives such simple but startling treatment in *Breath*, permeates every play. In *Waiting for Godot*, Pozzo says, 'They give birth astride of a grave, the light gleams an instant, then it's night once more,'[5] and shortly afterwards Vladimir takes up the image 'Astride of a grave and a difficult birth. Down in the hole, lingeringly, the grave-digger puts on the forceps. We have time to grow old. The air is full of our cries.'[6]

We are born astride the grave, and during the brief flicker of conscious-ness which we call our life, the darkness of death shrouds us. *Endgame* takes place in a small room at the edge of the world. All life has gone, or nearly gone. Some have taken the stage set to be a nuclear shelter. It isn't, but there is a sense of living, or rather dying, through the last minutes of time. Two of the characters on stage, Nagg and Nell, are toothless old folk stuffed into dustbins. During the course of the play one, or perhaps both of them, dies. But it makes no difference: everyone is dying anyway. The play begins with Clov saying tonelessly, 'Finished, it's finished, nearly finished, it must be nearly finished.' In due course, Hamm responds, 'Me – (he yawns) – to play.'[7] It is the last few moves of a game. Towards the end Clov hits Hamm with a dog and Hamm says, 'If you must hit me, hit me with the axe. (pause) Or with the gaff, hit me with the gaff.' Clov responds imploringly, 'Let's stop playing!' 'Never,' says Hamm, and, after a pause, 'Put me in my coffin.' 'There are no more coffins,' says Clov. 'Then let it end,' replies Hamm.[8] In Christian history, the preacher has tried to make people face up to the shortness of life and the inevitability of death, in order to summon them to their responsibilities before the God who will meet them after death to reward them according to their deeds. 'The end is nigh,' say the placards. 'Prepare to meet thy God.' 'Live each day as if thy last,' says the hymn. But the nearness of death in Beckett's plays is not something that people have to be reminded of. They are fully aware of the fact. Nor is it something they want to stave off. Death is near but still too far away; soon, but it cannot come too soon ('It must be nearly finished,' says Clov).

Meanwhile there is the problem of getting through until death does come. In Beckett's world, our main device for getting through until the end comes is talking. In *Waiting for Godot*, Vladimir and Estragon toss remarks back and forth like the circus clowns they in some ways resemble. At one point they have a rapid-fire dialogue, with each sentence only six words or fewer. Then they run out of conversation and a long silence ensues. 'Say something,' says Vladimir; 'I'm trying,' replies Estragon, but there is another long silence. 'Say anything at all,' says Vladimir in anguish. 'What do we do now?' responds Estragon; and so it goes on, in little bursts of three or four sentences followed by silence. They then get going for a couple of pages, and after another silence Estragon remarks, 'That wasn't such a bad little canter.' 'Yes,' says Vladimir, 'but now we'll have to find something else.'[9] And so it continues.

In *Happy Days*, the curtain goes up, revealing Winnie in a heap of sand up to her waist and lit with a hellish light. In the second act, the sand reaches her neck. Winnie spends the whole play talking and occupying herself with the objects of her handbag, which she lays out around her. Behind her, in a trench, for the most part unseen and silent, is her husband Willie:

Is not that so, Willie, that even words fail, at times? (Pause. Back front) What is one to do, then, until they come again? Brush and comb the hair if it has not been done. Or if there is some doubt, trim the nails if they are in need of trimming. These things tide one over. (Pause) That is what I mean.[10]

The play opens with the words 'Another heavenly day' and Winnie saying her prayers 'For Jesus Christ's sake Amen.' Again she prays, 'World without end. Amen,' and continues, 'Begin, Winnie.' (Pause) 'Begin your day, Winnie.' And so, with the aid of encouraging clichés, prayers, snatches from hymns and the objects from her handbag, Winnie tries bravely to get through:

> Ah well – can't complain – no, no – mustn't complain – so much to be thankful for – no pain – hardly any – wonderful thing that – nothing like it – slight headache sometimes – ah yes – occasional mild migraine – it comes – then goes – ah yes – many mercies – great mercies – prayers, perhaps not for naught – first thing – last thing.[11]

One way in which characters get through is by telling their story, spinning a tale which illuminates their own situation and reveals, in an oblique way, what they feel about it. 'What now? (Pause) What now, Willie? (Long pause) There is my story, of course, when all else fails.' And so she begins to tell her story about a girl called Mildred who had a doll, and who came downstairs one night. In telling the story, she breaks off for a while to look at Willie, who she suspects may be crying out. 'I do of course hear cries. (Pause. With finality) No no, my head was always full of cries (Pause) Faint confused cries.'[12] Then she talks about her song, which she sings every day to help her keep her spirits up, before returning to her story:

> Suddenly a mouse ran up her little thigh, and Mildred, dropping Dolly in her fright, began to scream. (Winnie gives a sudden piercing scream) – and screamed and screamed (Winnie screams twice) – screamed and screamed and screamed and screamed till all came running, in their night attire, papa, mamma, Bibby and . . . old Annie, to see what was the matter . . . (pause) . . . what on earth could possibly be the matter?[13]

The cries are there all the time. So is the hostility: hostility to the universe that causes such pain. In *Endgame*, Nagg tells a story about a man who asks his tailor to make some trousers. Some days later he comes back and finds that the tailor has made a mess of the seat. The man is understanding and returns in due course to find that the tailor has made a mess of the crotch. Again, he is understanding and comes back ten days later to find that the tailor has made a mess of the fly. And so it goes on. At last in exasperation the man says:

There are limits. In six days, do you hear me, six days, God made the world. Yes, Sir, no less, Sir, the WORLD! And you are not bloody well capable of making me a pair of trousers in three months!' (Tailor's voice, scandalised) 'But, my dear Sir, look! (disdainful gesture, disgustedly) – at the world – (pause) – and look – (loving gesture, proudly) – at my TROUSERS!'14

This brilliant story, though seriously meant, is genuinely funny and light-hearted in its tone. *Endgame* also has another story which is much grimmer and in which the merciless element in life is laid bare in a far harsher way without the humour.

Religious imagery, and references to religion, suddenly appear in much of Beckett's work. At the beginning of *Waiting for Godot*, for example, the two tramps suddenly turn to the Gospels. Vladimir says, 'Two thieves, crucified at the same time as our Saviour. One.' But he is interrupted by Estragon, 'Our what?' 'Our Saviour. Two thieves, one is supposed to have been saved and the other . . . damned.'

'Saved from what?' says Estragon. 'Hell,' answers Vladimir,15 who continues to puzzle about the fact that only one of the four Gospels reports the story. It matters to him that it is true, that one of the thieves was saved. Their life is a confused, hellish waiting for they know not what, but something that might save them. Meanwhile they suffer. 'But you can't go barefoot!' blurts out Vladimir. 'Christ did,' responds Estragon. He receives the reply, 'Christ! What's Christ got to do with it? You're not going to compare yourself to Christ!' 'All my life I've compared myself to him,' says Estragon. 'But where he lived it was warm, it was dry!' says Vladimir. 'Yes and they crucified quick,' responds his companion.16 Life is a waiting, a waiting for someone to come and put things right; but that person does not seem to come. We are in a state from which we need saving, but there does not seem to be a saviour. We suffer and it's not over. Religious imagery is used to heighten the aspects of our human situation for which religion has traditionally provided a solution. But no solution is offered. Indeed the possibility of a solution looks unlikely. So the religious references, which arouse expectation, in fact underline our predicament and intensify the awareness of our need. Beckett repeatedly had to deny that it was God they were waiting for, but admitted that it was probably because of this overinterpretation that the play was such a success. He said he did not know what they were waiting for, nor did the characters in the play. He was, however, deeply moved when a group of prisoners put on a performance.17

In *Not I*, all the audience sees is a luminous mouth in the middle of a darkened stage and a shadowy figure in the corner who hardly moves. The mouth talks very rapidly, in staccato fashion. The effect is extraordinarily powerful. After ten minutes, my wife and I had to look away and I wonder if we would have been able to last for more than the 20-minute length of the play. The effect is difficult to describe – words like panic, tension, terror, come to mind. The mind, which is projecting itself through this mouth, could be losing consciousness as a result of drugs, or because the person is dying. On the other hand, it could be coming back into consciousness. Certainly it is coming back into the non-stop flow of words. The mouth tells her story. Abandoned by both mother and father, she was brought up in an orphanage. Nothing of note happened until coming up to 70, the traditional allotted span, when on an early April morning all went out. She began to think she had died. The script says:

> for her first thought was . . . oh, long after . . . sudden flash . . . brought up as she had been to believe . . . with other waifs . . . in a merciful. . . (brief laugh) . . . God . . . (good laugh) . . . first thought was . . . oh, long after . . . sudden flash . . . she was being punished . . . for her sins.[18]

Then a few lines further on the same reference to what she had been taught as a child is repeated with the same laughs. A few pages later there is this dialogue, which again is repeated:

> Seventy?
> . . . Good God! . . . On and on to be seventy . . . something she didn't know herself . . . wouldn't know if she heard . . . then forgiven . . . God is love . . . tender mercies . . . new every morning . . .

Out of the mouth pours a torrent of tight words. The text refers to the experience of losing and regaining consciousness; and what happened on that April morning is being relived. If it is an experience of dying it is also an experience of coming to consciousness. And all the suffering of going impregnates the experience of coming. The title is *Not I*, and the mouth is desperately trying to confine the stream of consciousness to talk about itself only in the third person, to avoid being 'I'. The terror reveals the suffering, not emphasized but implied in almost every line:

> Dusk . . . sitting staring at her hand . . . there in her lap . . . palm upward . . . suddenly saw it wet . . . the pain . . . tears presumably . . . hers presumably . . . no-one else for miles . . . no sound . . . just the tears . . . sat and watched them dry . . . all over in a second.

Also on the stage there is a helpless figure, who moves slightly three times. The stage direction reads:

Movement; this consists in a simple sideways raising of arms from sides and their falling back, in a gesture of helpless compassion. It lessens with each recurrence till scarcely perceptible at third. There is just enough pause to contain it as MOUTH recovers from vehement refusal to relinquish third person.

Traditionally, dying is a time when the soul comes in judgement before God. But in *Not I* this may also be an experience of being born, or at least of coming to self-consciousness. In any case, it is an experience which is resisted, in which Mouth suffers and, as a result of which the reference to a merciful God brings forth a bitter laugh. The unknown hearer makes gestures of helpless compassion. *Not I*, like all Beckett plays, is many-layered, and it resists easy summary. But there is no doubting the centrality and subversion of religious imagery and ideas.

In Beckett's play entitled *Play*, three characters sit in urns. A spotlight focuses on each face in turn and is the signal for the person to speak. They are two women, and a man who has been involved with both of them. They each rehearse the story of what has happened to them from their own partial point of view, a sentence or two at a time, when the spot switches to the next. It could be some kind of judgement. Certainly they are conscious of going through something, of being answerable. 'Is it that I do not tell the truth? Is that it? That someday somehow I may tell the truth at last and then no more light at last for the truth?'[19] But the eye that observes them is, as they gradually realize, mindless – 'Mere eye. No mind. Opening and shutting on me,' says the man. 'Am I as much . . . am I as much as . . . being seen?'[20] In *Not I*, Mouth had a sense of being judged, of being answerable. This theme here is more explicit; of being answerable but with no one apparently to be answerable to. The spotlight is not the light of Christ but the flicker of consciousness with its baffled suffering sense of being answerable to someone or something. Although the characters have died and are in urns, and it seems like Sheol or purgatory, Beckett is not giving us his idea of what happens after death, any more than Sartre was in *Huis Clos*, in which the characters meet supposedly after death in a bare room. We have here something related to the life we know now; and this life is not just one that the characters would like to end; it is one they wish had never been:

> Yes, peace, one assumed, all out, all the pain, all as if . . . never been . . . no sense in this, oh I know . . . nonetheless one assumed peace . . . I mean . . . not merely all over, but as if it . . . never been . . .[21]

This appears to have been Beckett's own position when, for example he regrets God having a soft spot for Noah.[22]

The underlying assumption of all Beckett's plays can be brought out by two contrasting attitudes to existence. There are those that believe that at all times and in all circumstances life is a blessed gift. For Beckett, like the narrator in *The Unnamable*, 'Life is a punishment for having been born.'[23] In *Endgame*, Hamm puts his hand against the wall of this enclosed room and says, 'Old wall! Beyond is the . . . other hell.'[24] But what about the traditional consolations of life, available to all, believer and non-believer alike, human love and art? The characters in Beckett's plays need one another. Estragon says to Vladimir, 'Don't touch me! Don't question me! Don't speak to me! Stay with me!'[25] Winnie in *Happy Days* needs Willie, even though he utters only one grunt in the whole play. Being with another person is marginally less hellish than being on one's own. But these relationships are characterized by patterns of tormenting and being tormented. Among the belongings in Winnie's handbag in *Happy Days* is a revolver. As the poet Browning, with his mixture of doubt and religious comfort, was there for Victorians to quote, so is Winnie's Browning revolver. She brings it out and says, 'You'd think the weight of this thing would bring it down among the last rounds. But no, it doesn't. Ever uppermost, like Browning.'[26] At the end of the play Willie crawls out of his trench and up the heap of sand. He reaches out his arm to Winnie and they both look at each other. The revolver is on the sand between them. In *Not I*, Mouth tells the story of her conception and start in life: 'Parents unknown . . . unheard of . . . he having similarly . . . eight months later . . . almost to the tick . . . so no love . . . spared that . . . no love such as normally vented on the . . . speechless infant.'[27]

What about art? Beckett's characters tell stories which illuminate their situation. Their stories are one of the devices which keep them going. When all else fails, there is still their story to tell. Is that Beckett's view of art, of his own art? He has said that 'Every word is an unnecessary stain on silence' but also 'I couldn't have done it otherwise. Gone on, I mean, I could not have gone on through the awful wretched mess of life without having left a stain upon the silence.'[28] 'A stain upon the silence.' No more significance than that? But both love and art hint at more. In *Krapp's Last Tape*, a man on his sixtieth birthday is speaking into a recording machine and playing back old tapes. Every year he has recorded himself a birthday message, a review of how he has got on in the year, and now he is commenting on his previous views of himself. It is an ingenious device. Once again the religious themes are present: the three-score-years-and-ten nearly over; the review of the life; twice Krapp sings words from a hymn, 'Now the day is over, night is drawing nigh, shadows of the evening steal across the sky. The play focuses on the replay of what Krapp recorded on his thirty-ninth birthday, and on his present attitude to what he was then. In that year, he exults for what he calls 'a moment of vision, a miracle . . . for the fire that set it alight'. It was, he says, 'clear to me at last that the dark I have always struggled to keep under is in reality my most . . ', then he switches off impatiently and winds the tape forward. His voice on the tape speaks of a relationship with a girl: he is lying with her in a punt and they decide they cannot go on: 'He lay there without moving. But under us all moved, and moved us, gently, up and down, and from side to side.'[29] Krapp reviewing his life is a mixture of savagery and regret for this crucial year. It contained a beautiful moment of love. Times of happiness in Beckett's plays are rare. The occasional lyrical moment is quickly snuffed in the all-engulfing darkness. Love is deliberately put aside for the pursuit of the artistic vision, a vision which, on the approach of death, he feels has not been fulfilled. At the end of the tape he stands motionless and silent.

This moment in the play is a crucial one for understanding the nature of Beckett's art. This is not just the memory of a moment of love, tender though that is, but the reference to a moment of vision, a miracle. It was 'clear to me at last that the dark I have always struggled to keep under is in reality my most . . .' Although the romantic setting of the play is different from when Beckett did in fact have a personal moment of revelation, the revelation that came to him during a time of depression in Dublin, the insight was indeed that the dark, his failure, his inability to say what he wanted, was in fact what he had to write about.[30] This was the crucial turning point in his career as a writer. In 1956, he wrote to say that his little world was a closed one, with no outside to it. 'Aesthetically the adventure is that of the failed form 'no achieved statement of the inability to be'.[31] This helps to make sense of his statement 'Fail again, fail better'.[32] There is, however, a strange paradox here, for this method of drawing on failure, on his inability to say what he wanted, in the end brought him huge international success. Even then, however, failure was the theme of his letters, which are studded with a savage dismissal of his work and his inability to write anything. He corresponded, too, about his declining health, which had never been good.[33] This was also his strategy for living. When the estranged husband of his friend Barbara Bray died, Beckett wrote to her a letter of deep feeling in which he said:

> Somewhere at the heart of the gales of grief (and of love too, I've been told) already they have blown themselves out. I was always grateful for that humiliating consciousness and it was always there I huddled, in the innermost place of human frailty and lowliness.[34]

Beckett knew much suffering in his own life as well as being acutely sensitive to the suffering of others. He had a powerful mother from whose emotional clutches he took a long time escaping. He went through long periods of depression. It was many years before he achieved any degree of success. When his mother was dying, this is how Deirdre Bair describes the effect on him:

His days passed in an exhausting, crushing depression brought on by long hours at her bedside. His nights were spent walking and talking with Geoffrey Thompson, to whom he complained bitterly of the so-called God who would permit such suffering.[35]

This theme, the suffering of humanity, permeates all the plays. 'There's something dripping in my head,' says Hamm in *Endgame*, 'a heart, a heart in my head.'[36] And there are bitter laughs at the thought of a loving God in *Not 1* and elsewhere. Krapp's tape reviewing his life has the line 'Sneers at what he calls his youth and thanks God it's over. (Pause). False ring there. (Pause). Shadows of the opus . . . magnum closing with a – (brief laugh) – yelp to Providence.'[37] And the stage direction reads, 'Prolonged laugh in which Krapp joins.'

Beckett uses everyday language: (almost the whole of *Happy Days*, for example, is made up of clichés) which Beckett orders into an object of great beauty. He does this with such accuracy that they precisely convey the emotion of an experience. This beauty is related to the intensity and sensitivity with which Beckett himself experiences life. The effect on others can be overwhelming. Billie Whitelaw, who gave the first, astonishing performance of Mouth in *Not I*, has said, '*Not I* came through the letter-box. I opened it, read it and burst into tears, floods of tears. It had a tremendous emotional impact upon me.'[38] Beckett thought that an authentic work of art, in any form was a prayer.[39] George Devine wrote of Beckett, 'This man seemed to have lived and suffered so that l could see, and he was generous enough to pass it on to me.'[40]

There is a profound *challenge* to Christian faith in Beckett. But is there any *support* for it? First, despite the antagonism shown to God, or at least the idea of a merciful God, the question of God is never quite closed. It is a measure of Beckett's genius that you cannot say for certain, on the basis of his plays alone, that he is an atheist. Indeed he refused to be pinned down on the question. When he had to appear in court in 1937 in connection with a libel trial, he was asked whether he was a Christian, a Jew or an atheist and he replied 'None of the three.'[41] In the plays, there are many layers of meaning. 'The meaning', if there is such a thing, cannot be pinned down. If you think you understand a play, you can go back to it and discover you have misunderstood it; that another meaning suggests itself. It is this continuously suggestive power which the plays have that makes the question of God not finally closed. There is mystery in them, as in life itself, so that every interpretation opens out into the possibility of another somewhat different one. Second, there is the strange paradox that, despite everything, Beckett's characters do not commit suicide. Camus said that the great problem in life is suicide – and it is indicative of something that most people do not in fact kill themselves. Beckett's characters are tempted to do so. Vladimir and Estragon in *Waiting for Godot* talk about hanging themselves from the tree, but get in a muddle about who should go first. Winnie in *Happy Days* has her Browning revolver always handy: 'You remember Brownie, Willie, I can see him (pause) Brownie is there, Willie, beside me.'[42] In *Endgame*, Hamm says, 'It's the end of the day like any other day, isn't it, Clov?' 'Looks like it,' replies Clov. 'What's happening, what's happening?' asks Hamm, and Clov answers, 'Something is taking its course.' 'All right, be off . . . I thought I told you to be off', says Hamm, and Clov replies, 'I'm trying. Ever since I was whelped.'[43] The going-off refers to Clov's leaving Hamm, but there is also the hint of leaving the life which they both regard as hell. Yet they allow matters to take their course. Why *should* they struggle on? No reason is given. Beckett regarded suicide as an unacceptable kind of surrender. It belonged to the fundamental integrity of his being, partly derived from his Protestant upbringing, to soldier stoically on to the end. The end of one of his novels puts the matter vividly: 'Where I am, I don't know, I'll never know, in the silence you don't know, you must go on, I can't go on, I'll go on.'[44] This choosing to go on seems more than an animal will to survive. It is as though there is something big at stake.

Third, there is, despite the harshness, hardness and grotesque nature of many of the scenes and of some of the dialogue, a deep underlying compassion. A helpless compassion, as indicated in the gesture of the shadowy figure in *Not I*. But it is still compassion. Winnie, in *Happy Days*, is not a figure of fun. As a sense of horror grows in the audience at her plight, the mortality we all share, and our desperate attempts to keep going with a brave front, the pathos is intense. You don't admire Winnie, but neither is she the product of cynicism. 'Pity' is too weak a word for her predicament (also ours), but something akin to it is called forth by her struggle to keep going.

Finally, perhaps, Beckett's art itself is a sign of hope – the fact that out of all that he has experienced himself and been sensitive to in others, he has produced works of art which will undoubtedly endure. Once, Harold Pinter suggested to Beckett that his writing was a constantly courageous attempt to impose order and form upon the wretched mess mankind has made of the world. 'If you insist on finding form, I'll describe it for you,' Beckett replied. 'I was in hospital once. There was a man in another ward, dying of throat cancer. In the silence I could hear his screams continually. That's the only kind of form my work has.'[45] Nevertheless the form of Beckett's work, the dense poetic texture, the ordering of experience that he thinks of as absurd, is what makes it art.

Some words that Beckett used about his old master Joyce have often been used about Beckett himself: 'Here form is content, content *is* form.'[46] Literally speaking, this remark is not true either as a generalization or about Beckett. All art has some content and Beckett's plays have strong recognizable themes running through them. But these themes are inseparable from the way they are expressed, and it is this, the form, in which Beckett's genius is revealed. The form that Beckett uses is a simple one, repetition. Ruby Cohn has analysed the plays in detail and isolated many different kinds of repetition – simple doublets, that is, a word or sentence repeated immediately in order to sow doubt or express hesitancy; interrupted doublets; distanced doublets, echo doublets, triplets and refrains. In *Waiting for Godot*, for example, the dialogue 'Let's go. We can't. Why not? We're waiting for Godot. Ah' recurs six times, and each word in the sequence occurs in other groups. One play, *Play*, is repeated a second time straight through, and then begins a third time, indicating that this is a pattern that recurs without end. Endless repetition can convey a sense of the futility of life. It is famously put in the book of Ecclesiastes:

> Vanity of vanities . . . All is vanity . . . The sun rises and the sun goes down, and hastens to the place where it rises. The wind blows to the south, and goes round to the north; round and round goes the wind and on its circuits the wind returns. All things are full of weariness; a man cannot utter it . . . What has been is what will be, and what has been done is what will be done, and there is nothing new under the sun.
>
> (Eccles. 1.2, 5–6, 8–9, esv)

It is this biblical writer rather than any other that Beckett seems close to. Porter Abbott, the author of two books on Beckett, has written that repetition can mean 'no conclusion (and hence no redemption), or it can mean renewal'.[47] The dominant effect of Beckett's repetition is no conclusion, and hence no redemption. But, as always with Beckett, it is never as simple as that. *Not I* ends, 'God is love . . . tender mercies . . . new every morning . . . back in the field . . . April morning . . . face in the grass . . . nothing but larks . . . pick it up . . .' – words which have been repeated before, and which, you are led to believe, will be repeated again. What is picked up? It may be flowers, words, a body, a spirit, her return to consciousness, her telling of her story. There is endless repetition but it is part of the mystery with which Beckett leaves us – that the possibility of renewal cannot be totally ruled out.

In the Old Testament, God is the Creator who imposes order on chaos. He shapes the primeval chaos into life and then conscious life. An artist, through his attempt to impose form and order on experience, shares a similar vocation. The beauty of Beckett's works is, for those who are predisposed to see it, a sign of the capacity of creatures to share in their Creator's power and skill. It would be absurd of course to try and make Beckett a crypto-Christian, an anonymous believer. And nothing of the kind is being attempted. But the mystery in his plays is akin to the mystery of life itself, with the door not finally closed. There is the way the characters struggle on without killing themselves, the compassion, and the art itself, with its unique blend of truthful insight and poetry. These are for the believer signs which are underpinned and have their proper place in a view of the world that includes more than Beckett brings into his plays. Beckett was influenced in *Waiting for Godot* by an alleged saying of St Augustine: 'Do not despair; one of the thieves was saved. Do not presume; one of the thieves was damned.'[48] Reading Beckett's plays, a person is not likely to presume. And although the element of despair is always close to the surface, hope is not finally quenched. In the 1662 burial service, the minister is bidden to pray, 'We give thee hearty thanks, for that it hath pleased thee to deliver this our brother out of the miseries of this sinful world.' Beckett's world, grim and bleak as it is, would have been recognized by the writer of that prayer. And if it does not have the hope of that prayer, neither does it completely extinguish that hope. Beckett once wrote to a struggling writer friend, 'Don't lose heart: plug yourself into despair and sing it for us.'[49] Beckett himself did just that, for in his singing is a strange hope.

One of the intriguing might-have-been relationships of history is that of Beckett and Samuel Johnson, so unlike in so many ways, Johnson with his fear of hell, Beckett with his sense of hell in this life. But Beckett regarded Johnson as a soul mate. He had what he described as a 'passion' for Johnson, and collected anything he could about him.[50] He planned to write a play in four acts dealing with Johnson and Hester Thrale from the time of her husband's death until she ran off with her music teacher. He had clearly got behind the façade painted by James Boswell to know the Johnson of the diaries and prayers in which his tormented soul was bared. Johnson too suffered from depression, though it did not stop him producing what would have taken others many lifetimes. I think what really united them, however, was the struggle to get through, to fill up the time, what Johnson called vacuity. For Johnson it was holding forth to friends; for Beckett it was the words spilling from his mind. In the end, despite filling three bound octavo notebooks and struggling for years to focus on what he wanted, the multiple miseries of Johnson's inner life, he failed and produced only an unsatisfactory fragment of a play.[51] But it is fascinating that he felt so close to Johnson, despite Johnson's Christian faith.

In the introduction to this book, I quoted a remark by Francis Warner, who knew Beckett, that he was 'A Christ haunted man, a secular mystic.' The extent of Christian imagery in Beckett's work has been illustrated above, and other examples could have been given, from *All That Fall*, and *Ill Seen, Ill Said*, for example.[52] What about the claim that he was a secular mystic? In the Christian mystical tradition, as represented by St John of the Cross, for example, there comes a point when the contemplative has to go into unknowing, ignorance, failure and darkness and simply wait in silence. This was the state that Beckett was in all his life, and out of which, as discussed above in relation to *Krapp's Last Tape*, he made his art. In his recent book on different types of atheism, John Gray discusses what he calls 'the atheism of silence' or what Fritz Mauthner termed 'godless mysticism'. Gray notes that Samuel Beckett kept Mauthner's four-volume work by his bedside.[53]

8

W. H. Auden
'Bless what there is for being'

Introduction

W. H. Auden (1907–73) studied at Oxford, then lived in Berlin for a period before becoming a teacher. His talent as a poet emerged early and his first volume was published by Faber in 1930. His ability was quickly recognized by T. S. Eliot, who regarded him as the outstanding poet of the younger generation. His radical, edgy poetry made him the leading poetic voice in an age of anxiety, the title of one of his major poems. In 1940, he went to the USA and his reputation suffered for a number of years as a result. At this time he began to return to the Anglican faith in which his devout mother had brought him up and his poetry took a different turn, becoming celebratory of life in all its minute details. In 1956, he was elected Professor of Poetry at Oxford and a few years later started to live in a cottage in Christchurch. In the USA, he had met Chester Kallman, who became his lifelong friend and companion, and with whom for many years he shared a house in Austria. Auden was a total master of a wide range of verse forms. His wide idiosyncratic learning, extraordinary verbal dexterity and playful wit gave his poetry great authority. He collaborated with Benjamin Britten and wrote a number of librettos. He also wrote perceptive criticism and arresting prose on a range of unlikely subjects. The 1994 film, *Four Weddings and a Funeral*, with its haunting use of Auden's poem beginning 'Stop All the Clocks', suddenly put his name in public circulation again, this time to a wider circle than it had ever been before.[1]

Return to faith

During the 1930s Auden, like those associated with him such as Stephen Spender, Louis MacNeice and Cecil Day-Lewis, was thought of as politically committed and writing from the standpoint of the left. When Auden died in 1973, *The Times* obituary said that to anyone who was young in the 1930s and troubled by the state of the world at that time, it meant that something of their past had died too. He was for many the voice of their younger selves.

In 1940, Auden returned to the Christian faith, which he had left when he was 15 and his poetry came, after the Second World War, to embrace a wider range of subjects from a more accepting perspective. Critics are divided on the relative merits of his earlier and later poetry. Auden was not militant in his faith and it is mostly hidden in what he wrote. But what is surprising is that so many have totally ignored or underplayed the fact that everything he wrote after 1940 is undergirded and suffused by it. That influence has been acknowledged in an outstanding work of dispassionate scholarship, *Auden and Christianity* by Arthur Kirsch,[2] but commentators still tend to airbrush it out.[3]

Auden was the most prodigiously talented of all twentieth-century poets, possessing a technical virtuosity bordering on wizardry. This was combined with an amazingly wide, often esoteric culture. However, he recognized that the generation before his own, Stravinsky in music, Picasso in art, Joyce for the novel and T. S. Eliot in poetry, had made the decisive break with traditional norms and, as he put it, rather modestly, he was a colonizer of that tradition.[4] The modernism of the previous generation had radically shaken everything up. Without going back on that Auden saw himself as crafting poetry in the most disciplined way possible. He did this in an amazing variety of forms using a relaxed discursive style that could accommodate the language of prose and a concern for science, as well as moments of exalting lyricism.

Auden was brought up in a devout Anglo-Catholic home by parents who did in fact practise what they preached. However, like many an adolescent he did not so much rebel against religion as lose interest in it at the age of 15 to 'enjoy the pleasures of the world and the flesh'.[5] He became caught up in the fun of living and loving, the hectic social life of Oxford, the heady insights of Freud and Marx and the excitement of being at the centre of the literary avant-garde. There are a number of factors which led to his return to faith.

First, a gradual recognition during the 1930s that the great problems faced by the world were not going to be solved by political solutions alone. He had never been a fully paid-up member of the Communist Party, always aware that there were other factors in addition to politics that needed to be taken into account, and the crisis of the 1930s sharpened this awareness. The rise of Fascism in so civilized a country as Germany shocked him and it posed the question about the grounds on which he would oppose it. So in his poem 'September 1st 1939', a poem that once again became famous when it was read and reprinted widely after 9/11, he wrote of 'a low, dishonest decade'.[6]

Second, when teaching in an English public school he had an experience that affected him deeply. One balmy evening in June 1933 he was sitting outside with some colleagues. They had not been drinking and they were not sexually attracted to one another. They were talking quite casually about everyday matters when, as he wrote:

> I felt myself invaded by a power which, though I consented to it, was irresistible and certainly not mine. For the first time in my life I knew exactly – because, thanks to the power, I was doing it – what it means to love one's neighbour as oneself . . . My personal feelings towards them were unchanged – they were still colleagues, not intimate friends – but I felt their existence as themselves to be of infinite value and rejoiced in it.[7]

Third, when negotiating with the Oxford University Press over a book of light verse, he met someone, Charles Williams, who struck him as unqualifiedly good. Again, as he himself put it, 'He was a saint of a man. It was nothing he particularly did or said, and we never discussed religion. One just felt ten times a better person in his presence.'[8]

Fourth, there was the shock he felt when he was in Spain supporting the Republican cause, to find all the churches closed. Although he had been outside the church for many years, it surprised him how shaken he was. Then, finally, when he was in New York, where German films were still being shown before the Americans came into the war, he was even more shaken to find ordinary members of the German community in New York shouting, 'Kill the Poles!'[9]

I do not think there is anything unique about the kinds of reasons that brought Auden back to the Christian faith in which he had been nurtured as a child. What was decisive for his whole understanding of the nature of faith was what happened not long afterwards. When Auden arrived in the USA, he fell in love with an 18-year-old student, Chester Kallman. Before that, he had always doubted if he would find true love, indeed if anybody could ever love him. All went well for two years and then he discovered that Chester Kallman was being unfaithful to him. Auden had the highest ideals of marriage, and had seen his relationship to Chester as a true marriage involving a total, lifelong faithfulness. But as he came, bitterly, to understand, Kallman was temperamentally promiscuous, and was not prepared to have Auden on those terms. Auden himself, despite other physical affairs, continued to love Chester Kallman for the rest of his life and in a profound sense to be faithful to him. They lived together and collaborated on work. But this fundamental unhappiness at the heart of his life shaped his whole understanding of faith. In short, he came to believe, through great pain and grief, that his vocation was to love, even if he was not loved in the same way in return, and to be a poet. As he wrote:

> If equal affection cannot be,
> Let the more loving one be me.[10]

When Auden wrote about his return to faith, he said:

> And then, providentially – for the occupational disease of poets is frivolity – I was forced to know in person what it is like to feel oneself the prey of demonic powers, in both the Greek and the Christian sense, stripped of self-control and self-respect, behaving like a ham actor in a Strindberg play.[11]

That is a strong statement and we can only guess at the anguish and rage that lay behind it.[12] But it had the effect of making down-to-earth love of neighbour fundamental to Auden's understanding of religion, beginning with love for his immediate, unfaithful neighbour Chester Kallman, who caused him so much pain and grief.

Edward Mendelson, whose life's work has been to collect Auden's voluminous writings and writing about them, has argued that love of neighbour was not only the overriding element in Auden's religion, but its sole element, and that he rejected the transcendent, vertical dimension.[13] That is, I believe, wrong. It is always difficult to get the right balance between love of God and love of neighbour, and there is no doubt that for Auden the love of God not only had to be expressed in love of neighbour but love of neighbour was the touchstone of that love. It was what in the end mattered, the only serious thing in life. But he did not think that the Christian faith amounted only to this. Undergirding it for him, first of all, was a sense of gratitude for existence. In a poem called 'Precious Five', celebrating the five senses, he wrote:

> I could (which you cannot)
> Find reasons fast enough
> To face the sky and roar
> In anger and despair
> At what is going on,
> Demanding that it name
> Whoever is to blame:
> The sky would only wait
> Till all my breath was gone

And then reiterate
As if I wasn't there
That singular command
I do not understand,
Bless what there is for being,
Which has to be obeyed, for
What else am I made for,
Agreeing or disagreeing?[14]

Auden had a naturally happy temperament. 'Even when one is hurt and has to bellow, still one is always fundamentally happy to be able to,' he wrote, but he was hurt: Chester Kallman treated him like a doormat. He often faced the sky and roared in anger and despair, when people were not looking. Stephen Spender records sitting at a table with Auden and Chester Kallman when Chester got up and crossed the street to make advances to a young man. Auden went on talking but Spender saw that there were tears running down his cheeks. However, Auden knew that in the end there was no alternative but to bless what there is for being. 'Let your last thinks all be thanks' he wrote at the end.[15]

In facing up to the predicament of humanity, and the desperate need for us to love one another, he knew that he himself, like every other human being was part of the problem. First of all he had to face himself without self-deception or illusion:

O look, look in the mirror,
  O look in your distress;
Life remains a blessing
  Although you cannot bless.
O stand, stand at the window
  As the tears scald and start;
You must love your crooked neighbour
  With your crooked heart.[16]

Celebrating all life

The idea of life as a blessing had an extraordinary richness for Auden because of the amazing width of his natural interests. His father was a doctor who became Professor of Public Health in Birmingham and who was also a keen amateur archaeologist. Auden's great love as a child was the rocks and landscapes of Yorkshire, with its disused lead mines. One of his brothers became a professional geologist. He originally went up to Oxford to read science with a view to becoming a mining engineer and only there switched to English. There was almost nothing that did not genuinely arouse his curiosity and interest. So, as he wrote:

> Let us hymn the small but journal wonders
> Of Nature and of households.[17]

One of his best-known and loved poems is called 'In Praise of Limestone', which does just that, relating the landscape with its different features to the human condition, and ending up:

> When I try to imagine a faultless love
> Or the life to come, what I hear is the murmur
> Of underground streams, what I see is a limestone landscape.[18]

Many poets, in many different ways, have of course celebrated nature. Fewer have celebrated the wonders of households, but that also is what Auden did, most obviously in his collection called *Thanksgiving for a Habitat* in which he celebrates the different rooms in the house.

The wide range of things in which Auden took a delight does, I think, bring out an interesting and important aspect of his understanding of the Christian faith which stands in contrast to another strand, represented for example by T. S. Eliot. Auden was, in both a denigratory and a celebratory sense, a worldly person. He drank a lot, he smoked heavily, he loved parties, he even gave a positive value to gossip. As he wrote somewhat mischievously:

> How often I have worked off ill-feeling against friends by telling some rather malicious stories about them and as a result met them again with the feeling quite gone. When one reads in the papers of some unfortunate man who has gone for his wife with a razor, one can be pretty certain that he wasn't a great gossip . . . Gossip is creative. All art is based on gossip. Gossip is the art-form of the man and woman in the street, and the proper subject for gossip, as for all art, is the behaviour of mankind.[19]

It is not surprising that with this attitude to the world about him people found it difficult to think of him as deeply or seriously religious. But they are wrong. Indeed he argued, rightly, that those who come across as serious are often in fact frivolous, and it is surprising to find that he regarded the sombre and portentous Eliot, much as he admired him, as in the end frivolous. Apparent frivolity, apparent light heartedness, and sheer enjoyment often cover up a genuine seriousness about life. Philip Larkin wrote about a later collection of Auden's poetry, 'In some way Auden, never a pompous poet, has now become an unserious one.' In the light of that, it is not surprising that he included virtually none of Auden's later poetry in his *Twentieth Century Book of English Verse*. Larkin was mistaken in his judgement. As Auden wrote, 'A frivolity which, precisely because it is aware of what is serious, refuses to take seriously that which is not serious, can be profound.'[20]

So, in a world of self-consciously serious people it is 'the smoking-room story alone' which ironically enough stands for 'our hunger for eternal life'.

The contrast with Eliot is an illuminating one.

Eliot, in his poetry, is an advocate of the *via negativa*. This suggests that the way to God is through a negation of all we think we know about him, letting go all we hold on to for security, and experiencing loss and darkness. It comes across strongly in his lines from the *Four Quartets*, which are themselves virtually a quotation from St John of the Cross, who is particularly associated with this way, and in particular with 'the dark night of the soul' with which it is associated. In these lines, the poet tells himself not to hope, love or even think, for each would be for the wrong thing. The soul has simply to wait on God in stillness. The faith and love and hope are all summed up and focused in the waiting.[21] In short, to use words we have to go by the way of ignorance and dispossession.

Auden, being a learned as well as a serious believer, would not of course have denied this, and he knew very well that all our human words and thoughts about God are, in one inescapable sense, human projections. When it comes to God, we always make an image of what we most want or most fear. He used to ram this truth home to himself and others by talking about 'Miss God' in remarks like 'Miss God has decided to keep me celibate this summer'. That said, what is fundamental and characteristic about him is that he deeply appreciated and delighted in the world about him in its every aspect. Like the Roman writer Terence he would have said, *Homo sum; humani nil a me alienum puto* (I am a man; nothing human is alien to me). So, although Auden celebrated nature, he was essentially a city dweller, and it was city life that he rejoiced in both poetically and religiously, even to the smallest details of a dinner party. 'Tonight at Seven-Thirty', after describing many details of the ideal party ends:

> men
> and women who enjoy the cloop of corks, appreciate
> dapatical fare, yet can see in swallowing
> a sign act of reverence,
> in speech a work of representing
> the true olamic silence.[22]

This is a truly sacramental view of existence in which the outward and visible can be a sign of the inward and spiritual, so swallowing is 'a sign act of reverence', and the talk a touch of the eternal. Other Christian poets, notably Thomas Traherne and Gerard Manley Hopkins, have celebrated the *via positiva*, but none, I think, have done it in such a bold, inclusive and, well, utterly worldly way, as W. H. Auden.

Although the foundation of Auden's religion is rooted in his sense that the givenness of life, despite everything, is a blessing, there is no doubt, as Edward Mendelson emphasizes, that love of neighbour is the essential touchstone for the reality of that religion. Duty is not a word that is in fashion today, but it was a key word for Auden and he was not embarrassed to quote the old Anglican Catechism that the Christian vocation is 'To do my duty in that state of life, unto which it shall please God to call me.' He believed that the state of life to which he had been called was that of a poet, and his duty was to work on his talents to the best of his ability. He saw himself as a craftsman, in some ways like a carpenter, and he had no time for sloppy ideas of inspiration; all his work, in such a variety of styles and forms, is meticulously crafted.

This outlook is reflected in a poem he wrote beginning, 'Let us praise our maker, with true passion extol him', for it goes on in a wonderful paean of praise to celebrate a universe in which a proper order allows each individual to flourish in a 'grand givenness of gratitude and joy':

> When, in love and in laughter, each lives itself,
> For united by its Word, cognition and power,
> System and order, are a single glory,
> And the pattern is complex, their places safe.[23]

Although Auden had a heavily lined face and crumpled appearance and lived in some squalor, he was fanatical about timekeeping and could get irritated if meals were not served at the time expected. In a poem written for a friend's marriage, he recommends not only strong nerves but 'an accurate wrist-watch too / can be a great help'. In short, he unashamedly championed the bourgeois virtues. Acknowledging that bourgeois society is in a mess he does not think that Dostoevsky will help us get out of it: 'I would rather take the bourgeois hero, Sir Walter Scott, who worked himself to death to pay his creditors, than Alyosha or any other of Dostoevsky's seedy enthusiasts.'[24]

Paying your debts, keeping promises, turning up on time, observing the courtesies, improving your poetry – this was the more surprising side of a man who was known for his louche lifestyle, warm generosity and many good friends but which was all part of how he saw his duty to love God and neighbour. So duty is a key word. He kept going with Chester Kallman, because he continued to love him, because he had seen their relationship as a marriage and because happiness for him was not in the end about pain and pleasure. As he put it:

> Happiness consists in a loving and trusting relationship to God; accordingly we are to take one thing and one thing only seriously, our eternal duty to be happy, and to that all considerations of pleasure and pain are subordinate. Thou shalt love God and thy neighbour and Thou shall be happy mean the same thing.[25]

One of the sayings of Auden that has become quite well known is:

> There is no such thing as a Christian politics, or a Christian art, or a Christian science, any more than there is a Christian diet. There is only politics, or art, or science, which are natural activities concerned with the natural and historical man.[26]

This sentence occurred as part of a lecture at Yale Divinity School which was later published in the British journal *Theology*. It is a serious, theologically wide-ranging, somewhat conservative piece, in response to a request to speak about the vocation of a Christian layman, and set within the framework of rendering unto Caesar the things that are Caesar's. In the article, he sees the fall of humanity, eating from the tree of the knowledge of good and evil, as a desire for autonomy 'It is a desire to become one's own source of value, to become *as* God while still remaining a man.'[27] This results in a condition of guilt and anxiety from which we try to escape by our own efforts through natural religion. 'Such efforts were bound to be self-frustrated since they were rooted in a self-contradictory desire to find an Absolute which at the same time should be controllable by man.'[28] But with a revealed knowledge of God in Christ, this natural religion is no longer needed, if it ever was. The job of the church, in particular the priest, is to transmit this unchanging truth, and for this task the particular human gifts of the priest are not strictly speaking relevant. The layperson on the other hand still participates in the wider world, perhaps mostly mixing with non-Christians, and in that world the things of Caesar have to be rendered to Caesar. This includes art, as well as politics and science. They belong to the historical and natural realm and the poet has to use such gifts as he has in that realm, without claiming the special revelation of God any more than a government can.

This is not the place to examine in detail what I regard as an over-sharp distinction in Auden's overall view on the relation of Christian faith and wider culture, as expressed there, but it is worth pointing out that there is in fact such a thing as Christian art, in the sense that in Western culture for example, until recently, much if not most art was inspired by Christian themes and images. The Christian faith has been an integral part of our culture and until the Enlightenment its beliefs seeped into and saturated music, poetry and the visual arts. Of course it is right that a poet like Auden who had a Christian faith should not and would not claim that his poetic gifts and craft were more directly inspired, or more from God, than say, the communist Bertolt Brecht. They both had to work with the talents they had been given according to the norms of their literary crafts. In that sense, the arts are a realm that belong to Caesar. But Auden not only felt accountable to God for the way he used his talents, but his faith shaped how he viewed the world and how he celebrated it. In that sense, it is a Christian art. Sometimes, though not often, he used Christian imagery in this task.

It is not surprising, given people's stereotype about what does and does not count as religious, that people should have had difficulty thinking of Auden as a religious man and have missed the all-pervading religious dimension of his poetry. This hiddenness he made something of a creed. One of his poems is called 'The Truest Poetry Is the Most Feigning', which is a quotation from *As You Like It*. It celebrates the way that genuine poetry is bound to have a clever, artful, contrived aspect to it, and ends:

> What but tall tales, the luck of verbal playing,
> Can trick his lying nature into saying
> That love, or truth, in any serious sense,
> Like orthodoxy, is a reticence?[29]

The phrase 'Truth, in any serious sense, like orthodoxy, is a reticence' was a favourite of Auden.[30]

There were a number of reasons for his reticence. One is the traditional Englishman's reluctance to bring religion into polite conversation. This reluctance is particularly marked when it comes to what might come across as public display, for example in politics, but also in the arts. Most recently that attitude was shown by Tony Blair, who said he did not talk about his religion when he was Prime Minister, for fear, as he put it, of coming across as a nutter. Given the suspicion of religion in the kind of intellectual circles that Auden moved in, this motive would have been quite strong. So, when he wrote to T. S. Eliot, and said that he now shared Eliot's religious beliefs, he urged him not to tell anyone. Once, when someone came into the room and found him praying, Auden was extremely irritated. Then there was the reason, already suggested, that true seriousness is so serious, that it often disguises itself with surface humour or light-heartedness. This was certainly so in the case of Auden, for people sometimes could not make out whether he was being serious or not. He often was, but people did not grasp it. Then, perhaps most important of all, when it comes to some of the big things in life, especially religious truth, words can only hint at what it conveyed, not tie it up in a neat parcel. Quite simply, neat parcels of religion totally fail to convey the ultimate mystery of God, a mystery which is at the heart of Christian orthodoxy. As the great bastion of orthodoxy, with both a lower-case and an upper-case 'O', John of Damascus put it in the eighth century, 'What God is in himself is totally incomprehensible and unknowable.' So all the words we use to convey this mystery will, as it were, be in inverted commas, will be metaphor or analogy. He would strongly have agreed with the words of Emily Dickinson quoted in Chapter 2:

> Tell all the truth but tell it slant-
> Success in circuit lies[31]

In the lines of Auden quoted earlier, there are several other characteristic features of Auden's approach. Our nature is a lying nature. He had no illusions about himself or others. What tricks this lying nature into revealing the truth is 'the luck of verbal playing', a very modest way of talking about his massive poetic gifts.

The 1930s, when Auden was the leading young literary figure, was a time of unbelief as marked as our own. It is true that the crisis of those times, followed by the Second World War, made religious faith a more serious option for many, as it had for Auden. Nevertheless the *zeitgeist* in literary circles in his time, as in ours, is not on the whole sympathetic. So, telling it slant is often the only way in which an initial misunderstanding and resistance can be circumvented. But in Auden's case, this aspect was reinforced by the fact that in any case he understood the Christian faith as requiring us to celebrate this world in every aspect and in all its quirkiness. His faith was to be seen in that appreciation and celebration.

Unlike some people, Auden did not, so far as we know, have a great intellectual struggle to return to the faith of his childhood. He left it to pursue pleasure and he returned to it when he realized that the world was in a terrible state, and this was not just because of wrong political policies but because, as the psalmist put it, the heart is deceitful above all things.

This did not lead him into self-righteousness. Just the opposite. He knew it was his own crooked heart that had to be faced first. In this faith, he found a degree of stability that he did not have before. However, as is clear from his relationship with Chester Kallmann, he knew personal anguish as well as a world wracked by cruelty and deceit. It was this anguish which drove him to affirm that despite everything life is a blessing and all that exists is cause for praise.

One of the issues it is not always easy to get right from a religious point of view is the relationship between the pleasures of life and its pain. If some religious people have given the impression of letting the balance fall on the pain side, Auden is the opposite. Although he knew real personal anguish, I am tempted to say, because he knew personal anguish he was not prepared to offer an easy apologia for suffering. His poem entitled 'Epistle to a Godson' is precisely what its title suggests, advice from Auden to one of his godsons. In it, he asks what nourishment he, as a godfather, should offer his godson for the Christian way and writes nothing obscene or unpleasant: only

> the unscarred overfed enjoy Calvary
> As a verbal event. Nor satiric: no
> > scorn will ashame the Adversary.
> > nor shoddily made: to give a stunning
>
> display of concinnity and elegance
> is the least we can do, and its dominant
> > mood should be that of a Carnival.
> > Let us hymn the small but journal wonders
>
> of Nature and of households, and then finish
> on a serio-comic note with legends
> > of ultimate eucatastrophe,
> > regeneration beyond the waters.[32]

It should not of course be thought, because of that reference to Calvary as a verbal event, that the reality of Calvary as torture meant nothing to Auden. He took this and its implications for our understanding of human nature with the utmost seriousness. At one point he engages in a traditional Good Friday thought and wonders what he himself would have been doing at that time. He decides that at best he would have been an ancient philosopher walking by and remarking to a companion how disgusting the crucifixions were, and why couldn't the authorities put people to death humanely, before continuing to engage in their fascinating discussion of truth, beauty and goodness. But in his advice to his godson he rightly says that only the unscarred overfed enjoy Calvary as a verbal event. What we can do is use all our skill to create 'a stunning display of concinnity and elegance'. We should do this in a mood of carnival, praising the little things of the world, and with an ultimate hope that in the end all shall be well.

Auden loved to mint neologisms, and here we have one in the word eucatastrophe: but it is not difficult to work out its meaning. Catastrophe is an overturning that brings disaster. The Greek word *eu*, meaning 'well', therefore suggests an overturning, bringing its opposite, a good state of affairs. This is the ultimate outcome of the universe, in theological parlance the eschaton, regeneration beyond the waters, but even here it is put forward in terms of 'a serio-comic note with legends'. It is utterly serious, but the comic side can be seen and enjoyed as well. So, for him, in the end, all will be well, and with this hope in mind we are to do our job as well as we can 'to give a stunning display of concinnity and elegance is the least we can do', concinnity meaning 'skilfully put together', all in a mood of carnival with a perpetual hymn to the small but journal wonders of nature and of households.

Theologically Auden was well read, thoughtful and conservative. Those who developed theologically after the catastrophe of the First World War and its aftermath tended to take a very definite line against what they regarded as the mishmash of alternative views that then prevailed. Certainly Auden's tone of voice was no less confident and authoritative when writing on theology than it was when he was writing on literature. When he returned to faith as an adult, he was influenced by Søren Kierkegaard, the fountainhead of twentieth-century existentialism, and by Reinhold Niebuhr, the most influential American theologian of the twentieth century, with whom Auden became good friends, as he did with Niebuhr's wife, Ursula, also a theologian. They shared a strong sense of the propensity of human beings to deceive themselves and collude in illusions, particularly moral illusions. From this stage of his theological reading, he was reinforced both in his understanding of the dark side of human nature and the crucial importance of individual choice. He never lost that sense of the importance of the individual and personal choices. Names were crucially important for him because he believed that it was in the name that you became aware of the uniqueness of the individual. God, being God, was able to name every particle of the universe, and see its relation to every other.[33] Prayer for him was above all an act of attention to each unique individual, perhaps being influenced by Simone Weil in this, for whom this was fundamental.

However, Auden also came to stress the importance of Christ for the city, for organized human life. This comes out in what is perhaps the most profoundly Christian set of poems he wrote, 'Horae Canonicae',[34] seven poems based on the seven monastic hours. They are concerned with our life together as human beings, our life in the urban jungle. So although from one point of view the poem is about an individual getting up and going about his ordinary day, from another angle it is about the city in which Jesus is going to get killed in order to redeem the world.

'Prime' begins with a wonderful description of what it is to wake up in the morning but it goes on to include the whole world waking up to something sinister in the 'lying self-made city'. The hours continue with the same mixture of the personal and the universal, with all somehow rooted in a terrible event elsewhere:

> For without a cement of blood (it must be human, it must be innocent)
> No secular wall will safely stand.

The city, in the poem, is our organized life together, but what we hope for is something much more relaxed and carefree:

> (And I shall know exactly what happened
>> Today between noon and three)
> That we, too, may come to the picnic
>> With nothing to hide, join in the dance
> As it moves in perichoresis,
>> Turns about the abiding tree.

'Perichoresis' is a technical term in theology referring to the way the different persons of the Holy Trinity dwell in one another, but here it seems to suggest that in the dance of humanity round the abiding tree there is a mutual indwelling of the divine and the human.

This verse sums up so much of Auden as a Christian and a poet. For him life is essentially life together, life with one another, social life; and this took its most essential form, at once sacramental and enjoyable, in the meals we share. But it is noticeable here that the meal is a picnic, an image that conveys something relaxed and carefree. There is a conviviality in the fresh air that brings together the city and the country. But there is nothing sentimental or escapist in Auden's view on how this wonderful end state is achieved. 'It depends on what happened between noon and three'. It is this breaking down of the barriers of our pride before the cross that brings us before others 'With nothing to hide' and leads us to join in the dance of humanity. But this dance is at the same time the dance of God in humanity, for the perichoresis of the Blessed Trinity comes, through Christ and the Holy Spirit, to be an indwelling of God in us, and us in him. God and humanity are at one in that dance, a dance which turns about the tree, at once the tree of life and the cross as the definitive statement of divine love.

Auden is a poet of Christian reticence, his Christian faith is so transmuted into appreciation of the world that people can fail to see it glinting there. He could also be called a poet of Christian praise, for this is what much of poetry is about. In one of his best and most famous poems in memory of W. B. Yeats, he ends with the words

> Follow poet, follow right
> To the bottom of the night.
> With your unconstraining voice
> Still persuade us to rejoice;
>
> With the farming of a verse
> Make a vineyard of the curse.
> Sing of human unsuccess
> In a rapture of distress;
>
> In the deserts of the heart
> Let the healing fountain start,
> In the prison of his days,
> Teach the free man how to praise.[35]

This poem was written in 1939, not long before he formally returned to the Christian faith, and sums up so beautifully how he saw his craft as a poet, and how he thought human beings should respond to life.

9

William Golding
Universal pessimist, cosmic optimist

Introduction

William Golding (1911–93) studied at Oxford and served in the Second World War in the navy. He then taught English at Bishop Wordsworth's School in Salisbury. *Lord of the Flies*, written in 1954, was rejected by numerous publishers and was about to be put into the reject tray at Faber & Faber, when its genius was recognized by Charles Monteith, who still had a hard struggle to convince the directors to publish it. However, it was a critical success and, after a slow start, a commercial success as well. Becoming a set text in many schools it became one of the best-known novels of the last half of the twentieth century and has been made into a film and a play. Golding taught until 1961, when his financial success as an author enabled him to retire and concentrate on his writing. He was awarded the Nobel Prize for literature in 1983 and the Booker Prize in 1980 for *Rites of Passage*. Primarily known as a novelist he also wrote poetry and a play. In all, he wrote eight or nine major novels which, it could plausibly be argued, will stand the test of time.

Surprising success

Golding wrote *Lord of the Flies*, the novel which made him famous, while still teaching. The setting is an island paradise on which a group of school-boys, including some choirboys, is stranded when the plane evacuating them from a war is shot down. The boys quickly split up into gangs. There are disputes about leadership and power, leading to bullying, fighting and torture. Nice young children given perfect conditions descend into sav-agery. The wider setting of the novel makes it clear that the war which was going on in the wider world was simply this innate human brutality writ large. As a young man Golding was influenced by H. G. Wells, and shared the general optimism of a certain kind of person, that through education the world could get better and better. The war brought him up against the dark side of human nature. No doubt he also saw some of that behaviour among the boys he was teaching at the time. So Golding's dark novel can be seen as an alternative to *Coral Island* by R. M. Ballantyne, which reflected his own earlier more optimistic view of life. Indeed there are references to *Coral Island* in *Lord of the Flies*. John Carey, the literary critic and Golding's biographer, sums up a lecture on the novel which Golding gave in which Golding said that he came to recognize that '"man produces evil as a bee produces honey". He wrote *Lord of the Flies* out of a belief in original sin, derived not from books but from watching how people behave.'[1] Even more pertinently the Second World War made him see viciousness and cruelty not just in the Nazis but in himself as a young man. 'I have always understood the Nazis because I am of that sort by nature.' It was 'partly out of that sad self-knowledge' that he wrote his novel.[2]

In the original manuscript, the religious themes were very explicit, but Charles Monteith wanted them toned down, which they were; but they are still present in various ways. Simon, a key figure in the novel, is regarded by the others as somehow different. He looks after the young boys, tries to stop the bullying and spends time on his own in meditation. He is certainly a martyr and can be seen as a Christ figure. 'Lord of the Flies' is a literal translation of Beelzebub, from the first chapter of 2 Kings. There is fear of the supernatural, a sacrifice and also an authoritative moral voice to be heard. Again, this is based on Golding's own experience. He claimed a mythical or mystical experience while writing the book. The words spoken by the pig's head to Simon were dictated by something beyond himself. 'The pig's head spoke. I know because I heard it.'[3]

The Second World War engendered a new seriousness in the life of the nation. In contrast to what W. H. Auden was to call a 'low dishonest decade', it brought out a spirit of courage and self-sacrifice in many people. In opposing the Nazis, they realized something big was at stake. It also made many people rethink religion. Owen Chadwick, the distinguished historian, went up to Cambridge a non-believer. He said that Hitler made some of his contemporaries Communists; it made him, he said, a Christian. One of the effects of this was to bring about a mini religious revival after the war. This was nothing very dramatic but by 1958 ordinations in the Church of England were numbering something like 800 a year, compared to the 500 or so a year at the moment. Golding was one example of someone who experienced this shift in himself. It brought about what he termed 'a sort of religious convulsion' and gave him 'a kind of framework of principles which I still hold mainly even when I am untrue to them'.[4]

You do not have to believe in the literal truth of the story of Adam and Eve to recognize that something is fundamentally askew in human life, that something has gone wrong. This is not just about the survival of our animal instincts, for the most devastating evils come about as a resulted of twisted ideologies and religions. Christianity has always recognized the reality of sin and argued it is basic to any true understanding of life. For example the State is, in part, at once a result of and a remedy for the fall. The boys on their paradise island find they cannot live without some proper form of governance which holds a monopoly of power. Without it they tear themselves apart. If they had survived long enough they would have had to devise some such form of government. It would have been at once the result of their anarchy and a way of containing it.

If human beings have 'fallen' then when did that occur and what would an imaginative picture of that period look like? These were the implicit questions in Golding's next novel, *The Inheritors* (1955). It is a brilliantly imagined picture of one tribe on the threshold of human consciousness, and the other tribe just over it. The first group, who have the imagined characteristics of Neanderthals, do not use language, but have pictures in their heads. They have a form of telepathic communication and the group moves very much as one. They have an appealing innocence. The second group, who speak and have the characteristics of *Homo sapiens*, have discovered fire, alcohol, sacrifice and cruelty. They wipe out the Neanderthals, except for one infant whom they kidnap. The rewrite of the book that Golding did makes it clear that the book is not just about the loss of innocence but the evolutionary drive to a more advanced form of existence which is part of nature and which leads *Homo sapiens* to destroy what went before. The book has great emotional power as well as sensory originality. For some people it is their favourite novel by Golding.

Pincher Martin, which followed in 1956, was another remarkable tour de force. Like all Golding's writing it conveys an extraordinary emotional intensity. In this novel, the intensity is created by a sailor's struggle to survive after his destroyer has been torpedoed. He manages to climb on to a rock in the Atlantic and the whole novel is his battle to stay on it and not be swept back into the sea. Then, at the end there is a remarkable twist and we see all that has happened up to that point in a completely new way. We see that the book is about a different kind of struggle, one that has to do with the self and self-knowledge. Towards the end we read:

> The lightning crept in. The centre was unaware of anything but the claws and the threat. It focused its awareness on the crumbled serrations and the

blazing red. The lightning came forward. Some of the lines pointed to the centre, waiting for the moment when they could pierce it. Others lay against the claws, playing over them, prying for a weakness, wearing them away in a compassion that was timeless and without mercy.[5]

It is a vivid image of the self as a pair of lobster claws being worn away by a relentless compassion.

John Carey has written that *Pincher Martin* 'is one of the most profound and original novels of the twentieth century'.[6] As he points out, it draws significantly on Golding's harsh judgement about his own character. In the notebooks Golding kept before he wrote the book, he jotted down among other points that 'running away from God is running away from helplessness and death towards power and life'.[7] When the novel was adapted for the Third Programme in 1958, Golding said that Christopher Martin Hadley, the central character,

> had no belief in anything but the importance of his own life, no love, no God. Because he was created in the image of God he had a freedom of choice which he used to centre the world on himself. He did not believe in purgatory and therefore when he died it was not presented to him in overtly theological terms. The greed for life which had been the mainspring of his nature, forced him to refuse the selfless act of dying. He continued to exist separately in a world composed of his own murderous nature. His drowned body lies rolling in the Atlantic but the ravenous ego invents a rock for him to endure on.[8]

Lord of the Flies reveals the desperate need for redemption in the social order and *Pincher Martin* the origin of that need in our rocklike egos. But *Pincher Martin* also suggests that there is 'a compassion that was timeless and without mercy' wearing away that ego. This raises the question of how that compassion might have its effect. Have we the capacity to receive it, and if so how? *Free Fall* (1959), Golding's next novel, is about an artist, Samuel Mountjoy, who was a prisoner in the Second World War. In an extended self-examination, Mountjoy was conscious of genuine freedom of choice. He knew freedom 'like the taste of potatoes' and he realized that somewhere in his life he had, because of his nature, done something really mean. At some point however he had also been released from his inner prison. He locates this in the moment when he was a prisoner of war, when he cried out for help:

> My cry for help was the cry of the rat when the terrier shakes it, a hopeless sound, the raw signature of one savage act. My cry was no more, was instinctive, said here is flesh of which the nature is to suffer and so thus. I

cried out not with the hope of an ear but as accepting a shut door, darkness and a shut sky.

But the very act of crying out changed the thing that cried. Does the rat expect help? When a man cries out instinctively, he begins to search for a place where help may be found; and so the thing that cried out, struggling in the fetor, the sea of nightmare, with burning breath and racing heart, that thing as it was drowning looked with starting and not physical eyes on every place, against every wall, in every corner of the interior world.

'Help me!'[9]

The mean act which Samuel Mountjoy perpetrated is based on something Golding himself did as a young man.[10] There is every likelihood that the cry for help, the crying out that changed the thing that cried, also reflects Golding's own experience. It is after all a well-known phenomenon. Rabbi Lionel Blue wrote about just such an experience in his own life when, feeling desperate, he wandered into a Quaker Meeting house and cried out.[11] Francis Thompson, the nineteenth-century Roman Catholic poet, described such an experience memorably in his poem 'The Kingdom of God':

> But (when so sad thou canst not sadder)
> Cry; and upon thy so sore loss
> Shall shine the traffic of Jacob's ladder
> Pitched betwixed Heaven and Charing Cross.[12]

When a person cries out for help like Samuel Mountjoy, he or she may develop a religious faith. But religion is, from one point of view, a human creation and as such can become the vehicle of human egoism like any other human construction. Indeed worse than this, because people think they have the truth it can go along with a terrifying lack of self-knowledge and self-delusion. This was the theme of Golding's next novel.

The Spire (1964) concerns the ambition of the dean, Jocelin, to build a 404-foot tower on his cathedral. The detail of medieval cathedral building is so riveting that it is natural to think that Golding did a great deal of research for this book. But he didn't. Teaching in Bishop Wordsworth's School he saw the great spire of Salisbury Cathedral daily. He was able to go inside it and simply imagine how it would have been built. Not only did he have his extraordinarily powerful imagination, he had inherited his father's practical ability. His father, whom he greatly admired, was able to turn his hand to anything requiring practical expertise, and Golding himself was a very skilled sailor, with a knowledge of blocks and tackles in lifting heavy weights. So he imagined how he would have built the spire had he been there.[13] Opposing the dean was the master mason, Roger Mason, who thought the whole idea was dangerous and could not be done safely because of insecure foundations. The dean, however, believed that he had been given a vision to build the spire in order to bring the town nearer to God. There are also several subplots of love and lust. The reader is drawn into this vast act of hubris, stone by stone, until the dean loses his reason and receives a final humiliation.[14]

Darkness Visible (1979) is perhaps the least known and least understood of Golding's works. All were ambitious but this could claim to be the most ambitious of all, at least up to this point. It was 24 years in the writing and there were elements in the story that clearly meant a great deal to Golding. The plot is complicated but in John Carey's view quite apart from the writing it was a technical marvel uniting the various elements into a single narrative that is at once gripping and elusive.[15] The central character is Matty, who emerges out of a fire in London's Blitz most terribly disfigured. From his earliest days and throughout his life, people cannot bear even to look at him. Matty's mind is a strange one, scarred as it is by his terrible experience but it keeps formulating a pressing question, 'Who am I?' The question is never answered but Matty comes to reformulate it as 'What am I for?' and begins to feel he exists for something. When he is working as an odd-job man in a smart prep school, there is a terrorist attack as part of an attempt to kidnap some boys and he is killed. But he seems to become one of the flames in the fire, fire being a key image in the book. The flames of fire force one of the terrorists, who is fleeing with a boy, to let him go. Even more remarkable is what happens next. As a child Matty had met Mr Pedigree, a paedophile, who'd been revolted by Matty, but Matty through some strange misreading of the relationship had become devoted to Mr Pedigree. At the time of Matty's death Mr Pedigree is in the grip of one of his compulsive cycles and is waiting outside a public lavatory to seduce some children. In a vision of hazy golden light, Matty appears to free him from his enslavement. Pedigree explains to him that he is terrified he might kill one of the children he molests just to keep him quiet and he begs Matty for help:

He came and stood before Pedigree and looked down at him. Pedigree understood that they were in a park of mutuality and closeness where the sunlight lay right on the skin.

'You know it was all your fault, Matty.'

Matty seemed to agree; and really the boy was quite pleasant to look at![16]

John Carey has written:

> Matty's final appearance to Pedigree is Golding's greatest piece of religious writing, yet it allows the reader no fingerhold in certainty. Everything is as you interpret it. Pedigree may have been dreaming, or he may have had a vision of celestial reality.[17]

In the novel, there is a contrast between two worlds. When the terrorists attack the school in order to kidnap the children, the media are focused on all the outward events, with television cameras and reporters rushing everywhere. The death of an obscure, strange odd-job man is not noticed. But while the world watches these dramatic outward happenings another plot is all the time being worked out. Matty is an agent of redemption. He knows his life exists for something and his death releases him from the constraints of time and space for the redemption of Mr Pedigree.

Darkness Visible was the one novel which Golding refused to talk about, but his many notebooks reveal a great deal about the various stages of writing over the 24 years it took him to bring the book to fruition. He was quite prepared to acknowledge that he had intended Matty to be 'a saint' – like, he said, Simon in *Lord of the Flies*, St Jean Vianney, the Curé d'Ars, and St Thérèse of Lisieux. 'It's a figure I've tried for again and again and I suppose Matty in Darkness Visible is as near as I shall ever get.'[18]

Rites of Passage (1980), which won the Booker Prize, was the first of three nautical novels, the other two being *Close Quarters* (1987) and *Fire Down Below* (1989), to form a trilogy later named *To the Ends of the Earth*. They see the world through the eyes of a young aristocrat, Edmund Talbot, who sails out to Australia on a six-month voyage in the early part of the nineteenth century. He begins by keeping a journal for his uncle, who has arranged for him to go out there. During the voyage, there is a violent episode in which a naive clergyman is subjected to a homosexual act, in which Edmund seems somehow to be implicated. On the way back, the ship is found to be unseaworthy, and there are various episodes through which Edmund comes to a greater self-knowledge. The books bring to the fore Golding's love of sailing and his skilled seamanship, as well as his wartime experience in the navy. The themes are less obviously metaphysical compared with the novels previously discussed here, and what the author is attempting is ambitious and subtle: Edmund Talbot's deepening understanding of himself.

Edmund Talbot as a young aristocrat had all the sense of entitlement, the narrowness of outlook and *naïveté* which one might expect of a person in that position. It is interesting that Golding should have wanted to make such a character central to the trilogy and to see the world from his perspective. For Golding had gone to a grammar school in Marlborough, which was the town of a major public school. He developed a sense of resentment towards privilege which, according to Carey, remained with him for the rest of his life. So it is a major exercise in imaginative self-positioning to depict Talbot, whose *naïveté* always had a certain appeal and who develops into a not unattractive person. But, in short, he has to grow up. He is made aware of the brutal world of which he is a part and comes to a dawning realization of his own drives. Golding himself was ruthlessly honest with himself and others about his own lust, potential for cruelty, desire for praise and vulnerabilities. It's as though he wants to bring young Edmund through that process. And though this is a necessary part of any human life and there is nothing religious in itself about it, any healthy religion will have at its forefront bringing about such self-insight. Edmund Talbot is forced to face himself in a way that Dean Jocelin in *The Spire* resists doing.

One of William Golding's less well-known novels, *The Double Tongue*, published posthumously, concerns a woman who acted as the Oracle of Delphi.[19] In reality, her job is simply to pass on the interpretation given by the high priest, who is manipulating her for his own political ends. However, she does sometimes go into genuine prophetic trances and eventually at the end of her long service the authorities want to erect a statue to her on one of the altars of the Field of Mars. She declines and asks instead for a simple altar inscribed with the words 'To the unknown God', words with which the novel ends. Most readers will know that this is a reference to Chapter 17 in the Acts of the Apostles, which describes Paul's preaching the Christian faith to assembled philosophers in Athens when he draws their attention to this inscription. His claim is that the unknown God has made himself known in the life, death and resurrection of Jesus Christ.

Golding's own religious position is not easy to fathom and it is likely to have varied during the course of his life. Furthermore, when he had had too much to drink, as he did on occasions, he was prone to put things in a vivid way which might not have represented his considered position the following morning.

As a student at Oxford, Golding was a scientific rationalist like his father.[20] When he was on the staff of Bishop Wordsworth's School, however, he taught religion, not only as a form of knowledge with which the boys needed to be familiar, but as a way of Christian life including prayer and self-examination. The boys got the impression he was a 'devout Christian' and they detected in him 'a living spirituality' which had a profound effect on some of them.[21]

Tony Brown, a great friend of Golding, was not a Christian, and when he asked Golding whether he was one, Golding replied, 'No, but I like to think of myself as a religious person.'[22] Why he thought of himself as religious but not Christian can only be guessed at. It may have to do with the centrality of the cross in Christian faith. He told the literary scholar Stephen Medcalf, that he could not endure the crucifix. It was a 'horror to be veiled'. But that might have been because of the depiction of suffering, not because of its meaning in Christian theology.

It was after a late night's drinking and talking session with Medcalf that Golding said he could imagine a longing for absolution so great that you would create the world. Medcalf did not know what he meant but was sure he said it. On one of Medcalf's visits to Golding, he was accompanied by Tom Braun, a Merton don from the University of Oxford, who said at breakfast, 'Last night you said you weren't a Christian; but it strikes me your novels are much more Christian than those of many who would claim to be.' This brought forth a retort from Golding's wife, Ann, 'Oh Bill, you didn't say you weren't a Christian did you?' 'That was last night,' Golding replied.[23]

Golding's father, Alec, whom he hugely admired and whom he claimed was a major influence on his life, was an atheist. When he died, it was the greatest grief of Golding's life. Later he wrote that he had wept for Alec 'the most tears I ever had'. It hurt him to think of his father's atheism because it meant he had 'died in no hope'. His father was 'a profoundly religious man who remained a grieving atheist until the last days of his life'.[24] Then, in an interview in 1959 with Frank Kermode broadcast on what was then called the Third Programme, Golding described himself as 'a religious though possibly incompetently religious man' and insisted that Simon in *Lord of the Flies* was a saint.

Golding went through a very bad period in his life, suffering both from writer's block and doubts about the value of his work and, like many people having a hard time, turned in desperation to prayer. In Golding's case, this prayer took a very personal and idiosyncratic form: 'Dear God,' he asks 'if you are the One who can properly be supplicated on this question – let me write a major novel.'[25]

Interestingly it was Golding who suggested the name Gaia to James Lovelock, for Lovelock's increasingly fashionable view about the importance of mother earth.[26]

It can be seen from the above paragraphs that it would be foolish to draw any firm conclusions about Golding's personal faith, which can be safely left to the one 'To whom all hearts are open'. What is likely however is that his views fluctuated in the course of his life, that different people brought out different aspects of his personal faith and that as he got older the less definite he wanted to be. As John Carey put it, his faith became 'more tenuous as time went on until it was belief in something that could not be named. Yet it was still belief.'[27] In Christian terms, this is a form of negative theology. When interviewed for the *Sunday Times* in 1989, he said, 'I believe in God, but God is not even that which I believe in,' a statement which can only leave one guessing. More positive was his response to the Hebrew blessing, 'Blessed art thou, our Lord God, King of the universe, who hast made the creation,' quoted by Stephen Medcalf in a conversation with him: 'There's nothing else to say is there?' replied Golding.[28]

What is inescapable is that Golding's major novels disclose a classic-ally Augustinian view of the world, with their brutal disclosure of sin in both social and personal life, the need for divine help in overcoming this and the availability of this grace for those who will open themselves to it. As mentioned earlier, Golding's preparatory notebooks for *Pincher Martin* reveal one of the themes to be 'Running away from God is running away from helplessness and death towards power and life.'[29] The sculptor Michael Ayrton brilliantly likened Golding to 'a cross between Hornblower and St Augustine' and said Golding felt the world's evils as if they were a personal guilt. 'I don't know any man', he said, 'with a more intense and passionate sense of sin.' He was struck too by Golding's unpretentious-ness.[30] A final endorsement can be taken from T. S. Eliot. When an elderly Eliot was told by someone worried that Faber & Faber had published *Lord of the Flies*, he read it and found it a splendid novel that was morally and theologically impeccable.[31]

A revealing disclosure of how Golding saw his own philosophy of life in relation to his writing was given in a lecture he delivered in Hamburg in 1980.[32] In this, he admitted to being subject to great rages, one of the greatest being directed against what he described as 'the three most crashing bores of the Western world', Marx, Darwin and Freud. In fact, it was not the writings of these men themselves which enraged him but the simplistic reductionism which had been so widely adopted in the Western world as a result of them. We see that revolt against reductionism in all his novels, for they concern people who make genuine choices in a mysterious, baffling world. This points to the second conviction out of which Golding wrote: 'The bare act of being is an outrageous improbability. Indeed and indeed, I wonder at it. A mental attitude to which both heredity and upbringing have made me prone is a sense of continual astonishment.' He then adds that his epitaph should be 'He wondered',[33] and continues that the major theme of his novels is an exploration of 'What man *is*, whatever man is under the eye of heaven.' So he has put man, with his little light of consciousness, at extremities, and has tested him to the limit.

In this exercise, his great preoccupation, he has had the label 'pessimist' pasted on him. In fact his position is that of 'a universal pessimist but a cosmic optimist', and he goes on to explain what he means by this: 'I guess we are in hell', he says, and continues, 'If this were the only world, it would be not only hell but also the only possible damnation.' But it may be, and he hopes this to be the case, 'that the universe, the hell we see for all its beauty, vastness, majesty is only part of a whole which is quite unimaginable', and the human act of creativity 'is a signature scribbled in the human soul, a sign that beyond the transient horrors and beauties of our hell there is a Good which is ultimate and absolute'.[34] There is a remarkable affinity here in his view of hell and redemption with the view of T. S. Eliot discussed earlier in this book.

10

R. S. Thomas
Presence in absence

Introduction

R. S. Thomas (1913–2000) read Latin at Bangor University, North Wales, and after training at St Michael's College, Llandaff, was ordained in the Church of Wales. He served in a number of increasingly remote parishes, ending up at Aberdaron on the Llŷn Peninsula, finally retiring to Y Rhiw, on the south-west tip of the peninsula in 1978. His first three volumes of verse were largely included in *Song at the Year's Turning*, published in 1955 to great critical acclaim. He continued to publish slim volumes of verse throughout his ministry as a parish priest. He was awarded the Queen's Gold Medal for Poetry in 1964 and was nominated for the Nobel Prize for literature in 1966. Brought up in an English-speaking family in Liverpool he taught himself Welsh at the age of 30. He regretted that Welsh was not deeply enough part of him for him to write Welsh poetry but he preferred to converse in Welsh and wrote some prose in Welsh, including an autobiography of himself in the third person. He was a fierce Welsh Nationalist, and wrote bitterly about the loss of the Welsh language and culture, castigating both the English, for their takeover, and the Welsh, for their subservience to this.

Looking west

When R. S. Thomas's collection of poems *Song at the Year's Turning*, was published in 1955 it had an introduction by John Betjeman containing the words 'The "Name" which has the honour to introduce this fine poet to a wider public will be forgotten long before that of R. S. Thomas.'[1] Betjeman remains popular, but the reputation of Thomas has indeed grown, and will endure as long as people continue to explore the mystery of life in poetry. As mentioned, he was nominated by the Welsh Academy for the Nobel Prize for literature in 1996. Through a combination of fashion and ill luck this particular award never came his way, but he regarded all such things with total disdain anyway. What is certain is that after the deaths of W. H. Auden and T. S. Eliot he was the major English-language poet writing on religious themes in a way that resonates with unbelievers and believers alike. For the last part of the twentieth century his poetry spoke more clearly than any other for, and to, the condition of all who raise the question of God in any serious way.

Thomas's father was a sailor. In a poem about his parents' marriage, he wrote

> The voice of my father
> in the night with the hunger
> of the sea in it and the emptiness
> of the sea. While the house founders
> in time, I must listen to him
> complaining, a ship's captain
> with no crew, a navigator
> without a port; rejected
> by the barrenness of his wife's
> coasts, by the wind's bitterness
> off her heart. I take his failure
> for ensign, flying it
> at my bedpost, where my own
> children cry to be born.[2]

It is a poem that immediately brings home one of the strengths of Thomas's poetry: its vivid, sustained imagery. Different aspects of a sea captain's life are used to accentuate the emptiness of his parents' marriage. It is also a poem that indicates both the harsh honesty of his own approach to life, and the source of that hardness within himself.[3]

The influence of his mother led Thomas to be ordained,[4] and after training he served as a curate in two parishes on the Welsh Borders. But from here he could see the Welsh hills in the distance, and this unsettled him. He knew he needed to be living in the deep Welsh countryside, so he set about learning Welsh and in 1942 went to Manafon in the Welsh hills, then totally remote from the industrial world with not a single tractor. There he observed the Welsh hill farmers and wondered aloud in poetry what went on in their heads:

> Iago Prytherch his name, though, be it allowed
> Just an ordinary man of the bald Welsh hills,
> Who pens a few sheep in a gap of cloud.
> Docking mangels, chipping the green skin
> From the yellow bones with a half-witted grin

Of satisfaction, or churning the crude earth
To a stiff sea of clods that glint in the wind –
So are his days spent, his spittled mirth
Rarer than the sun that cracks the cheeks
Of the gaunt sky perhaps once in a week.
And then at night see him fixed in his chair
Motionless, except when he leans to gob in the fire.
There is something frightening in the vacancy of his mind.
His clothes, sour with years of sweat
And animal contact, shock the refined,
But affected, sense with their stark naturalness.
Yet this is your prototype, who, season by season
Against siege of rain and the wind's attrition,
Preserves his stock, an impregnable fortress
Not to be stormed even in death's confusion.
Remember him, then, for he, too, is a winner of wars,
Enduring like a tree under the curious stars.[5]

There is a brutal realism in the description of that farm labourer, yet at the same time the onlooker is warned off any attitude of superiority, and there is an ungrudging admiration for Prytherch's fortitude and endurance. It was poems like these that first caught people's imagination, and with which he is often associated because a number have been reproduced in school textbooks and anthologies. But this was not an approach to life likely to win many friends in the parish. This is his poem about a funeral:

There was a death, yes; but death's brother,
Sin, is of more importance.
Shabbily the teeth gleam,
Sharpening themselves on reputations
That were firm once. On the cheap coffin
The earth falls more cleanly than tears.
What are these red faces for?
This incidence of pious catarrh
At the grave's edge?[6]

Like Wordsworth, Thomas found inspiration both for his poetry and his spirit in nature. But he has a less idealistic view of day-to-day rural life, and he focuses far more on the harsher aspects of lives which are 'mortgaged to the grasping soil'.[7]

Thomas's poetry never lost this element of bleak realism, this stark, painful honesty. It matched photos of his face that began appearing in the press, gaunt, unsmiling, uncompromising. But if he was hard on other people, he was even harder on himself. He continually castigates himself for his emptiness and how little he has to give. He warns himself and town dwellers not to think of themselves as superior to the peasant farmers he wrote about.

Interviewed towards the end of his life Thomas said he was disqualified from major status by his 'lack of love for human beings', adding, 'there is a kind of narrowness in my work which a good critic would condemn'.[8] Yet in fact the element of sensitive compassion does often come out in his poems. He knows that the hill farmers to whom he ministers have hands that have 'bruised themselves on the locked doors of life' and that their hearts are 'full of gulped tears'.[9]

This bleak and uncompromising honesty does not sit well with people's image of the average parish priest, and there is no doubt that the majority of people found him aloof and cold. When the BBC made a film about him a few years ago, they interviewed the churchwarden of one of the parishes where he had served, and received the response 'Aye, I knew him – and a right miserable bugger he was too.' The first paradox about Thomas is that someone of his temperament ever became a parish priest at all, let alone remained one. The second paradox is even stranger: the contrast between his grim image and what is revealed in the biography of Thomas by Byron Rogers about his humour and pastoral care. This suggests a picture, with a great deal of supporting evidence from people who knew Thomas well, that strongly contradicts the public impression of him.[10] First, Thomas could be extremely funny. The BBC Wales arts correspondent said he had met only three really funny men in his life. The first two were Ken Dodd and Lenny Bruce; the third was R. S. Thomas. Second, when Thomas felt that people were in real need, he was sensitive and unstinting in his support for them. There are many testimonies in the book to this.

Another major paradox in his life was in his attitude to Wales and the Welsh language. His love of Wales was passionate, as was the other side of this, his hatred of English domination both in history, and even more through the influx of caravans and the domination of the English language. He compared the destruction of Wales by the English to the destruction of the Native Americans in the USA.[11] Indeed he achieved notoriety in the 1960s when he failed to condemn the burning of English second homes in Wales, even though he was a lifelong pacifist and a member of the Campaign for Nuclear Disarmament. Although he deplored killing, he did say that 'even if one Englishman got killed, what is that compared to the killing of our nation'.[12]

Years later he denied that this was encouraging violence, and was quite clear that he would say it again. He defended it on the grounds that when you are dealing with a nation you are dealing with a spiritual concept, in this case the very soul of Wales, which was being eroded more and more.[13] He resigned from Plaid Cymru, the Welsh Nationalist political party, because he thought they compromised too much with the English. He taught himself to be fluent in Welsh, and he published prose in Welsh. Yet despite this he did not teach his son Gwydion to speak Welsh, and sent him to be educated in an English Public School, while R. S. Thomas himself in fact sounded like an upper-class Englishman. A good number of his poems are critical of the English invasion, but even more powerful are the ones which castigate the Welsh for caring so little about it. 'Through indifference, lack of backbone, snobbishness and laziness' they had chosen to speak English and to cast away their inheritance, a culture older than that of the English. They were, he wrote in 1955

> An impotent people
> Sick with inbreeding
> Worrying the carcass of an old song.[14]

However, when Thomas died most Welsh people realized that he had in fact been their austere, fierce conscience and from most of them he evinced the same grudging respect we reserve for our consciences. As one put it, he was 'the one who urged us down the difficult road of duty and responsibility to our past when our feet danced towards the primrose path of compromise, accommodation and forgetfulness.'[15]

A further paradox is that of his first marriage to Mildred Eldridge, a talented artist. While getting on perfectly well, they seem to have lived somewhat separate lives, for she liked to stay at home and paint, while he liked to be out and about in the countryside, particularly bird watching, which was his greatest passion in life. There were no newspapers in their house, still less a television, and virtually no heating. Thomas himself was clearly something of a recluse, but his wife was a very private person as well. When she died, a journalist asked him whether he missed his wife. 'I suppose so,' he replied. 'Was he lonely?' 'I was lonely when I was with her,' he said. Yet after her death he wrote what must be some of the loveliest of all poems about marriage in the English language:

> We met
>   under a shower
> of bird-notes.
>   Fifty years passed,
> love's moment
>   in a world in

servitude to time.
   She was young;
I kissed with my eyes
   closed and opened
them on her wrinkles.
   'Come' said death,
choosing her as his
   partner for
the last dance. And she,
   who in life
had done everything
   with a bird's grace,
opened her bill now
   for the shedding
Of one sigh no
   heavier than a feather.[16]

The bird image occurs in another poem about their marriage, where he writes:

   She is at work
always, mending the garment
of our marriage, foraging
like a bird for something
for us to eat.[17]

The other extraordinary aspect of this side of Thomas's life is that a few years after his wife died he was seen going around hand in hand with another woman. At the age of 83 he married Betty Vernon, of Irish-Canadian extraction, not much younger than himself. This lady, Betty Vernon, was a member of the English squirearchy, with attitudes very different from those of Thomas himself. But apparently he was like a young boy, joyous and bubbly.

Earlier he had written a poem called 'Self-Portrait':

That resigned look! Here I am,
it says; fifty-nine,
balding, shirking the challenge
of the young girls. Time is running out
now; and the soul
unfinished. And the heart knows
this is not the portrait
it posed for. Keep the lips
firm; too many disappointments

have turned the mouth down
at the corners. There is no surgery
can mend those lines; cruelly
the light fingers them and the mind
winces. All that skill,
life, on the carving
of the curved nostril and to no end
but disgust. The hurrying eyes
pause, waiting for an outdistanced
gladness to overtake them.[18]

However, that gladness did seem to overtake him at the end.

Thomas was hardly original in finding nature itself a great source of spiritual sustenance, but this source must be stressed because it was true. He had happy childhood memories of the sea.[19] He loved to imagine the nativity scene as set in the countryside.[20] He loved watching birds and he is on record as saying that to sustain his faith he wanted nothing other than contact with God through nature.[21] A poem called 'The Moor' has rightly become popular:

It was like a church to me.
I entered it on soft foot,
Breath held like a cap in the hand.
It was quiet.
What God was there made himself felt,
Not listened to, in clean colours
That brought a moistening of the eye,
In movement of the wind over grass.

There were no prayers said. But the stillness
Of the heart's passions – that was praise
Enough; and the mind's cession
Of its kingdom. I walked on,
Simple and poor, while the air crumbled
And broke on me generously as bread.[22]

One of his most telling images is that of a field on the hillside lit up by the sun, which he writes about both in an essay and a poem. This he calls 'the pearl of great price'.[23] And he described how nature had sometimes come to him like the first day of creation and he had fallen to his knees to praise God.[24]

There was nothing sentimental about his view of nature, as can be seen in his poetry about hill farmers. He knew the hardness and cruelty of natural life at first hand.[25] A very short poem reads:

Who said to the trout,
You shall die on Good Friday
To be food for a man
And his pretty lady?

It was I, said God,
Who formed the roses
In the delicate flesh
And the tooth that bruises.[26]

This brings out his holistic view of nature, both its beauty, the roses in the delicate flesh of the trout, and the pain – the tooth that bruises. But it also indicates his great lyrical gift, which he used only sparingly because, like Beckett, he was suspicious of the power of language to seduce us away from the truth. For this reason he was particularly wary of the influence of poets like Yeats on him. He clearly had the gift of a lyricist, but lyrical elements in his poetry are very rare. He sought instead a spare, austere language to tell the hard truth as he saw it, without consolation.

While imagery drawn from nature was natural to Thomas, he also tried seriously to use metaphors from science and technology, not always successfully. The negative side of this was that he hated what he termed 'the machine', the mechanization of life, all that technology brings. His dislike of this was as strong as his bitterness towards the English language and English caravans destroying Welsh culture, and it is a theme that was very prominent in his middle period.

In one poem, he writes:

The idiot goes round and around
With his brother in a bumping-car
At the fair. The famous idiot
Smile hangs over the car's edge,
Illuminating nothing. This is mankind
Being taken for a ride by a rich
Relation. The responses are fixed:
Bump, smile; bump, smile. And the current

Is generated by the smooth flow
Of the shillings. This is an orchestra
Of steel with the constant percussion
Of laughter. But where he should be laughing
Too, his features are split open, and look!
Out of the cracks come warm human tears.[27]

It is a poem which brings out a number of characteristic features of Thomas's poetry. First, a simple vivid image; and it is important to remember that Thomas, according to his own account has always tried to make his poetry as accessible as possible and deliberately eschewed the obscure. Then that image is developed with several subsidiary images which are all related to the main one. It expresses his hatred of the mechanization of human life in the service of mindless sensation. But also his sensitivity to human anguish: 'Out of the cracks come warm human tears.' More positively he tried to use the language of physics in some of his poems to bring out the immensity and mystery of the universe.

His awareness of the harshness of nature and the extent of suffering in human life led him to write some extraordinarily bitter poems about God, for example in 'H'm':

> and one said
> speak to us of love
> and the preacher opened
> his mouth and the word God
> fell out so they tried
> again speak to us
> of God then but the preacher
> was silent reaching
> his arms out but the little
> children the ones with
> big bellies and bow
> legs that were like
> a razor shell
> were too weak to come[28]

The title gets it right: 'H'm', a quizzical, sceptical questioning of all the answers. The poem has no punctuation, no capital at the beginning or full stop at the end. It is, as it were, a fragment of an unending sentence.

Against this background it is not surprising that for Thomas the image of the cross was crucial. Indeed he has said that the reason he is content to call himself a Christian is because the Christian belief that God has taken suffering into himself is the most profound and satisfactory answer to the great problem of suffering.[29] The image of the cross occurs in a number of poems. It was a conviction he expressed in his poem 'The Coming':

> And God held in his hand
> A small globe. Look, he said.
> The son looked. Far off,

As through water, he saw
A scorched land of fierce
Colour. The light burned
There; crusted buildings
Cast their shadows; a bright
Serpent, a river
Uncoiled itself, radiant
With slime.
     On a bare
Hill a bare tree saddened
The sky. Many people
Held out their thin arms
To it, as though waiting
For a vanished April
To return to its crossed
boughs. The son watched
Them. Let me go there, he said.[30]

This, we might say, however hard, is Christian orthodoxy, powerfully conveyed. But in the 1970s the poetry of Thomas went through an even stranger, more disconcerting phase. A number of poems accused God of egomaniacal sadism, as in his poem 'The Island':

And God said, I will build a church here
And cause this people to worship me,
And afflict them with poverty and sickness
In return for centuries of hard work
And patience. And its walls shall be hard as
Their hearts, and its windows let in the light
Grudgingly, as their minds do, and the priest's words be drowned
By the wind's caterwauling. All this I will do,

Said God, and watch the bitterness in their eyes
Grow, and their lips suppurate with
Their prayers. And their women shall bring forth
On my altars, and I will choose the best
Of them to be thrown back into the sea.

And that was only on one island.[31]

It is possible to see this and other poems infected with a hatred of God as a kind of poetic therapy, as Thomas's getting something out of his system. But it is more than that. As has been well said, Thomas seems to be pursuing a kind of *via negativa*: 'Stating the worst that can be said against the anthropomorphic notion of God, he also traces a discipline of deliberate spiritual emptying.'[32] And this leads us into the main religious theme of Thomas's poetry, the absence of God, which is at the same time his presence. In 1964, R. S., as he was always known, not Ronald, his name, and certainly not Ron, moved with his wife to Aberdaron at the end of the Llŷn Peninsula. Although he moved homes on retirement, he remained in an isolated spot on the edge of the British Isles. This move marked a change in the direction of his poetry. As he wrote:

> I have become more interested in what somebody termed semi-abstract ideas. It coincided with moving out to the end of the Llŷn Peninsula in Wales, away from the hill country and the hill farmers, where I became conscious of the large horizons, the sea, the Atlantic thrusting itself into the Irish Sea, and the starry sky at night.[33]

Poems speak of the silence of God and tell of the many hours he spent kneeling in the chancel of the church and no word coming; of questions addressed to which no answer is given. Images include that of the church building as a trap in which the great God might be caught but who somehow always eludes him; of a record which picks up nothing but the natural background; of a camera which films the landscape but whose film shows a blank as far as God is concerned. By the time of his 1972 collection he seems to have accepted this:

> Why no! I never thought other than
> That God is that great absence
> In our lives, the empty silence
> Within, the place where we go
> Seeking, not in hope to
> Arrive or find. He keeps the interstices
> In our knowledge, the darkness
> Between stars. His are the echoes
> We follow, the footprints he has just
> Left.[34]

That last image was developed in an interview on the radio, where he said:

> Being something of a naturalist myself, I know how I have found a hare's form on the hillside and I have been able to put my hand in it and feel it still warm, and this is my feeling of God – that we don't actually find him but we find where he has been, we find the place still warm with his presence, but he is absent, and we find his footsteps, his footprints, but we never actually come upon him because how can we? If we could comprehend God we would be God ourselves.[35]

This absence, however, had a powerful effect on him:

> It is this great absence
> that is like a presence, that compels
> me to address it without hope
> of a reply.[36]

Here we need to pause and refer more widely than Thomas himself to this theme. The philosopher and mystic Simone Weil once wrote that 'God can only be present in creation under the form of absence.'[37] This is because God is not a thing in the world of things. He is not a reality that can be put in any category of which we are aware. Anything that we could categorize in that way would not be God. He upholds all things, fills all things and includes all things within his infinity, but is not anything that we can point to or describe. So it is that, paradoxically, the more aware we are of the absence of God from creation, in the sense that he cannot be pinpointed by either finger or word, the more aware we are of what it is for God to be God.

The fact that this absence is not an ordinary kind of absence reveals itself by the way it does not let us go, but haunts us. Thomas has written both an essay in Welsh and a poem in English on the theme of Abercauwg. Literally this means something like 'the place where the cuckoos sing'. But it is a place we can never find. Wherever we look, it is not there; but this is not cause for despair. In the poem, he wrote:

> An absence is how we become surer
> Of what we want. Abercauwg
> Is not here now, but there And
> There is the indefinable point . . .[38]

In the essay, he said:

> The fact that we go to the Machynlleth area to look for the site of Abercauwg, saying 'No this isn't it', means nothing. Here is not cause for disappointment and despair, but rather a way to come to know better, through its absence, the nature of the place we seek . . . through striving to see it, through longing for it, through refusing to accept that it belongs to the past and has fallen into oblivion; through refusing to accept some second-hand substitute, we will succeed in preserving it as an eternal possibility.[39]

Thomas hated being pressed to give sound-bite answers. Once, when he was giving a public reading of his poems in the University Church in Cambridge, he went into the pulpit with a great sheaf of papers, and after a certain amount of shuffling through them read a number of poems in his dry voice, all the more powerful for being expressionless, and then showed himself willing to answer questions. 'Which poet has most influenced you, Mr Thomas?' 'I never answer that question.' And that was the kind of answer all the questions got. He did not like oversimplifications, or being categorized: 'No, friend, that is *not* what I said. I am not one of those people who have a ready answer.'[40] This is most obviously so in questions relating God, who is by definition mystery beyond anything we can say about him and in relation to whom all words are partially misleading. This makes all the more surprising the interview he gave to Naim Attallah for *The Oldie*,[41] in which he says that while his crisis of faith is a continual one, he has never ceased to believe in God, and puts his trust in 'this great presence' and, as far as his own future is concerned, trust for whatever might come after death, oblivion or a continued existence in some form.

Barry Morgan, the Archbishop of Wales, went to see Thomas shortly before his death. He wrote:

> I tentatively asked him how he felt about death. 'We came from God and go to God', he replied, 'that was good enough for Augustine and it is good enough for me. For He who created us will at the last receive us'. That is eloquent testimony of his deep faith at a critical time as was the deeply reverential way in which he received the sacraments.[42]

So we are not talking about atheism here, but of an ultimate mystery which can never have been fully fathomed. I think he would have had a lot of sympathy with what Gerard Manley Hopkins wrote to his friend Robert Bridges, 'You do not mean by a mystery what a Catholic does. You mean an interesting uncertainty . . . but a Catholic by mystery means an incomprehensible certainty.'[43] While it is natural to try to understand that mystery, that is, make it comprehensible, not only is our comprehension limited and limiting, unless we are very careful it has the effect of pinning down or tying up that which by definition must always elude such attempts. When those attempts at comprehension have been sanctified by authority and long usage, as in any established religion, this can also blind us to the limiting effect of the words used. So Thomas, as it were, lets go his religious anchorage in a tradition and launches out. As he put it in the words previously quoted:

> through striving to see it, through longing for it, through refusing to accept that it belongs to the past and has fallen into oblivion; through refusing to accept some second-hand substitute, we will succeed in preserving it as an eternal possibility.

What he wants to keep as an eternal possibility is God as God, not simply preserve a hallowed image which we can control.

The title of Simone Weil's best-known book is *Waiting on God*, which is the theme of one of the essays in it. The image of waiting is also central to one of Thomas's best-loved poems:

> Moments of great calm,
> Kneeling before an altar
> Of wood in a stone church
> In summer, waiting for the God
> To speak; the air a staircase
> For silence; the sun's light
> Ringing me, as though I acted
> A great role. And the audiences
> Still; all that close throng
> Of spirits waiting, as I,
> For the message.
>   Prompt me, God;
> But not yet. When I speak,
> Though it be you who speak
> Through me, something is lost.
> The meaning is in the waiting.[44]

This brings out well the fact that all words purportedly from God come to us through human words, and as such will inevitably be limited, that is in some way distorting: 'something is lost'. We can speak of God at all only through our human metaphors, and every metaphor or image we use is as untrue as it is true. So our human words that try to reach up and refer to God continually have to be made, and broken and remade. One image has to be set constantly against another, which contradicts and corrects it, and then this image in its turn has to be qualified in a new way.

Moments of hope

In the chapter on W. H. Auden, I contrasted his *via positiva* with Eliot's negative or apophatic way in which, realizing the radical limitation of all words, we simply wait upon God in wordless longing. In this stillness, this waiting on God, the meaning is in the waiting. As Thomas puts it:

> When I speak,
> Though it be you who speak
> Through me, something is lost.

Although the poetry of R. S. is brutal in its bleak realism, and though sometimes he has posited an egomaniacal and sadistic God, the dominant themes of Thomas's religious poems, the apparent absence and silence of God, have their proper place in the Christian mystical tradition. There are also other moments that keep hope alive. As I mentioned earlier, he was an expert birdwatcher. In one poem, he draws on the imagery of looking for birds over the sea:

> Grey waters, vast
> as an area of prayer
> that one enters. Daily
> over a period of years
> I have let the eye rest on them.
> Was I waiting for something?
> Nothing
> but that continuous waving
> that is without meaning
> occurred.
> Ah, but a rare bird is
> rare. It is when one is not looking,
> at times one is not there
> that it comes.[45]

So there is hope. The rare bird does come, even if it comes when one is not looking or not there. There might also be a moment of illumination that comes to us through nature:

> Suddenly after long silence
> he has become voluble.
> He addresses me from a myriad
> directions with the fluency
> of water, the articulateness
> of green leaves . . .
> I listen to the things
> round me: weeds, stones, instruments,
> the machine itself, all
> Speaking to me in the vernacular
> of the purposes of One who is.[46]

There is in the poetry of Thomas the occasional surprising moment of hope:

Not conscious
    that you have been seeking
        suddenly
        you have come upon it.
the village in the Welsh hills
        dust free
        with no road out
but the one you came in by.

           A bird chimes
    from a green tree
the hour that is no hour
    you know. The river dawdles
to hold a mirror for you
where you may see yourself
        as you are, a traveller
           with the moon's halo
        above him, who has arrived
        after long journeying where he
           began, catching this
        one truth by surprise
that there is everything to look forward to.[47]

It is a haunting poem with many of the same themes as Eliot, the timeless moment, the journey back to where we started, the echoes of joy, but put in a very different way from him.

These moments are rare, and not easily won. They emerge, if at all, out of the silence, which was at the heart of Thomas's approach to God: the silent waiting on the mystery that always eludes our words. For Thomas silence was fundamental to true religion. It was itself a kind of invitation to enter into the unfathomable depths of God:

But the silence in the mind
is when we live best, within
listening distance of the silence
we call God. This is the deep
calling to deep of the psalm-
writer, the bottomless ocean
we launch the armada of
our thoughts on, never arriving.

It is a presence, then,
whose margins are our margins;
that calls us out over our

own fathoms. What to do
but draw a little nearer to
such ubiquity by remaining still.[48]

Finally a few lines from a poem in which he indicates how he was once attracted by the poetry of Yeats, and then came to distrust that kind of eloquence when faced by the harshness of life.[49] It ends:

Now

in the small hours
Of belief the one eloquence

to master is that
of the bowed head, the bent
knee, waiting, as at the end

Of a hard winter
for one flower to open
on the mind's tree of thorns.[50]

So the final paradox of R. S. Thomas is that few poets have been so fierce in their disbelief in a God of love, or in the presence of any kind of God with us. Yet he, more than any other modern poet since Eliot, has conveyed the reality of belief in a time of unbelief, has kept open the possibility of faith in God in a hard time. The winter may be long, and the mind scratched by thorns of continual self-questioning, but the poet waits in hope for that one flower to open.

11

Edwin Muir and George Mackay Brown
Light from the Orkneys

Introduction

Off the north coast of Scotland lie the Orkneys, with their remarkable Neolithic and Iron Age remains, including the village of Skara Brae, some 5,000 years old. In the capital, Kirkwall, is the magnificent twelfth-century red-and-white sandstone cathedral of St Magnus, and in a small corner of the cathedral are the names of about a dozen distinguished Orkneymen. Two of those men are among the finest poets of the twentieth century, Edwin Muir and George Mackay Brown.

Edwin Muir (1887–1959) lived in the Orkneys until he was 14, when his family moved to Glasgow. He married Willa Anderson and in 1921 they moved to Prague, where they did translations, especially of Franz Kafka. He was Director of the British Council in Prague and later in Rome. This move to Europe released his imagination and he published a number of books of poems, including a collected edition in 1952. He also wrote three novels. He was Norton Professor of English at Harvard in 1955. Muir lived through traumatic times but what mattered to him was the inner journey, which is reflected in his poetry and autobiography.

George Mackay Brown (1921–96) was brought up in Stromness in the Orkneys, where, except for short periods as a mature student on the mainland, he remained all his life. Born into a poor family and suffering from ill health he started to write poetry and prose. The quality of this was eventually recognized by Edwin Muir, and his first volume of poems was published in 1954. He wrote articles for the local press, short stories, plays and novels. His work is deeply steeped in Norse saga and local folk-lore, and is imbued with both the beauty of the natural world around him and its suffering. He himself became an influence on the composer Peter Maxwell Davies, who set a number of Mackay Brown's works to music for the St Magnus Festival.

By the late 1960s his work was internationally renowned and the American poet Robert Lowell travelled to the Orkneys with the express purpose of meeting him. Brought up as a Presbyterian, he became a Roman Catholic, a faith which helped him hold together a very fragile life.

Edwin Muir

Edwin Muir lived the first 14 years of his life in the Orkneys. This is how he describes that pre-industrial time, which always had an enchantment for him:

> The Orkney I was born into was a place where there was no great distinction between the ordinary and the fabulous; the lives of living men turned into legend. A man I knew once sailed out in a boat to look for a mermaid, and claimed afterwards that he had talked with her. Fantastic feats of strength were commonly reported. Fairies, or 'fairicks', as they were called, were encountered dancing on the sands on moonlight nights. From people's talk, they were small, graceful creatures, about the size of leprechauns, but pretty, not grotesque. There was no harm in them. All these things have vanished from Orkney in the past fifty years under the pressure of compulsory education.[1]

It was a community that was uncompetitive, in which the farmers helped one another. It was a shock to him when he was later precipitated into a highly competitive world. Unfortunately, because of heavy exactions the family had to move from one farm to another and then to Glasgow. There in quick succession his father, mother and two brothers died. Muir did a number of unpleasant jobs in factories and offices, including working in a factory that turned bones into glue. Glasgow was a devastating experience, one which shaped the whole of his life and set going in his mind the first great myth around which his life story was organized: expulsion from the garden of Eden.

In Glasgow, it wasn't just the loss of this earthly Eden; it wasn't just the anguish of losing the closest members of his family. It was the stripping away of all sense of what for the moment I shall call 'enchantment': the value and dignity and worth that we recognize in human beings. He remembered the moment exactly. He was travelling in a tram on his way to work when he looked at the people sitting opposite him. Suddenly they seemed to him just animals: flesh and bone and no more. Jonathan Swift, the great Dean of St Patrick's Cathedral, Dublin, had a similar feeling about human beings, which he turned to good effect in his satirical writings. But it left Edwin Muir totally devastated. It set for ever in his mind the myth that he had been thrown out of Eden into a kind of hell. As he wrote:

I was returning in a tramcar from my work; the tramcar was full and very hot; the sun burned through the glass on backs of necks, shoulders, faces, trousers, skirts, hands, all stacked there impartially. Opposite me was sitting a man with a face like a pig's, and as I looked at him in the oppressive heat the words came into my mind, 'That is an animal.' I looked around me at the other people in the tramcar. I was conscious that something had fallen from them and from me; and with a sense of desolation I saw that they were all animals, some of them good, some evil, some charming, some sad, some happy, some sick, some well. The tramcar stopped and went on again, carrying its menagerie; my mind saw countless other tramcars where animals sat or got on or off with mechanical dexterity, as if they had been trained in a circus; and I realized that in all Glasgow, in all Scotland, in all the world, there was nothing but millions of such creatures living an animal life and moving towards an animal death as towards a great slaughterhouse. I stared at the faces, trying to make them human again and to dispel the hallucination, but I could not.[2]

The outward course of Edwin Muir's life can be told quite quickly. In 1919, he married Willa Anderson, about which he wrote simply 'My marriage was the most fortunate event in my life.' One of the reasons it was so fortunate is that Edwin Muir suffered from devastating fears and terrors. These came up in vivid, amazing dreams and daylight trances and bouts of depression. He sought help from psychoanalysis, which did help in the long run, but which brought about dreams that took him even closer to the edge. Willa clearly helped him through all this. There is a poem called 'The Annunciation', the first lines of which read:

Now in this iron reign
I sing the liberty
Where each asks from each
What each most wants to give . . .[3]

After their marriage, the Muirs moved to London and then lived in cities on the continent, Prague, Dresden, in Italy, Salzburg and Vienna, returning to England in 1924. Muir had no formal education to speak of, but had come to read voraciously and teach himself languages and an appreciation of music. He and his wife collaborated on highly acclaimed translations of various writers like Kafka and Thomas Mann. Between 1925 and 1956 he published seven volumes of poetry, which were collated and published as a complete collection after his death. He also published three novels and after he came to St Andrew's in 1935 a controversial book, *Scott and Scotland*, which argued that Scotland could create a national literature only by writing in English.

From 1946 to 1949, Muir was the Director of the British Council in Prague and Rome, a time which was important for his spiritual journey. In 1950, he became Warden of Newbattle Abbey College, a college for working-class men, half an hour south of Edinburgh. Due to his influence George Mackay Brown became a student there, much to the benefit of Brown. Muir loved the task of teaching and encouraging people from very similar backgrounds to himself. After Muir's death, George Mackay Brown wrote a play about him in which he says of his students:

> Never be hard on them. Never let them feel they're wasting their time. My time as well. The whole treasury of literature is there for them to ransack. Open their minds to the old wisdom, goodness, beauty. Arm them against the gray impersonal powers. They press in on every side. More and more.[4]

Everyone agrees it was difficult to capture Muir's personality or what there was about someone whom Maggie Fergusson, George Mackay Brown's biographer, has described as 'This serene, withdrawn, deeply private man that inspired such love.'[5] For everyone saw that it was love that the students had for him. T. S. Eliot thought Muir had complete integrity: 'I cannot believe that [he] ever uttered one disingenuous word in speech, or committed one disingenuous word to print.'[6] Then in 1955 he became Norton Professor of English at Harvard University. He returned to England in 1956 and died in 1959.

So it was a varied, somewhat peripatetic, life. But for Muir, what happened outwardly was not as important as what happened inwardly. For his whole life was a spiritual journey, an attempt to recover that which he had lost when he was precipitated out of Eden. It is significant that when his autobiography was first published in 1940 it bore the title *The Story and the Fable, an Autobiography*. This gives a much better idea than the bare title *An Autobiography* that was later used, because he saw his life in terms of a story and a fable. The story, the outward course of events, has already been outlined. But for Muir, it was the fable that mattered. The first part of the fable was the loss of paradise. The second part he described in various images. But in essence it was a rediscovery of what he had lost during that tram journey, the essential dignity of human beings, their spiritual nature, and for him this was connected with an awareness of the immortal. He had gone through various phases, an evangelical conversion as a teenager (which he quickly came to despise), an ardent Nietzschean materialism, a passionate socialism, but finally he achieved a sense of the immortal self. As he put it:

> I realized that immortality is not an idea or a belief, but a state of being in which man keeps alive in himself his perception of that boundless union and freedom, which he can faintly apprehend in time, though its consummation lies beyond time.[7]

Again:

> My belief in immortality, so far as I can divine its origin, and that is not far, seems to be connected with the same impulse to know myself. I can never know myself; but the closer I come to knowledge of myself, the more certain I must feel that I am immortal, and conversely, the more certain I am of my immortality the more intimately I must come to know myself.[8]

Muir's psychological distress led him to undergo Jungian analysis in London, and this lent itself to an archetypal or mythical way of looking at life in a way that Freud does not. But whether or not one is in sympathy with Jung, Muir's poems of what we might call discovery and return are of importance. What had happened to him, he believed, was not just about him, but was in principle true of all human beings. He thought that the life of every individual was an endlessly repeated performance of an archetypal person and that we live out this myth almost without knowing it.

Some of Muir's poems also suggest a Platonic view of life and time. But Platonism, though often regarded as an ally of Christianity, is not Christianity. But Muir went beyond Platonism as a result of some powerful experiences. While in Rome running the British Council, Muir was struck by the little religious statues and plaques around the city. One of them, depicting the annunciation, inspired a lovely poem of that title. In this poem, he describes the angel and Mary gazing at each other, each face reflecting heaven in a timeless moment as outside 'the destroying minutes' flow'. Outside this trancelike moment time continues on its unrelenting way:

> But through the endless afternoon
> These neither speak nor movement make,
> But stare into their deepening trance
> As if their gaze would never break.[9]

That was clearly a magical moment, the stillness of that gaze seeming to lift the viewer beyond this world. But it was scenes like this that changed Muir's whole approach to religion, and made him look for the spiritual within the materiality of *this* world. He had been bought up in the Orkneys with a rather severe form of Presbyterianism. As he wrote in his autobiography:

I was aware of religion chiefly as the sacred word, and the church itself, severe and decent, with its touching bareness and austerity . . . but nothing told me that Christ was born in the flesh and had lived on the earth.[10]

But when in Rome he saw plaques like that of the annunciation, as he put it:

A religion that dared to show forth the mystery for everyone to see would have shocked the congregations of the North, would have seemed a sort of blasphemy, perhaps even an indecency. But here it was publicly shown, as Christ showed himself on earth . . . This open declaration was to me the very mark of Christianity, distinguishing it from the older religions. For although the pagan gods had visited the earth, they did not assume the burden of our flesh, live our life and die our death.[11]

Edwin Muir's outward life traversed some of the key events of the previous 200 years. For, as he said, he was brought up in a pre-industrial Eden, and in his move to Glasgow travelled 150 years. He lived in a city that at that time had some of the worst slums in Europe, and experienced some of its most demeaning working conditions in office and factory. In the course of his life, although he lived for periods in St Andrew's and Edinburgh, he experienced what was happening on the continent, in a way only few others had the opportunity to do, both the rise of Nazism before the war and the ascension of communism in Prague afterwards. In short, he witnessed first hand some of the terrible evil of one of the worst centuries in human history. Without formal education, he became, through his own reading, highly educated, and an educator of others. He went through the intellectual pilgrimage of so many intellectuals of his generation, first as a Nietzschean materialist, and then as a socialist. He underwent psychoanalysis. Yet for him all this was secondary. What was primary was the mythical life, the loss of Eden and the gradual recovery of it over a lifetime's living.

Earlier in his life Muir had had a kind of vision of creation, of creation as it ought to be. His whole life after that was a kind of working out of the second part of the fable. If the first part was his expulsion from Eden, the second part was his return from exile. It was a return that, he came to believe, was opened up for us by the movement of the divine to the human. This had implications not just for humanity but for the whole of creation. One aspect of the traditional myth was that the expulsion of humanity from our primeval paradise ruptured the whole of creation, set everything against everything else; and one aspect of redemption would be this healing in nature itself. One wonderful poem, which describes life

after a nuclear holocaust, suggests a new world, in which we are recon-
nected with the animal kingdom. In this devastated world, even the radios
become dumb. The poem says that the survivors do not like to hear the
radios again, which will only bring news of the bad old world. Now they
live as they can, tractors rusting in the fields. And then horses suddenly
appear, like fabulous steeds from an ancient world. They have waited
shyly and now seek humans out for a 'long-lost archaic companionship'
in which they freely offer their services. That free servitude 'pierced our
hearts' and changed our lives.[12]

It is a brilliant updating of the ancient myth of the restoration of nature,
another aspect of the fable that he thought human life lived out. So we
come to perhaps the most important form of the fable of all. It is expressed
in his poem 'One Foot in Eden'.

In terms of Muir's own experience, he still has part of him in that
Orkney childhood Eden, 'One foot in Eden still, I stand'. Now, however
he looks at the world about him so full of love and hate. Yet, he continues:

> Blossoms of grief and charity
> Bloom in these darkened fields alone.
> What had Eden ever to say
> Of hope and faith and pity and love . . .

He ends

> Strange blessings never in Paradise
> Fall from these beclouded skies.[13]

Here we have to be very careful not to suggest that suffering is in itself a
blessing, and I think Muir got it right when at the end of his autobiography
he reflects on his own periods of depression. He writes:

> Now and then during the years I fell into the dumps for short or prolonged
> periods, was subject to fears which I did not understand, and passed
> through stretches of blankness and deprivation. From these, I learned
> things which I could not otherwise have learned, so that I cannot regard
> them as mere loss. Yet I believe that I would have been better without
> them.[14]

I love that statement – its understated pain and honesty. He wrote that out
of the blankness and deprivation came things which otherwise he would
not have learned, but nevertheless it would have been better to have been
without them. He did not have an easy life, and in one poem he writes
about his depression in terms of devastations. He knew what it was like
to live with famished field and blackened tree. He would rather not have

gone through all that, yet recognized that without them his insight into life would have been poorer. In his wonderful words, already quoted:

> Strange blessings never in Paradise
> Fall from these beclouded skies.

George Mackay Brown

George Mackay Brown spent the whole of his life on the Orkneys apart from a short spell as a mature student at Edinburgh University and one at Newbattle Abbey College when, as mentioned earlier, Edwin Muir was Warden. It was these islands, their scenery, history, legends and people that provided the inspiration for his poetry, short stories and novels.

On his mother's side, he came from Gaelic-speaking Highlanders. His mother, Mhairi Mackay, had come over from their croft in Sutherland when she was 16 to work in a hotel. His father, John Brown, came from a family that had lived in the Orkneys for centuries. They had six children, George being the youngest.

The family lived in Stromness, which George liked to call 'Hamnavoe', the Old Norse name meaning 'haven inside the bay'. The family were poor, and, as well as being a postman, John Brown had two other jobs. Being a postman meant that he had a new uniform every year, and this had the great advantage that the old one could be cut and remade for the children. Even so they had to apply for grants from the poor fund for shoes for their children in the winter. They went barefoot in the summer. Nevertheless they were basically happy and George had a stability and routine of life which he loved. Mhairi Mackay was a warm, generous, unfailingly buoyant soul, gently singing Gaelic songs about the house, to whom George was absolutely devoted throughout the whole of his life. His father, 15 years older than his mother, short and fat, had a sharp wit, was a good mimic and was clearly something of a frustrated actor. This combination of Mhairi's songs about the house and his father's wit and sense of drama helped to create an environment in which George's imagination and poetry were nurtured. His environment was also helped by his sister, Ruby, 10 years older than him, who loved telling melodramatic stories with unhappy endings. As George said in response to this:

> I was beginning to learn that there was a thing in the world called evil; but I learned a thing even more important, that all the bad things in life, that happen to everybody sooner or later, could be faced, controlled, and even made beautiful by poetry.[15]

This stable childhood was rudely broken when an unkind landlady took against Mhairi and kicked the family out of their house. They went first to an ugly house with a drain under it, a factor that further undermined the health of George's father, John, and then to a council house. John became totally crippled with arthritis, and had to retire with no pension. Brooding and depressed in his room, he became convinced that his teeth were the cause of the trouble and persuaded the dentist to take the whole lot out. This was done without anaesthetic, John and his dentist drinking half a bottle of whiskey during the operation to help matters along.

In his mid teens George started to get into a bad way both physically and psychologically. He chain-smoked Woodbines from the age of 15, and was so frightened of being separated from his mother he used to follow her out shopping and hide in doorways to keep an eye on her. Then came the war. George applied for the forces, but was diagnosed with tuberculosis (TB) and sent to a sanatorium in Kirkwall. TB in those days inspired great terror – interestingly, it was believed that smoking was good for it, and that suited George very well – but he remained ill for a long time. The TB returned in later years when he was at Newbattle Abbey College, when again he had to go into hospital.

George's recurrent illnesses made it impossible for him to lead a normal working life but this is what gave him the space to write. Interviewed in 1996 he said, 'Sometimes I think . . . recurrent illness is a kind of refuge. When things are beginning to be too much, you suddenly become ill. Not desperately ill, but ill enough to avoid your responsibilities.'[16] He also wrote that 'there must be a secret wisdom inside us all that directs our lives, often against our wills and desires',[17] and he saw that wisdom at work in his illnesses. Of course some, like his sister, simply thought he was a lazy idler. She was often sharp with him, which she bitterly regretted later in life, not realizing at the time how ill her brother had in fact been.

George's mother cooked three meals a day for him and generally mollycoddled him. He got £1 10s a week paid by the government to TB sufferers, of which he gave £1 to his mother for his keep. With the ten shillings he bought cigarettes and a small library of 78-inch records, including T. S. Eliot's reading his own poetry. He played this so often and so loudly that those working in the house would loudly chant great chunks of *The Waste Land* and *Murder in the Cathedral* by heart.

The years immediately after the Second World War were difficult ones for George, who lived the life of a semi-invalid, his only outlet being occasional pieces for the *Orkney Herald*, in which he championed what we would call reactionary views, regarding every change of modern life as a change for the worse.

However, at about this time George became more disciplined, putting a mask over his depression, and spending hours working on his poetic technique. He saw poetry as a craft, and himself as a craftsman like a plumber or carpenter. His poetry did not just come, but he worked at it in ever more disciplined ways as he grew older. He also moved significantly closer to becoming a Roman Catholic. Brought up by his father to attend a Presbyterian church every Sunday, Presbyterianism never had much appeal for him and in his teens he started attending an Anglican church. Then during the war some Italian prisoners of war, in their own time, started to turn an old Nissen hut into a remarkable chapel which can still be visited. As George wrote in 1945:

> Where the English captive would build a theatre or a canteen to remind him of home, the Italian, without embarrassment, with careful devout hands, erects a chapel . . . The Italians, who fought weakly and without hope on the battlefield, because they lacked faith in the ridiculous strutting little Duce, have wrought strongly here.[18]

That chapel and his reading Newman's *Apologia* shifted him decisively towards Catholicism.

Another rather different change in his life at that time was the discovery of alcohol. The islanders had continually voted until 1947 against having pubs, but then, in 1948, the Stromness Hotel opened its bar for the first time in 27 years. George drank two glasses of beer and was hooked. They were, he wrote, 'a revelation; they flushed my veins with happiness; they washed away all cares and shyness and worries. I remember thinking to myself "If I could have two pints of beer every afternoon, life would be a great happiness."'[19] Unfortunately it did not stay at two glasses and he needed more and more to get that feeling again, until he had become an alcoholic. He frequently had to be carried home at night, where his mother would be waiting up for him, with his dinner ready cooked hours before, never complaining. As a local remarked, if George had died then he would simply have been remembered as the local soak.

It was at this time, however, that he had the good fortune to meet people who encouraged him; in particular Edwin Muir, who immediately recognized George's poetic gifts. As mentioned earlier Muir obtained a place for him at Newbattle Abbey College, where he was Warden, and persuaded George to publish his first book of poems. As Muir said about the poems, he was impressed 'by something which I can only call grace. Grace is what breathes warmth into beauty and tenderness into comedy; it is in a sense the crowning gift, for without it beauty would be cold and comedy would be heartless.'[20] And as George wrote, 'It was Edwin Muir who turned my face in the right direction: firmly but discretely – and gave me a pocketful of hope and promise for the journey.'[21]

Muir singled out a particular poem based on a true story of a Stromness lad, Thorfinn, a known poultry thief, who had rowed out beyond the harbour one evening, supposedly to collect his lobster creels, and had drowned. The poem poses the question whether it was someone seeking revenge on the lad for his thieving:

> Or whether Love, abroad in a seeking wave
> Lifted him from the creaking rowlocks of time
> And flung a glad ghost on a wingless shore.[22]

That poem is typical of the way George dealt with some of the hardness and sadness of life in the Orkneys, with its constant battle to survive. He never sentimentalizes what happens but strives to see it in terms of divine grace. There is a kindly total acceptance of life in all its aspects.

George Mackay Brown saw himself as writing for the crofters and fishermen of the Islands. Although at one stage he hero-worshipped T. S. Eliot, he turned against the whole world of what he called 'Kulture', for he believed that everyone could respond to poetry. Community was always important to him and he saw himself belonging to and writing for the local people.

At the age of 35 George enrolled at Edinburgh University, at a time when mature students were very rare indeed. Although he came to benefit from his studies, the place where he really came to feel at home was Milne's public house in Rose Street, the seediest bar in the seediest street in the city. For here well-known Scottish poets used to assemble to talk and drink, often presided over by the great Scottish literary figure of the time Hugh MacDiarmid. It was here he met Stella Cartwright, a girl who had been drinking whiskey in pubs since she was 15. They fell in love. It was the first time in his life he felt truly at home with someone and it helped release his poetic impulse. When they were together, and even after, through their letters, their isolated, suffering natures were helped by one another. As George put it in one of four poems dedicated to her, she transmuted pain into something quiet.[23]

After graduating, George started teaching, for which he was totally unsuited, and he rapidly went back into hospital. When he came out of hospital, he lost control of his class and the authorities recognized that this work was not for him. A friend obtained a research grant for him to do postgraduate work on Gerard Manley Hopkins as a shelter from the stormy blast of life, but it was not completed, and George returned home to his mother, supported by handouts from friends. A book of poems he submitted to a publisher was turned down.

Then things started to improve. George's poems began to appear in prestigious magazines. A book of poetry was published to critical acclaim. It contained a poem called 'The Poet', which reveals so much about the relationship between George's persona, his poetry and its source. It tells how he moves from 'the pool of silence' to going about the islands with a mask and guitar, inviting them to share in the dance before returning to his true vocation: 'interrogation of silence'.[24]

There is much of the poet himself in that poem: outwardly so cheerful, enabling people to dance through the guitar of his poetry, but behind the mask questions to the silence. How he found much silence in his mother's house, with the wireless going all the time, is difficult to imagine.

Then George's stories started being read on the BBC and a collection of them were published, again to very good reviews. He received an Arts Council grant and for the first time in his life was financially independent. But he was also drinking even more seriously than before, as was Stella. George continued to worry about her, write to her and regularly pray for her, but he felt guilty about her. Some think that a story he was writing at this time about a girl called Celia draws on her character. Celia is a beautiful, vulnerable creature, acutely sensitive to pain. She is also an alcoholic. When finally persuaded to talk to a minister, she says she drinks because she is frightened. As she says:

> I'm so desperately involved with all the weak things, lonely things, suffering things I see about me. I can't bear the pity I feel for them. Not being able to help them all. There's blood everywhere. The world's a torture chamber, just a sewer of pain. That frightens me.

She then tells of a horrendous incident of a gull and a water rat she saw at the harbour and remarks, 'It seems most folk can live with that kind of thing. Not me . . . I get all caught up in it.'[25]

Celia prostitutes herself with visiting sailors for alcohol but at the end is touched by some subtle indefinable grace and we are left believing all will be well for her.

George's wonderful mother Mhairi died leaving an estate of £5. On the anniversary of her birthday some years later, George wrote a poem about her life, her gentleness, her hospitality even though dirt poor, her singing and her courtesy.[26]

George felt lonely but he wrote to Willa Muir, Edwin's widow, that

there's a kind of happiness in the house too because I have the feeling that a notable victory has been won for goodness . . . I have faith that the goodness of people like her is not lost at all, and is not just gathered up in heaven (though it is that too) but when their small faults and frailties are urged away their sweetness will infuse itself into the lives of the living also.[27]

He became more sober, and found doing the kitchen chores both soothing and a way of keeping depression at bay. He was also hard at work on *An Orkney Tapestry*, which became one of his best-appreciated books.

One copy of that book was to have a dramatic effect on another person's life, and, through him, on George also.

In 1970, aged 36, Peter Maxwell Davies took a holiday in Scotland. Writing music that was explosive, atonal and iconoclastic he had burst on the musical scene and produced a torrent of work. Exhausted by this and the fact that his cottage in Dorset had burnt down with all his books and possessions, he came to Kirkwall. One evening in the hotel he opened a copy of *An Orkney Tapestry* and read till 3 a.m. totally transfixed. Next day he caught a ferry to Hoy, where George Mackay Brown had discovered Rackwick, an enchanted valley at one end of the island, and by chance met a friend of George's who was also over there for the weekend. They met, and from then on, as Peter Maxwell Davies recorded, 'everything happened as if preordained'.[28] In Rackwick, they chose a deserted croft up on the cliffs, and there Peter Maxwell Davies lived for 24 years before moving to the Orkney island of Sanday in 1998. A great deal of his music composed after the time he came to the Orkneys was shaped by the sounds and silence and landscape of the islands as well as the words of George Mackay Brown.

George had written a novel about St Magnus and from this came Peter Maxwell Davies's opera *The Martyrdom of St Magnus* and the establishment of the first annual St Magnus Festival in 1977.

Over the years Peter Maxwell Davies was to set many of George's poems to music, continuing to do so after his death.

Outwardly things for George became better and better. But inwardly he was a man in deep despair. In addition to the physical ailments such as bronchitis that afflicted him from time to time, he suffered from agoraphobia, and going out was a nightmare for him. Then of course there was his depression, which led him to play with feelings of suicide and which required unceasing antidepressants. People sought him out at all hours of the day and night; and though he had a note on his front door asking people not to disturb him until after 2 p.m., it was to no avail. At this time he fell in love with another girl, Nora Kennedy, and it seems this was consummated, but it was not an easy relationship and the result was that his sense of guilt and torment were only increased. He also felt that his work was worthless or worse. When he went about Stromness chatting to people, they would not have guessed at his problems. He put up a good front, and worked in a disciplined way, which helped also to keep the depression at bay for periods. He was not willing to take part himself in the annual festival but invited other poets to come and read their poetry. When Seamus Heaney came, he said that Ted Hughes had once suggested to him that 'poetry is derived from a place of ultimate suffering and decision in us' and he went on, 'Despite George's social sweetness and his geniality and kindness and deference as a social creature, you did recognise that there was a solitude there . . . that there was a place of suffering and decision.'[29]

One of George's best-known poems, written in 1952, appeared as the prologue of his first collection of verse. In it he says that he sings for the islands, for Scotland, 'the Knox-ruined nation' which must be rebuilt by poet and saint, and for workers in the field, mill and mine. He sends his songs on their way to be as gay as they can, but also with permission to weep:

> Praise tinker and saint,
>> And the rose that takes
> Its fill of sunlight
>> Though a world breaks.[30]

It is a poem that expresses in lapidary form a philosophy of life that suffused all his writing. He sees his poetry as a form of singing – for friends, for Scotland, for those who toil for a living. He believes the poet and saint must rebuild a Scotland ruined by the Calvinism of John Knox. There is suffering in the world, for it is a world that breaks, and we must weep if we have to. But it is still a world in which we can praise the tinker and the saint, those able to sit light to the world's usual preoccupations. This despite everything was for him a world in which the rose takes its fill of sunlight.

Both Edwin Muir and George Mackay Brown struggled against depression; in addition Brown had the burdens of his alcoholism and unemployability. Both Muir and Brown knew at first hand the harshness of life in the Orkneys; in addition Muir knew it in Glasgow and the turmoil of central Europe between the wars. Both moved away from Presbyterianism to a sacramental Christian faith as adults and reflected that faith in their writing. Their struggle with the dark side of human existence and the anguish of life is reflected in their poetry, as is the light they found in the Christian faith.

In 1996, George Mackay Brown died, and some words from one of his poems, 'A Work for Poets', were carved over his grave:

Carve the runes
Then be content with silence.[31]

For both Brown and Muir those words seem wonderfully apt.

12

Elizabeth Jennings
Poet of pain and praise

Introduction

Elizabeth Jennings (1926–2001) moved to Oxford when she was six and remained there all her life. She discovered her passion for poetry while still at school, as well as a seriousness about the Roman Catholic faith in which she had been brought up. Her talent was recognized early and she published volumes of her poems throughout her life. She was given the Somerset Maugham Award in 1955 and her *Collected Poems* (1986) gained the W. H. Smith Prize. She was made a Commander (of the Order) of the British Empire in 1999 and an honorary Doctor of Divinity by Durham University in the year of her death. In the words of Michael Schmidt, her publisher from 1975, she was 'the most unconditionally loved' writer of her poetic generation.[1]

Mental distress

Although Elizabeth Jennings lived in Oxford from the age of six until her death, her poetry is not the poetry of place. There is no strong sense that it was written in Oxford rather than anywhere else. Rather, her themes are very personal ones, exploring different moods and states of mind, memories, hopes and fears as well as the changing seasons of the year. She was born and brought up as a Roman Catholic and this faith was fundamental to her life and being. It expresses itself in the poetry in some obvious ways, in poems about the liturgical year and through the imagery of the mass for example. But more deeply than that it is a feature of all her poetry as revealed in her self-questioning and honest self-disclosure. Perhaps above all it is disclosed in her capacity to work through pain to appreciate and praise the world and its people in all their rich variety. She considered herself a Christian, and more specifically a Catholic, poet, and gave thought to what this meant for herself and others she placed in that category in *Christianity and Poetry*.[2]

The poems of Elizabeth Jennings reflect a happy upbringing, both her very early years when the family lived in Lincolnshire[3] and in Oxford where she remembers playing in a hayfield, later to be built over, adjacent to her house.[4] The time when she was ten seemed to be a particularly happy one, when she went to her new school and discovered the power of words,[5] and when she used to go prawning with her grandfather off the Devon coast. But even here there was a cloud ahead which she was blissfully unaware of at the time:

> The age of ten's a treasured time for me,
> I could not see the clouds ahead, the turning
> Inward for years.[6]

One of the most touching poems, 'One Flesh', is about her aged parents:

> Lying apart now, each in a separate bed
> He with a book, keeping the light on late
> She like a girl dreaming of childhood . . .
> Strangely apart, yet strangely close together,
> Silence between them like a thread to hold
> And not wind in.[7]

In Oxford, she went first to the Roman Catholic school of Rye St Antony and then to the prestigious Oxford High School for girls. It was here, just before the Second World War at the age of 13 that she discovered her talent for writing poetry and when she became consciously devout in her Christian faith. From there, she went to St Anne's College in Oxford to read English, where, according to contemporaries, she was sociable and popular, acting and listening to jazz. She became briefly engaged to another student but never married.

Her poetic gifts were recognized early and some of her poems were published in *Oxford Poetry* in 1949 along with other promising poets of the time. Kingsley Amis, who was co-editor of the volume, said she was the star of the show. *Oxford Poetry* was one of the main launch pads for the university's poetic talent in these post-war years; another was the series of short-run editions published by Oscar Mellor's Fantasy Press, where Jennings's first slim collection, *Poems*, appeared in 1953. By this time, after a short period working in advertising, she had become an assistant at Oxford City Library, where she remained until 1958.

Her poems appeared with other young poets like Donald Davie, Thom Gunn, Kingsley Amis and Philip Larkin in Robert Conquest's *New Lines* (1956), the anthology which established 'the Movement' as the predominant grouping of English poets during the 1950s. According to Neil Powell 'a typical Movement poem combined formal discipline and intellectual lucidity with an ironic and often mildly disaffected view of contemporary life'. However, 'Jennings, the only woman in the group, was also exceptional in being immune to irony; her vision was, from the start, both steadily focused and unfashionably spiritual.'[8]

Her 1955 collection *A Way of Looking* won the Somerset Maugham Award which enabled her to travel to Italy. A number of her poems reflect her love of that country, especially Rome,[9] as well as her appreciation of painting.

Elizabeth Jennings's vulnerability, hinted at in some of her poems, became obvious in 1962. It was a time of great success for she was one of three writers included (with R. S. Thomas and Lawrence Durrell) in the first volume of *Penguin Modern Poets*. At this point, however, she suffered a major breakdown and was hospitalized in Oxford, the beginning of a period of mental illness which was to last for 20 years. This was before the time when skilled use of modern drugs could keep people prone to mental illness out of hospital for much of the time, and when periods within such hospitals became much shorter. It was also the time when large mental institutions built in Victorian times were still the main repository for such people, many of whom remained in them for many years. This period in hospital resulted in some experimental poems, later suppressed, but also 'Sequence in Hospital', from her 1964 collection, *Recoveries*).[10] Not in the least self-indulgent, self-pitying or hysterical, but deeply felt in its restraint, it could usefully be compulsory reading for anyone working with the mentally ill. 'I. Pain' evokes well her overwhelming fear, 'My storehouse of dread', and also how 'I still fight the stronger / terror-oblivion-the needle thrusts in', the needle being thrust in to make her unconscious. 'II. The Ward' recounts the snatches of conversation among the patients about grandchildren and gardens as well as the spring outside the window:

> The great preservers here are little things –
> The dream last night, a photograph, a view.

This is indeed what the eighteenth-century poet William Cowper found in his depression. It was the little things in life which kept him going. 'III. After an Operation' is presumably about the effect of electroconvulsive therapy (ECT), which was more widely used for depression then than now. The poem contrasts the time when her fear was absolute and general to the time after ECT, when it becomes more particular again and her nerves become

like shoots which hurt while growing, sensitive
To find not death but further ways to live.
And now I'm convalescent, fear can claim
No general power. Yet I am not the same.

'IV. Patients in a Public Ward' evokes the picture of each patient full of fear, lying in a 'sealed-off nest', and 'V. The Visitors', the pain and difficulty of someone who is deeply depressed making conversation. It also mentions one particular visitor whose absence was the strongest pain of all, 'in that sick desert, you were life, were rain'.

'VI. The Hospital' is in some ways the bleakest of the sequence with its evocation of the shrieks and silences, 'the muffled cries, the curtains drawn'. 'VII. 'For a Woman with a Fatal Illness' is followed by 'VIII. Patients', in which she is tempted to violence: to 'crash my voice into the silence, flout / the passive suffering here'.

There are a number of other poems about her stay in hospital. One, 'Night Sister',[11] is an expression of admiration for someone able to see so much pain without getting hard or cynical:

you listen and we know
that you can meet us in our own distress.

Another poem, 'On a Friend's Relapse and Return to a Mental Clinic', is about someone who is gentle and wounded, with its realization that 'it is the good who often know joy least'.[12]

Gracious moments

Many of her poems are about relationships: how much they mean to her and how they can go wrong. She was aware she could be awkward and she knew she could be badly hurt. Some poems suggest she knew the fulfilment and peace of passionate physical love,[13] but more often love had come to her and been lost. In so many poems, there are hints of love unrequited, thwarted, longed for or frustrated. Friends who are so dear can still let her down. People can be cruel. She can feel alone and inward turned. Through all this she seeks to resist cynicism and bitterness, and to retain hope through every disillusionment.[14] The pain of all this is a fundamental feature of her poetry. It is muted, not shouted, but none the less real for that. 'I must know dark and carry it about'.[15] Yet out of this pain comes first a sensitivity to what lasting relationships require. One aspect, for example, is knowing how to give the right gifts to someone, not only carefully chosen and not too large but which betray

some lack that you have
Which I can help to heal and make you whole,
Like shyness, dark moods and even lack of love.[16]

This acute sensitivity to human relationships resulted in her beautiful poem 'Friendship':

Such love I cannot analyse;
It does not rest in lips or eyes,
Neither in kisses or caress.
Partly, I know, its gentleness

And understanding in one word
Or in brief letters. It's preserved
By trust and by respect and awe.
These are the words I'm feeling for.

Two people, yes, two lasting friends.
The giving comes, the taking ends.
There is no measure for such things.
For this all nature slows and sings.[17]

'Gentleness' is a word that recurs in a number of her poems.

At the Christian centre of her poems is the daily discipline of following Christ by turning away from self to others and to God. This is the struggle in the soul of all Christian life and which the poems reflect. Sonnets to Narcissus recognize that mirrors are essential in the world, where we may learn to see ourselves, but they are also where we turn inward:

Did selfishness
start here, and pride, in this so shining showing?

Perhaps. It makes good sense. Such happiness
We gain indeed when our selves start going
Outward. Be wise and break the looking glass.

Holy people search beyond themselves to be united with the living god.
At the same time
Satan, of course, always sought them out
Would turn them inward to themselves alone.[18]

What helped her to look outward was her imagination. 'Imagination' is a key word which recurs and is itself the subject of some poems. At its most literal she used it in the middle of Oxford when feeling oppressed by tourists: 'Lift up your eyes, I say', a clear echo of Psalm 121, in which we are urged to lift up our eyes to hills to the God from whom our help comes. She lifts her eyes above the crowds to the spires and towers:

> So I say look up only a few rungs
> Of imagination's ladder
> And you will find a city inviting you
> To hear all its bells and enter.[19]

She prizes storytellers above books because they

> let their imagination go
> Imagination will always walk off
> With the golden trophies, the prizes, with the best
> Their listeners can afford.[20]

She uses this imagination in church to bring the familiar scenes and stories alive:

> Surely an Act of the imagination
> When a doubt brushes us.
> Helps more than one of faith.[21]

She uses this imagination to take her into the scenes and people around her. And this leads to the next great expression of her faith – grace. Indeed the title of her 1979 collection is *Moments of Grace*. She sees flashes of grace in so many aspects of her life:

> And grace is caught in seconds unexpected –
> Beads of light hung on a chain of stars,
> The child's goodnight look.[22]

Particularly successful is

> I count the moments of my mercies up.
> I make a list of love and find it full.
> I do all this before I fall asleep.
>
> Others examine consciences. I tell
> My beads of gracious moments shining still.
> I count my good hours and they guide me well
>
> Into a sleepless night. It's when I fill
> Pages with what I think I am made for,
> A life of writing poems. Then may they heal
>
> The pain of silence for all those who stare
> At stars as I do but are helpless to
> Make the bright necklace. May I set ajar

The door of closed minds. Words come and words go
And poetry is pain as well as passion.
But in the large flights of imagination

I see for one crammed second, order so
Explicit that I need no more persuasion.[23]

Here a number of ideas central to her poetry gather together: gracious moments, appreciation and gratitude for them; her vocation as a poet and the imagination which makes this possible. It is important to stress that for her it was a disciplined imagination. The order she sees as so explicit in the universe she sought to recreate in her poetry. So many of her poems are acts of imaginative sympathy when she has turned outwards from herself to see and appreciate the lives of others, the parents who care for a Down syndrome child, the teenagers who question her at a poetry reading. This in turn leads to a sense of gratitude and praise. 'Gratitude' is a word and theme which often occurs: 'I want a music of pure thankfulness'.[24] Her 1998 collection was entitled simply *Praises*. She has poems about nature in all its aspects, the changing seasons, especially spring and others on a whole range of creatures including ants and rooks. Like Rupert Brooke in his poem 'The Great Love', with its theme 'These I Love', Jennings has a list beginning

I praise those things I always take for granted: –
The tap my sister turns on for my bath
Every time I stay, the safety pin –
And who invented it? I do not know –
The comb, the piece of soap, a shoe, its shine . . .
I praise the yawning kind of sleep that's coming,
And where the spirit goes, the sheet, the pillow . . .[25]

What kept her going through all her difficulties, in addition to her faith, was her sense of vocation as a poet, her belief that this was a gift, and the satisfaction that she had in writing poems. She believed that the mystic and the artist drew from the same source, and in her the two vocations were fused.[26] Her soaring imagination, disciplined by her poetic skill, resulted in moments of revelation when the world suddenly seemed transformed and translucent. So it was that she felt much at home with fable and myth, which can also create another kind of world. She says to herself:

You own
    a gift that few possess.

Somehow you know how to make magic happen.
It's here before me with the curtains open.[27]

There are poems on biblical themes, and here I select just one. One of the most dramatic stories in the Gospel of John is the raising of Lazarus which occupies a key position in the Gospel, where it anticipates the death of Jesus himself (John 11). Not surprisingly it was one of the main images in the early catacombs in Rome and gathered many legends to itself in the Middle Ages. In 1947–8, Jacob Epstein had carved a great Lazarus, which was eventually purchased by New College, Oxford, where it is placed in the ante-chapel. It is an evocative piece, with Lazarus shown looking back over his shoulder. As the Oxford theologian Austin Farrer said, 'This happy region of death from which he drags his eyes so unwillingly – what is it?'[28]

Death was always something of a preoccupation of Elizabeth Jennings and it is not altogether surprising she should have been drawn to write three poems on Lazarus. The first, 'Lazarus', paints a haunting picture:

> It was the amazing white, it was the way he simply
> Refused to answer our questions, it was the cold, pale glance
> Of death upon him.[29]

This Lazarus would not enter our world with words we could twist. As the poem continues, he just stood there:

> Cold like a white root pressed in the bowels of the earth
> He looked, but also vulnerable – like birth.

The second poem begins with the unwillingness of the bystanders, for whatever reason, to ask Lazarus questions but then focuses again on Lazarus himself:

> It seems more likely that you could not say
>
> What after-death can yield and mean and show,
> that there were no words for
> That place or time when human spirits know
> This whole vast what? There was no metaphor.[30]

The third poem, 'A View of Lazarus', in which there is movement, like a film sequence, is the finest. The crowd, some silent and staring, others whispering, watch Lazarus' emerging. Gradually his senses set to work:

> A look of loss
> shows on his features but he does not speak.

Some try to question him but he remains dumb:

> Then it's odd,
> But we feel we should stop talking. Lazarus is,

Yes no doubt of it, now shedding tears,
And whispering quietly, God, O no, dear God.[31]

As mentioned earlier, there are a good number of poems by Elizabeth Jennings based on the Church's year or which use the imagery of the mass. The theme of God's coming among us in Christ to share our pain and beg our love is also prominent. But what is most striking is how in and through her pain she comes in the poetry to turn away from herself to the world around her other people and God. In that turning outward, she saw grace all around her and learned appreciation and gratitude which led to praise. There are visionary moments when all seems well. So there is a marked contrast in mood between the earlier poems, the poems of distress and her later volumes on grace and praise. It is in this turning and the poems that resulted from it that her work seems most deeply Christian as well as most humanly appealing.

13

Grace in failure
Four Catholic novelists – Graham Greene, Flannery O'Connor, Shusaku Endo and Evelyn Waugh

Introduction

Rowan Williams has suggested that there is a distinction between two kinds of Catholic novelist. There are those, like Graham Greene, whose works cannot properly be understood without some grasp of the Catholic faith, and which move towards a Catholic outcome. Then there are those, like Flannery O'Connor, whose faith works to show up the absurdities and flaws of humanity but who do not offer an obvious Catholic remedy.[1] Williams admits that someone like Evelyn Waugh straddles both categories. In this chapter, I will be discussing failure, a feature which both categories can have in common, together with the grace that can glimmer in it. There is no attempt to consider the writers in the round or their work as a whole. The focus is almost entirely on one work by each author, with some attempt to relate it to his or her personal faith and to a novel or short story by the other writers considered here.

Graham Greene

Graham Greene (1904–91) has said that some words of Robert Browning would best serve as an epitaph for his novels:

> Our interest's on the dangerous edge of things.
> The honest thief, the tender murderer,
> The superstitious atheist.
> The superstitious atheist, demirep
> That loves and saves her soul in new French books.[2]

This dangerous edge could also be taken as the theme of Greene's life. At school he played Russian roulette with a live bullet. Fortunately for his many devoted readers he survived one game and did not try another. During his career he travelled to many of the world's danger spots, often risking his life. Out of this came novels such as *The Quiet American*, based on his experiences in Vietnam. Greene was unusual in both having a vast international readership and being appreciated by literary critics.

After Greene left Oxford, he worked as a reporter in Nottingham. Here he became engaged to a Catholic girl. He went for instruction to a Father Trollope, who had once been an actor, and who convinced him of the reality of God. Greene was baptized. He wrote:

> I remember very clearly the nature of my emotion as I walked away from the cathedral; there was no joy in it at all, only a sombre apprehension. I made the first move with a view to my marriage, but now the land had given way under my feet and I was afraid of where the tide would take me. Even my marriage seemed uncertain to me now. Suppose I discovered in myself what Father Trollope had once discovered, the desire to be a priest . . . at that moment it seemed by no means impossible. Only now after more than forty years I am able to smile at the unreality of my fear and feel at the same time a sad nostalgia for it, since I lost more than I gained when the fear belonged irrevocably to the past.[3]

Later Greene wrote to say that his conversion wasn't simply because of his fiancée. It was a rational decision and a genuine conversion, based on the probability of the existence of God brought about during his many discussions with Father Trollope.[4] At the same time he emphasized he was a doubting Thomas. Although later he was unable to receive Holy Communion because of his irregular lifestyle, he remained a Mass-goer to the end of his life and retained a faith, even if it was a very doubting and paradoxical one. He was often interviewed about his faith, sometimes giving apparently contradictory answers. There was also a mischievous side to him which needs to be taken into account.[5] He once suggested towards the end of his life that his faith was a faith that his disbelief would be proved wrong. He said that as he grew older his doubts grew but his faith grew stronger:

> There's a difference between belief and faith. If I don't believe in X or Y, faith intervenes, telling me that I am wrong not to believe. Faith is above belief. One can say it is a gift of God, while belief is not. On the whole I keep my faith while enduring long periods of disbelief. At such moments I shrug my shoulders and tell myself I am wrong. My faith remains in the background but it remains.[6]

As the account of his baptism makes clear, Greene's God was not one for whom "happy clappy" poster-paint jollity was appropriate. In one of his short stories, a character muses on 'Our baseless human optimism that is so much more appalling than our despair'.[7] God is simply there, as the old troubler, pursuing us relentlessly, sometimes even with miracles. Indeed Greene himself claimed to have experienced a miracle.[8]

From the publication of *Brighton Rock* in 1938 to *The End of the Affair* in 1951, he was above all known as 'a Catholic novelist', a description he disliked. This implied some special features. First, a very strong sense of good and evil. You don't have to be a Catholic or a Christian to have that, for any novel that is at all worthwhile reflects the moral dimension and a moral struggle in some way. But Greene's special insight here was to refuse to divide the world into good and bad people. He knew that the division went straight through every human heart, as the Browning quotation suggests. This dichotomy was reflected in his attitude to the church. He seemed to relish stories of the failures of the institutional church; at the same time he recognized its power to produce saints, like Padre Pio, to whom he was drawn. It was however, the Christian insight about moral failure that more than anything led him to see its larger truth: 'For me, the sinner and the saint can meet; there is no discontinuity, no rupture. I believe in reversibility. But the basic element I admire in Christianity is its sense of moral failure. That is its very foundation.'[9]

This insight means that all of his central characters are ambiguous mixtures of good and evil, with their goodness deeply flawed and, more often, their immorality with an element of strange goodness about it. This is particularly marked in his great Mexican novel *The Power and the Glory*. No less marked in his writings, particularly his writings of his early period, is his strong sense of heaven and hell as just round the corner. 'Between the stirrup and the ground' is a saying that recurs in *Brighton Rock*. There is a split second before death to repent.

In *The Power and the Glory*, the protagonist is a 'whiskey priest', a term he coined. The novel came out of Greene's own experience, for he had visited Mexico when it was in the hands of a fiercely anti-Catholic government which sought to drive the Church out of the country and Greene had written a book about it, *The Lawless Roads*, in 1939. It was this experience which put steel into his newly baptized Catholic soul, for he saw at first hand the amazing faith of the peasants and the desperate efforts of priests to celebrate mass when under persecution.[10] 'I had attended masses in upper rooms where the sanctus bell could not sound for fear of the Police.'[11] The novel focuses on a priest who is on the run from the police. He is an alcoholic, and riven by guilt for having fathered a child. Yet he still seeks to minister to his people by saying mass and giving them communion. In the end, he even agrees to hear a man's confession, although he knows he is being led into a trap. Opposing the priest in the novel is a police officer who wants to get rid of a corrupt Church. There is a characteristic Greene theme, 'the idealistic police officer who stifled life from the best possible motives: the drunken priest who continued to pass life on'.[12] Especially here we see in very stark terms someone who is a moral failure in obvious ways: an alcoholic living in contradiction to his vow of priestly celibacy, but who despite everything tries to remain faithful to his priestly calling to minister the sacraments to Christ's people. Above all he has no pride, regarding himself as no better than the wretched person who betrayed him. The power in the title, which of course comes from the Lord's Prayer, belongs to the atheistic police state, but the grace and the glory can be seen in the priest despite his failures.[13]

Greene's last novel, *Monsignor Quixote*, is very different from *The Power and the Glory* with its lightness of touch and mellowness. The central character is a priest who claims to be descended from the famous fictional character Don Quixote. This fictional priest is based on a Spanish priest friend of Greene's with whom he used to go travelling.[14] Greene has said about him, 'He has a faculty for bringing people to life. He is not a conventionally pious person but he is possessed by an absolute faith.'[15] In the novel, the reference to Don Quixote annoys an American professor, who says, 'I haven't much time for fiction. Facts are what I like.' This draws the response 'Fact and fiction – they are not always easy to distinguish.' Such is the charm and power of the book, the reader is drawn in to share that point of view. Father Quixote is a mixture of innocence, shrewdness and goodwill, travelling with his friend the communist mayor. He has been forbidden to celebrate the Eucharist by his bishop but, dying and delirious, he insists on celebrating Mass without any bread and wine, getting his companion the atheist mayor to kneel. When the priest dies, the mayor reflects:

> Why is it that the hate of a man – even of a man like Franco – dies with his death, and yet love, the love which he had begun to feel for Father Quixote, seemed now to live and grow in spite of the final separation and the final silence – for how long, he wondered with a kind of fear, was it possible for that love of his to continue? And to what end?[16]

This is not a triumphalist conclusion. It ends with a question mark, with an open future ahead. But it suggests that what seems totally ineffectual in terms of the world is where truth lies, and in such a life there is grace to be seen. As has been written about this passage:

the danger of trying to say too much, of falling into sentimentality is avoided with great skill and self-control; and yet, by adhering to a simple narrative of fact and the simplest thoughts at the back of the mayor's mind, something is pointed at: the barest constituents have seeded another narrative that grows between the lines.[17]

Father Quixote is not an obvious moral failure like the priest in *The Power and the Glory*, but he is a failure in the eyes of the institutional church and the secular world. He is someone who can safely be disregarded, who counts for nothing. Yet the communist mayor can see something different about him. There is an innocence and loveableness about Monsignor Quixote – a grace that most often is denied to the successful of this world. It has been suggested that this was very different from the worldly wise and weary Greene. Yet in Greene himself there was a straightforwardness close to that quality of children which Jesus said that we must have in order to enter the kingdom of heaven. It was this grace that enabled him to see the grace in both the priest in *The Power and the Glory* and in *Monsignor Quixote*.

Flannery O'Connor

Flannery O'Connor (1925–64) was a much more obviously devout and practising Catholic than Graham Greene, as her letters and occasional prose make clear. She died at the age of 39 after years of suffering from lupus, a painful, incapacitating illness. She said a daily office and saw her illness as a special mercy of God:

I have never been anywhere but sick. In a sense, sickness is a place, more instructive than a long trip to Europe and it's always a place where there's no company; where nobody can follow. Sickness before death is a very appropriate thing and I think those who don't have it miss one of God's mercies.[18]

Two facts are fundamental to her writing: her Catholic faith[19] and the fact that she lived in and wrote about the American Protestant Bible Belt which she knew well. These were usually poor, white, uneducated and bizarre people caught up in fundamentalist religion, not the obvious milieu for a deeply serious Catholic author to write about. But this is related to what she wrote about the challenge of being a believing Christian novelist in a largely secular Western world. Although it was the 1950s, a time which we now tend of think of as religious, especially in the USA, she regarded it as a time of unbelieving. She has said, for example, that one of the reasons she writes about such unfashionable people is because their faith and passion reveal truths that are hidden from politer society. More deeply, in a time when Christian truth is ignored or rejected, to believe in the Incarnation and redemption makes a total difference to the way one sees things. As she put it, the Christian novelist 'Will have, in these times, the sharpest eyes for the grotesque, for the perverse, and for the unacceptable . . .'[20]

This is certainly borne out in *Darkness Visible* by William Golding, discussed in a previous chapter. O'Connor has also written:

> The Christian novelist is distinguished from his pagan colleagues by recognizing sin as sin. According to this heritage he sees it not as sickness or an accident of environment, but as a responsible choice of offence against God, which involves his eternal future. Either one is serious about salvation or one is not. And it is well to realize that the maximum amount of seriousness admits the maximum amount of comedy. Only if we are secure in our beliefs can we see the comical side of the universe.[21]

She believed that the Deep South of the USA still reflected this sense that our human condition is a broken one: that sin is a reality. And though the South was not Christ centred it was certainly Christ haunted. No less important to her is the working of grace in her characters. As she put it, 'My subject in fiction is the action of grace in territory held largely by the devil.'[22] So even when the central character of a story is what she terms a 'freak', she is trying to show what we have in us to become and what, through grace, we can become. There is in her stories, she says, an action that is totally unexpected yet totally believable. Such an action indicates that grace has been offered. Frequently it is an action in which the devil has been the unwilling instrument of grace.

Flannery O'Connor wrote novels and short stories. The focus here will be on just one of her short stories, which illustrates her basic philosophy of writing, called *Parker's Back*.[23] It is only 20 pages but she worked on it over many years and finished it as she was dying in hospital. It was her final accomplishment.[24]

Parker leaves school early and runs away to join the navy but, one leave, fails to return. So after nine months' punishment he is discharged. He does odd jobs to earn a living and marries Ruth, whom he finds ugly but whom, despite this, he still wants to attract to himself.

Parker's obsession in life is tattoos. His whole body, except his back, is covered in tattoos. One day after an accident on a tractor he goes to a local town and has his whole back tattooed with a Christ Pantocrator in mosaic design – the rather stern figure which is usually found on the ceiling of the dome of an Orthodox church which he just happened to see in a book of designs and about which he knows nothing. Parker goes home and in

expectation that his wife, who is religious, will be pleased, shows her his
back. She does not recognize the Christ of the Orthodox tradition, beats
him over the back with a broom and he goes into the yard to weep.

Parker's obsession with having his body tattooed is bizarre, but it seems
to be religiously important to him. When he was 14, he saw a man tattooed all over in a fairground, and the sight of his body, in its glorious
designs and colours was a moment of revelation for him. Then, although
his life seems all futile drift, with nothing achieved, he senses a destiny
behind it. This destiny is at once a reality pursuing him, from which he
wants to flee, and a glory in him which wants to be revealed. When he first
meets his wife, he sits on her porch looking across the highway to a vista
of hills. The story describes Parker's state of mind.

> Long views depress Parker. You look into space like that and you begin to
> feel as if someone is after you, the navy or the government or religion.

After he has had his back tattooed, he drinks a bottle of whiskey with
friends; then goes outside and sits on the ground to examine his soul.

> He sees it as a spiderweb of facts and lies that is not at all important to him
> but which appears to be necessary in spite of his opinion. The eyes that are
> now for ever on his back are eyes to be obeyed. He is as certain of it as he
> has ever been of anything. Throughout his life, grumbling and sometimes
> cursing, often afraid, once in rapture, Parker has obeyed whatever instinct
> of this kind has come to him – in rapture when his spirit has lifted at the
> sight of the tattooed man at the fair, afraid when he has joined the navy,
> grumbling when he has married Sarah Ruth.

Although Parker appears to dislike his wife, he has this strange desire to
please her. It is for her sake that he has his back tattooed with a religious
picture, because she is religious even though he is not. He thinks that
showing his back to her will make it all right between them. But she rejects
both the picture and him.

Parker is too stunned to resist. He sits there and lets her beat him until
she has nearly knocked him senseless and large welts have formed on the
face of the tattooed Christ. Then he staggers up and makes for the door.

His wife looks out and sees him crying like a baby. Suddenly we see the
longing and suffering of Parker; and the longing and suffering of Christ
in him. Parker, an ordinary, uneducated, unattractive, rather useless man
with a futile obsession, caught up in an apparently loveless marriage. Yet a
man who, almost totally uncomprehending, knows that God is ceaselessly
searching him out and who senses the glory of God to be revealed in him.

The Incarnation was fundamental to O'Connor's religion: the fact that God had become flesh, had taken a particular human form. The implication of this for her was that every life about which she wrote is a reflection of this divine taking particular flesh to disclose the divine glory. As has been written:

> Parker becomes obsessed with flesh at the age of fourteen when he sees a brilliantly tattooed man at a fair sideshow. Instead of seeing him as a freak, he sees him as beautiful, his ordinary flesh transformed into a miraculous vision by the colours and patterns needled into his skin. By contrast Parker's own flesh seems barren and lifeless. Thus begins Parker's quest for the perfect pattern of tattooing that will redeem his own body from the mortal curse of the ordinary.[25]

We can go beyond this and say that Parker's flesh is not just redeemed from the moral curse of the ordinary but transfigured to become replete with the possibility of the divine. We can also see how well this story fits in with Flannery O'Connor's philosophy of how a Christian writer has to respond to a time of indifference and unbelief with a narrative that is totally surprising and shocking. Parker is an abject failure in every aspect of his life, yet in him too there is grace. In the wretchedness of his life there is a hidden glory wanting to be disclosed.

Shusaku Endo

Shusaku Endo (1923–96) was baptized as a Catholic at the age of 12 as a result of the influence of his mother or aunt. After the Second World War, he studied in France for some years, edited a leading literary magazine and lectured at various universities. He suffered from poor health for most of his life. Christianity is a theme in nearly all his writing and, although he missed out on the 1994 Nobel Prize for Literature to a fellow Japanese author, he won a number of prestigious awards. He has been called the Japanese Graham Greene, who in turn much admired Endo's novels. One of his dominant images is of Japanese culture as a marsh which will absorb anything that is different, like Christianity, and make it impossible for its distinctiveness to be revealed.

Endo is best known for his two novels about Christians in Japan in the sixteenth and early seventeenth century. Christianity was brought to Japan in the middle of the sixteenth century, and by 1614 there were 300,000 Christians in a population of 20 million. Then the rulers turned against them and thousands were tortured and crucified to force them to renounce their faith. *Silence*, the title of one of Endo's novels, refers to the apparent silence of God at this time of terrible persecution. It was turned into a film in 2016 by Martin Scorsese. *The Samurai* is Endo's other novel, set in the early seventeenth century when things were just beginning to look ominous, and it is this which is considered here. It follows the fortunes of four Samurai, or minor gentry, who are on a diplomatic mission to Mexico and Europe to explore the possibilities of trade. Travelling with them as an interpreter is a Jesuit priest. As the politics of Japan fluctuate, the Samurai first embrace the Christian faith and then abandon it. Because they had earlier embraced it they went back to Japan knowing that torture and death awaited them. The novel brings out powerfully not only the universal self-seeking and misery of humanity but also the difficulty that Japanese culture has with finding any-thing admirable in Christianity, especially the figure of someone crucified.

In Mexico, the mission comes across a strange man, a Japanese living with the Native Americans. It turns out he had been brought up in Japan by a Christian priest and himself had become a believer, indeed a monk. But he had become disillusioned with the institutional church both in Japan and Mexico and now lives with the Native Americans, trying to help them. As he says:

> Wherever the Indians go, I shall go; where they stay, I shall stay. They need someone like me to wipe off their sweat when they are ill, to hold their hands at the moment of death. The Indians and I – we are both without a home.[26]

When the Samurai go home, one of them pulls out a piece of paper given to him by that strange Japanese person. Written on it are the words

> He is always beside us.
> He listens to our agony and grief.
> He weeps with us.
> And says to us,
> 'Blessed are they who weep in this life, for in the Kingdom of Heaven they shall smile.'

Then he reflects:

> 'He' was that man with the drooping head, that man as scrawny as a pin, that man whose arms stretched lifelessly out, nailed to a cross . . . for some reason he did not feel the same contempt for him he had felt before. In fact it seemed as though that wretched man was much like himself as he sat abstractedly by the hearth.[27]

Later he speaks to his servant Yoso, a Christian who has followed his master through thick and thin:

I suppose that somewhere in the hearts of men, there is a yearning for someone who will be with you throughout your life, someone who will never betray you, never leave you – even if that someone is just a sick, mangy dog. That man became just such a miserable dog for the sake of mankind.[28]

Then the Samurai leaves his home for virtually certain death:

The swirling flakes seemed like the white swans of the marshlands. Birds of passage which came to the marshland from a distant country and then departed for a distant country. Birds which had seen many countries, many cities. They were himself. And now, he was setting off for another unknown land . . .

'From now on . . . he will be beside you.'
Suddenly he heard Yoso's strained voice behind him.
'From now on he will attend you.'[29]

The novel deals with different kinds of failure. The failure of the once highly successful Christian mission to Japan. The failure of the Samurai to be loyal to the faith they once embraced. The failure of the institutional Church against which the strange man living with the Indians had reacted. He himself is a poor nobody. It is a novel that powerfully reinforces the point that in our time it is Christ crucified to whom we respond, however alien this is to Japanese culture. In Japan, of course, in addition to the catalogue of horrors described in the novel, there was the later bombing of Hiroshima and of Nagasaki, the traditional centre of Christianity in Japan. But the novel is not just about universal suffering and the failure of every human endeavour. In all this, 'From now on . . . he will be beside you . . . From now on he will attend you.' The Christian mission fails but the hidden presence of Christ remains and this can be seen both in the grace of the hidden ministry to the Native Americans and in the faith of the servant Yoso.

Evelyn Waugh

Evelyn Waugh (1903–66) was a devout Anglican at Lancing school but at Oxford and afterwards led an irregular life. He converted to Roman Catholicism in 1930. He made his name as a satirist, exposing the vanities and pretensions of the upper-class English world.[30] He is widely regarded as the greatest English prose writer of the twentieth century.

While capable of great acts of generosity, Waugh could be notoriously rude. Two anecdotes reveal an approach in his personal faith which is also reflected in his novels. When Randolph Churchill and Evelyn Waugh were serving together in Yugoslavia during the Second World War, they had a series of bitter quarrels. Eventually Churchill could stand it no more and shouted out, 'I thought you were meant to be a Christian and a Catholic?' To which Waugh replied, 'And think how much worse I would be if I wasn't.' On another occasion, he was walking with a friend when they passed a beggar. Waugh gave him some money, and his friend commented, 'He will only spend it on drink'; to which Waugh responded 'That's just what I was going to spend it on myself.'

The novel in which Waugh's Catholic faith is most pronounced is *Brideshead Revisited* (1945). Hugely popular when it first came out, critics later turned against it, and Waugh himself thought some of it was over-written. However, it remains a fine novel, and was made into one of the best ever television series in 1981.

In this novel, which covers the period from the 1920s to the early 40s, we view the world through the eyes of Charles Ryder, an agnostic from a middle-class family who has become entranced with an aris-tocratic Catholic family, the Flytes. All, however, are deeply flawed. Sebastian, the younger son, has an air of childhood innocence but becomes an alcoholic. Julia, his sister, is estranged from her husband. Lord Marchmain, who returns to Brideshead Castle to die, is a long-time adulterer, having lived for years in Venice with his mistress. The novel in its simplest terms is about the operation of divine grace on a group of diverse but closely connected characters. A focal point of the novel is when Lord Marchmain, on his deathbed, makes the sign of the cross and assents to the Christian faith. The chapter in which this scene appears is entitled 'A twitch on the thread', echoing a remark of a character in a Father Brown story, in which divine grace is likened to the line of a fisherman, luring us towards it. All the characters undergo change during the course of the novel, particularly Charles Ryder. Before the war, he had become estranged from the Flyte family, but during the war 'homeless, childless, middle-aged and loveless' he finds himself billeted at Brideshead. The house is in a bad state but the chapel, which was closed on Lady Marchmain's death, was later reopened for the soldiers' worship. Charles hears a bugle and the jaunty tune awakes in him a deeper happiness. He enters the chapel and muses that out of all the chaos and ruin in Europe, the dysfunction of the Flyte family and his own life, something unexpected has come about. He sees the lamp burning outside the aumbry where the blessed sacrament is kept. Charles Ryder reflects:

A small red flame – a beaten-copper lamp of deplorable design relit before the beaten-copper doors of a tabernacle; the flame which the old knights saw from their tombs, which they saw put out; that flame burns again for other soldiers far from home, farther, in heart, than Acre or Jerusalem. It could not have been lit but for the builders and tragedians, and there I found it this morning burning among the old stones.[31]

Earlier in the novel Charles Ryder had begun to think that perhaps his love, first for Sebastian, and then Julia, pointed beyond both of them:

I had not forgotten Sebastian. He was with me daily in Julia; or rather it was Julia I had known in him in those distant Arcadian days . . .
Perhaps all our loves are merely hints and symbols . . . perhaps you and I are types and this sadness which sometimes falls between us springs from disappointment in our search, each straining through and beyond the other, snatching a glimpse now and then of the shadow which turns the corner always a pace or two ahead of us.[32]

The cultured despisers of religion in the literary world were particularly antagonistic to this strong religious theme when the novel appeared, and also later when the paperback edition was published. Waugh believed that it had lost him such esteem as he once enjoyed among his contemporaries. There was particular antagonism to the barefaced way that the novel apparently arranged for its three most unregenerate characters – Sebastian, Lord Marchmain and Julia – to claim the highest spiritual honours.

The very language of such criticism, however, betrays a thin understanding of the Christian faith. The novel is not claiming the highest spiritual honours for the characters. It is just that Waugh believed that divine grace works in everyone, and sometimes those who have failed badly in their own lives are most open to its operation. The fact is that the criteria of the gospel are not those of the world. This is cleverly brought out in the description of the tabernacle as of deplorable design. Charles Ryder would have been particularly sensitive to this as before the war he had been an artist. But with the new movement of his heart he puts his aesthetic judgement aside to see the overwhelming importance of the presence of Christ in a broken world. In this novel, what matters above all is a person's conformity to the divine will, his or her vocation, a theme strongly brought out in Waugh's novel *Helena* about the mother of the emperor Constantine. Helena in great old age travelled to Jerusalem and, according to tradition, found the cross on which Christ was crucified. Afterwards she reflects:

She had done what only the saints succeed in doing; what indeed constitutes their patent of sanctity. She had completely conformed to the will of God. Others a few years back had done their duty gloriously in the arena. Hers was a gentler task, merely to gather wood. That was the particular, humble purpose for which she had been created. And now it was done.[33]

In *Brideshead Revisited*, the two most seriously devout Flyte children are Bridey, Sebastian's elder brother, and their younger sister, Cordelia. At one point Cordelia reflects on the theme of purpose and tells Charles Ryder what is meant by having a vocation:

It means you can be a nun. If you haven't a vocation, it's no good, however much you want to be, and, if you have a vocation, you can't get away from it, however much you hate it. Bridey thinks he has a vocation and hasn't. I used to think Sebastian had and hated it – but I don't know now.[34]

In fact the concept of vocation goes wider than that to include how all human beings align their lives with the particular divine purpose for them. Sebastian ends his days not as a priest but as a porter in a monastery in Morocco.[35]

Helena, though usually regarded as a minor work, contains one of his finest pieces of prose which illustrates well this understanding of faith. Helena, having found the cross, reflects on the coming of the three kings. They were late, but their gifts were still accepted: 'In that new order of charity that had just come to life, there was room for you, too. You were not lower in the eyes of the holy family than the ox or the ass.' She then prays:

for the great, lest they perish utterly . . . For his sake who did not reject your curious gifts, pray always for the learned, the oblique, the delicate. Let them not be quite forgotten at the throne of God when the simple come into their kingdom.[36]

Sebastian has something of that simplicity, which is why Cordelia sees something of holiness in him. The learned, the oblique and the delicate come into the kingdom, if at all, on their coat tails.

This is a novel about failure. The aristocracy, by which Charles Ryder, like Waugh himself, was so charmed, is finished. Lord Marchmain is an adulterer, Sebastian an alcoholic. Charles Ryder is 'homeless, childless, middle-aged and loveless'. Yet in all of them a different strand of divine grace gleams. The Flytes, though now counting for little in the post-war world, were trying to remain loyal to their Catholic faith, Lord Marchmain indicated faith by making the sign of the cross on his deathbed, and

Charles Ryder underwent a change of heart and mind even in the midst of a ruined world and an empty life.

Four novels by Catholic novelists, all indicating a different kind of failure, and in all of them the same divine grace working in richly diverse ways.

14

C. S. Lewis and Philip Pullman
Competing myths

Introduction

After serving in the army in the First World War, C. S. Lewis (1898–1963) became a world-renowned scholar of English literature. He was based in Oxford for most of his career where, with J. R. R. Tolkien and Charles Williams, he was one of 'The Inklings'. He transferred to Cambridge to be Professor of Mediaeval and Renaissance Literature at the end of his career. He wrote about his conversion from atheism in *Surprised by Joy* and during the Second World War became well known on the radio as a popular apologist for Christianity. He also wrote a range of essays of remarkable perception and power such as 'The Inner Ring' and 'The Weight of Glory'. His reputation grew with his science fiction and his Narnia series of books for children, all with strong Christian themes.

For much of his life he lived with the mother of a friend of his who had been killed in the First World War, but late in life he married an American poet, Joy Davidman, who died of cancer not long after. The devastating account of his bereavement, *A Grief Observed*, originally published anonymously, reveals how close he came to thinking the world to be the work of an evil power. A brilliant, vivid writer, his Christian apologetics was at its most sensitive in his later works, like *Letters to Malcolm on Prayer*. He remains by far the most popular Christian apologist of the past hundred years. A middle-of-the-road Anglican he is especially well received in Evangelical circles in the USA for his robust defence of Christian orthodoxy and his conservative social views.

After Oxford, Philip Pullman (1946–) taught for a number of years, at the same time keeping up his writing, beginning with school plays. The His Dark Materials trilogy was both critically acclaimed and hugely popular. It was adapted for the stage at the National Theatre in 2003. He became a full-time writer in 1996 and is the recipient of numerous awards and prizes. A further trilogy, The Book of Dust, with some of the characters from His Dark Materials, was published in October 2017.

Pullman is an outspoken critic of religion and this took literary form in his book *The Good Man Jesus and the Scoundrel Christ*.[1]

Two magical worlds

Both C. S. Lewis and Philip Pullman created brilliant worlds. But, as is well known, the His Dark Materials trilogy subverts the Christian universe of The Chronicles of Narnia at almost every point. So the spiritual worlds of the two authors are very different from each other.[2] But what about their moral worlds, the moral values that the readers will imbibe and find reinforced through these books? Pullman made it clear in his lecture at the 2002 Edinburgh Festival that fiction must carry what he termed 'a moral punch' if it is not to become petty and worthless: and it is certainly true that his trilogy carries a strong, even stern, moral message. Are the moral values he conveys so very different from the ones purveyed by The Chronicles of Narnia and, if so, in what way? Related to this are the criticisms of Lewis made by Pullman himself, as well as by other writers. Pullman has said of Lewis:

> When he wrote the Narnia books, he was expressing a vision of life that is ugly, mean, racist, misogynistic; a view that sees violence as the answer to most problems, and that glories in slaughter and bloodshed; a view that shrinks with timorous horror from the natural process of growing up and from a developing sexuality.[3]

This kind of criticism is not confined to agnostics or atheists.

Let me state at the outset that with some of the criticisms I am very much in sympathy. Lewis's attitude to women and girls; the way he allows sheer prejudice to bully its way into certain passages, for example against progressive schooling; his attitude towards punishment. But some of this criticism can only be called a rant, and it sometimes misses the humour in the stories. We also have to bear in mind that the two authors were born into and shaped in very different worlds, for Lewis it was the world of the respectable professional classes before the First World War. For Pullman it is the more liberal world that emerged in the youth culture of the 1960s.

That said, I believe that Lewis and Pullman have some very fundamental values in common. Both are concerned with the struggle of good and evil, conceived in terms of a battle or series of battles. Evil for Lewis is above all about cruelty and exploitation. In *The Magician's Nephew*, it is epitomized in the magician, Uncle Andrew, who is entirely self-centred, wanting to use his magic for his own advantage and willing to use other people for this purpose. In this, he reflects the witch who wants power and control and who is willing to destroy everyone and everything to get her way. In *The Last Battle*, it is symbolized in the ape Shift, who exploits the donkey Puzzle, through whom he seeks to enslave all the other creatures in his world. In terms of children's experience, it takes the particular form of bullying at school. *The Silver Chair* begins with some horrifying bullying at school and ends with Jill Pole and a changed Eustace returning to punish them. Evil, for Pullman, is not so different. In the His Dark Materials trilogy, the universe is in the grip of the Magisterium, who wish to control people and even torture them, in order to separate them from their daemon, so stripping them of their humanity and leaving them as zombies.

In this great struggle against those who would enslave and exploit others, the key value at first is courage. In the Narnia series, the children, girls as well as boys, have to be brave. They have to show both physical and moral courage: physical courage in the many battles and moral courage in resisting temptation and standing up to evil. The same is true of Lyra and Will in Pullman's work. Whatever they are feeling, they know they have to be brave, to risk injury and life itself.

Second, and no less crucial, there is loyalty. There is the loyalty of Lyra and Will to one another, the loyalty of Lyra to her old friend in Oxford, Roger, the loyalty of Will to his sick mother, and through all these specific loyalties, loyalty to the side of good. In the Narnia series again, what is at stake is the question of one's fundamental loyalty. This emerges constantly, not least through the possibility of its opposite, namely betrayal. Edmund, in *The Lion, the Witch and the Wardrobe*, begins by being extremely greedy. He is susceptible to flattery, he torments and bullies others in a spiteful way, he wants to make himself king, deceiving himself in the process. It all went fundamentally wrong from the beginning, when he refused to back up Lucy in agreeing that Narnia was real, although he knew it was because he, like Lucy, had been there before. So, as Lewis writes:

And now we come to one of the nastiest things in this story. Up to that moment Edmund had been feeling sick, and sulky, and annoyed with Lucy for being right, but he hadn't made up his mind what to do. When Peter suddenly asked him the question, he decided all at once to do the meanest and most spiteful thing he could think of. He decided to let Lucy down.[4]

This was betrayal: letting Lucy down and, behind her, the world of Narnia which he had encountered. One particular loyalty, shared by both series, is to a sick mother. In *The Magician's Nephew*, Digory goes through to another world in a desperate search for Aslan, to see if he can find a cure for his mother, who is dying. In Pullman's trilogy, Will's mother is mentally ill, and he is desperate to protect her. In the end, Will and Lyra give up their happiness with each other because of Will's love for his mother and sense of obligation that he should go back to his own world to look after her. They both accept this.

Closely related to this value of loyalty is the importance of keeping promises. One of the reasons that Lyra believes she must go back to her own world is the promise she made to her Oxford friend, Roger. It was her loyalty to him that made her undertake the dangerous journey to the abode of the dead to look for him in the first place. When she is told, 'While you are alive, your business is with life,' she replies, 'No, Iorek . . . our business is to keep promises, no matter how difficult they are.'5 It hardly needs saying that the value of promise-keeping is also basic to The Chronicles of Narnia.

So we can sum up two points at this stage. First, there is indeed a 'moral punch' in Pullman's trilogy. Absence of God, or rebellion against false gods, far from leading to an amoral universe, in his view leads to a reiteration of the importance of moral values. In Rose Macaulay's novel *The Towers of Trebizond*, there is a wonderful, breathless passage on the struggle of good and evil down the ages. When she gets to the Victorians, she writes, 'The weaker they got on religion, the stronger they got on morals, which used to be the case rather more then than now.'6 In the light of this passage, Pullman is a Victorian, in that his rejection of religion, far from leading to a downplaying of morality, leads to its strong affirmation. The former nun, who lost her faith and who is now a scientist but still finds herself troubled by moral questions, Dr Mary Malone, says to Lyra:

> Everything about this is embarrassing . . . Do you know how embarrassing it is to mention good and evil in a scientific laboratory? Have you any idea? One of the reasons I became a scientist was not to have to think about that kind of thing.7

Second, despite the criticism of Lewis's moral world mentioned earlier, there are certain fundamental values, ones that are absolutely basic to the Narnia stories, that totally overlap with Pullman: the powerful, difficult moral struggle of good and evil, courage, both physical and moral, loyalty and keeping of promises. None of this is surprising. For Pullman as much as Lewis, has been shaped by a culture in which such values are basic, values which became part of the culture because of the Christian faith.

One of the difficulties about writing books concerned with a great struggle between good and evil is that it is all too easy to slip into stereotypes: goodies against baddies. Philip Pullman's trilogy has deservedly won prizes for adult as well as children's literature. It is an absorbing read but even he does not totally avoid stereotyping. There is no sympathetic religious character; indeed religious characters and institutions are conveyed in the most odious terms – literally as far as the priest is concerned, who is described as smelly on top of everything else. The church is conceived in terms of the worst excesses of the Spanish Inquisition and the god emerges as an earthly creature who has seized power. Lewis's villains are hardly more rounded, and he is at his worst when he expresses extreme prejudice against a progressive school, ridiculing its co-education, vegetarianism and pacifism.

Real human beings are a mixture of admirable and less admirable qualities, with the two often being closely intertwined. This is not always the case with the fictional characters of either Lewis or Pullman. There are, however, one or two exceptions. In Pullman, I would point to the character of Mrs Coulter, Lyra's mother. Mrs Coulter begins by being in league with the enemy, a beautiful, sinister woman working for the oppressive Magisterium to capture Lyra and separate her from her daemon. But Mrs Coulter, cradling Lyra in her arms towards the end of the trilogy, finds that buried within her is a love for her daughter. So she switches sides in the great struggle. Or does she?

Then there is the character of Lyra, a wonderful creation, the most rounded and alive person in all the books under discussion. Pullman has made her much more than a cardboard figure representing good. When Will, a fierce fighter, who believes he accidentally killed a man who was trying to get at his mother, tells Lyra that he is a murderer; rather shockingly to the reader, she is pleased. Lyra herself, for all her deep-seated sense of truth, is in fact a great storyteller, liar and trickster, if these characteristics are needed to help her in the great struggle. So, although Pullman's religious figures lack depth and subtlety, this is certainly not true of the very alive and attractive Lyra.

In Lewis, for all his conventional moralism, this more nuanced approach, this sense of the ambiguity of so much good and evil, with some seed of evil in things good and some soul of good in things evil, emerges in a couple of ways. First, the witch in *The Silver Chair*, the Queen of the Underland, has real power to charm. Partly through the use of drug-like incense but even more by her soft, cajoling voice and her laugh, which is referred to in the words 'You couldn't have heard a lovelier laugh'.[8] She enchants the children and causes great confusion about whether and when the prince, tied to the silver chair, is really in his right mind or not. Even reading those few pages has a hypnotic effect.

Second, there is the capacity of Edmund and Eustace, originally the baddies, to change, to be redeemed and show heroic qualities. Edmund, originally the arch-betrayer is revealed to have turned nasty like this at his school. But once redeemed by Aslan's sacrifice for him he is the most valiant of all in battle and himself disarms the witch of her wand. In this, he also shows himself to be brighter than the others, in that he recognized the source of her power. Similarly Eustace, despite his formation in the terrible progressive school, comes really good in the end.

Some critics of Lewis focus on the theme of a great battle in which the righteous punish the unrighteous in what is for them an unacceptably harsh and aggressive way. There is truth in this. In a small book I wrote a few years ago, I questioned both Lewis's understanding of the role of pain in God's purpose and the picture of God lying behind it.[9] I have no doubt either that the early death of Lewis's mother and the appalling cruelty at the school to which Lewis was sent severely affected him and helped shape his outlook. But a number of points can be made which put this criticism in perspective.

First, the idea of a battle of good and evil in which the evil ones are decisively beaten and punished is hardly an invention of Lewis. However awkward the liberal mind feels about this theme today, it, together with a great deal of pretty ferocious imagery, is pretty basic to the Bible. Even at their fiercest Lewis's scenes do not match those of the Bible for dire punishment.

Second, if in the end there is a triumph of the good, and therefore of good people, and a defeat of evil and people caught up in evil, any imagery depicting this will have a toughness about it.

Third, there is more emphasis on mercy in the Narnia series than there is on punishment: on forgiveness, on not putting people to death, for example. If we take the scene at the end of *The Silver Chair*, where the children come back to punish the bullies at 'Experiment House', the progressive school, the children are specifically told by Aslan to draw their swords, 'But use only the flat, for it's cowards and children, not warriors, against whom I send you.'[10] That's what the children did: apply the flat of their swords. Moreover, all this is done in a kind of dream or vision, because when the police come to investigate they can find no trace of what has been reported to them; no lion, for example. One is reminded of the line in the Magnificat, 'He scattereth the proud in the *imagination* of their hearts.'

Fourth, the most pervasive idea of punishment in the books is in fact being made to look ridiculous. Uncle Andrew, the magician, is doused in water by an elephant; and a rebel lord who thinks he is all-powerful, and no one can touch him, is turned into a donkey. Ridicule is regarded as a powerful weapon: not to be used by the strong against the weak, a form of cruelty which is rejected, but a legitimate weapon of the weak against the strong, and one which has an ultimate status; for in the end, those who rebel and deny their creaturely status turn out to be simply absurd, and are shown up in all their ridiculousness.

This said, there is some truth in the criticism of Lewis: the element of righteous glee, for example. Lewis was a combative person, not only with the pen but in person. Apparently he used to challenge startled students to sword fights. Also, as Austin Farrer pointed out, he took too moralistic a view of pain. As Farrer wrote, 'Pain cannot be related to the will of God as an evil wholly turned into a moral instrument. Pain is the bitter savour of that mortality out of which it is the unimaginable mercy of God to rescue us.'[11]

In *The Horse and His Boy*, Aravis is torn by a lion, who later turns out to be Aslan. She is told:

> The scratches on your back, tear for tear, throb for throb, blood for blood were equal to the stripes laid on the back of your stepmother's slave because of the drugged sleep you cast upon her. You needed to know what it felt like.[12]

This understanding of pain, however neat its moral symmetry, is, I believe, subject to Farrer's criticism.

I now come to the fundamental difference between Pullman and Lewis, their overall perspective on human existence, to see what difference this makes to their respective moral worlds. The spiritual vision that comes across most strongly in Pullman's trilogy is that this life matters. It is wondrous, precious and, despite everything, good. When Will and Lyra lead the ghosts out of the abode of the dead, Pullman writes, 'The other ghosts followed him, and Will and Lyra fell exhausted on the dew-laden grass, every nerve in their bodies blessing the sweetness of the good soil, the night air, the stars.'[13]

Physical life, sensual life, is good. A corollary of this is that we should not try to escape into other worlds. Will in the end has to shut up all the windows that enable him to move into those worlds and break the subtle knife which opens up those windows. Most poignantly of all Will and Lyra, despite their love for one another, know they have to separate to return to their own worlds.

This life matters, and within this life we have to take responsibility for our own decisions. One of the most brilliant images in the book is the alethiometer, the truth meter. It helps them to make the right decisions on their quest. But when the children reach early adolescence, Lyra finds to her dismay she can no longer use the alethiometer to help her find her way. She now has to decide for herself. She is told, 'You read it by grace . . . and you can regain it by work.' In answer to the question of how long this will take, she is told it will take a lifetime:

> But your reading will be even better then, after a lifetime of thought and effort, because it will come from conscious understanding. Grace attained like that is deeper and fuller than grace that comes freely, and furthermore, once you have gained it, it will never leave you.[14]

One of the major debts which Pullman acknowledges is to an essay by Heinrich von Kleist, which he first read in a translation by Idris Parry in *The Times Literary Supplement*.[15]

This essay, entitled 'On the Marionette Theatre', describes how the writer saw sheer grace in puppets, greater grace than in dancing by humans. It also describes how a bear, through sheer, graceful instinct could outfence a human. It suggests, however, that when human beings as it were go round the full circle, they can, through knowledge, acquire that full and perfect grace which they lack now. We have, as it were, to find paradise by going through the experience of Genesis 3 again. This is what Will and Lyra do, through their love for one another and, as a result, dust which had been streaming out of the universe now reverses its flow: golden, glorious dust, which is matter having become conscious of itself, this life, in itself, fully appreciated.

The other two major influences, apart from Kleist, which Pullman acknowledges are John Milton's *Paradise Lost* and William Blake. The theme of rebellion against heaven is obviously fundamental to the trilogy and, as in Blake, is combined with a powerful affirmation of the joys of this life, a sense of infinity in a grain of sand. In order for this world to be fully lived in and appreciated, in order for us to take responsibility for our own lives and destiny, all religious institutions and the Authority that lies behind them have to be defeated and banished for ever. The destiny of Lyra is to be the agent through which this liberation from religion comes about.

Pullman's fictional world, like Lewis's, is a tough one. When Will learns he has to separate from Lyra, he asks an angel to help them. He is told:

> This is no comfort, but believe me, every single being who knows of your dilemma wishes things could be otherwise: but there are facts that even

the most powerful have to submit to. There is nothing I can do to help you change the way things are.[16]

Despite some strong values in common we have to face the fact that there is a fundamental difference between them in the way Lewis and Pullman understand the way things are. For Lewis the most basic, crucial fact of all is the reality of God, the ground of our being and the goal of our longing. A number of things follow from this, not all of them incompatible with Pullman's world view. But some are, and first, is the picture of God in Pullman's trilogy. One writer first encountered his work through the enthusiasm of his 12-year-old god-daughter. This girl simply said, 'Pullman's God is nothing like the God I worship.'[17] Pullman's God is not the creator of the universe but an early creature who seized control. He is not immortal, but shrivels away to nothing in total impotence. He is not the one whose heart and mind is known to us in Jesus, but more like Blake's Nobodaddy. Such a God has to be rejected.

It is morally necessary to rebel against the kind of God Pullman purveys, as well as against the tyrannical institutions through which he controls his world. Rejection of and rebellion against the kind of God that Pullman pictures is not only compatible with belief in the true God; it is a moral necessity in order to arrive at true faith.[18]

This presents a challenge to the Church. As Rowan Williams has written:

> If the Authority is not God, why has the historic Church so often behaved as if it did indeed exist to protect a mortal and finite God? What would a church look like that actually expressed the reality of a divine freedom enabling human freedom?[19]

But this, as Williams also says, raises a question for the non-believer as well 'of what exactly the God is in whom they don't believe'.

Then there is the question as to whether it is really necessary to rid oneself of religion in order to appreciate the beauty and joy of this life. While, of course, there have been religious people who have been world deniers and world haters, there have been those, like Traherne or Hopkins to take just two, for whom religious faith intensifies their sense of the glory of this life. It is true that some of Lewis's best writing is about heaven, or the hints of heaven we get here and now. In the Narnia series, the presence of Aslan brings fragrant scents, joyous sounds, beauteous scenes and Lewis is able to conjure up a wonderful, heavenly world. But that world is rooted in, and takes its description from, the world we actually know. Lewis was, in fact a person who relished the physical pleasures of life and tried to turn his relish of them into prayer. In short, though he believed heaven was the greater reality, he could only write about heaven in such an evocative way because he savoured the pleasures of this world so strongly. Lewis wrote that he came to 'read' every pleasure as a touch of heaven. For him to receive a pleasure and to recognize its divine source became a single experience:

> This heavenly fruit is instantly redolent of the orchard where it grew. This sweet air whispers of the country whence it blows . . . If I could always be what I aim at being, no pleasure would be too ordinary or usual for such a reception, from the first taste of the air when I look out of the window – one's whole cheek becomes a sort of palate down to one's slippers at bedtime.[20]

Lewis was a person for whom sensual pleasure mattered – he could not have written as powerfully as he did unless that was the case – and when he got married that included, according to his own account, great sexual pleasure. But there is a telling criticism by Pullman of Lewis's understanding of adolescent physicality. In *The Last Battle*, Susan is refused entry into the stable, the route to salvation and heaven on the grounds that she is 'no longer a friend of Narnia'. Jill comments, 'She's interested in nothing nowadays except nylons and lipstick and invitations. She always was a jolly sight too keen on being grown up.'[21]

As Pullman comments:

> In other words, normal human development, which includes a growing awareness of your body and its effect on the opposite sex, is something from which Lewis's narrative, and what he would like us to think is the Kingdom of Heaven, turns with horror.[22]

There is no doubt that there is in historic Christianity a Manichaean or Puritan element, one which entered Lewis through his Belfast upbringing, and which particularly reveals itself when faced by teenage sexuality. But I suspect that, certainly in the 1950s, this was also very much part of English cultural life as a whole, and we could just as well imagine an atheist schoolmistress at a leading school taking such an attitude, concerned that her pupil should be looking to 'higher things' like good exam results, rather than wasting time on frivolities. That said, it is clear that Pullman has a deep sympathy with children growing up, whereas Lewis sees everything in terms of a moral obstacle course on the route to heaven.

One other point can be made in Lewis's defence, which might also be seen as the defence of historic Christianity. There are indeed many good things in this life, a life about which God in Genesis is reported as saying, 'And behold it was very good.' But these good things, according to classical teaching, need to be ordered aright. Lewis was strong on this doctrine, but within it he was able to include some surprising pleasures – there is the great resurrection romp with Aslan, for example. More unusual is the way he brings Dionysian ecstasy and Bacchic revels into heaven. In classical mythology, these became a byword for unlicensed excess and orgiastic frenzy. By incorporating them into his heaven Lewis is suggesting that our desire for this kind of release and ecstasy is not in itself wrong. But it needs to be ordered aright and, if it is, there is a proper place for it.

We now come to the heart of the difference between the two perspectives: the central figure of Aslan, whom the children in the story are encouraged to see as Christ. It is made clear on a number of occasions that Aslan is no tame lion. Awe is regarded as the proper feeling to have in his presence. Aslan is beautiful and makes everything round him appear beautiful, but he also induces feelings of guilt in his presence, if one of the children has done anything wrong. Aslan is the great liberator before whom the frozen land melts, and who gives his life to save others. Not least, he is one who is to be obeyed. This is at its most evident in *The Silver Chair*, in which the children are given four signs by Aslan to guide them. They muff three, to use their word, and the fourth presents them with an agonizing dilemma. They have promised not to release the prince from the chair to which he is tied, on the grounds that if they do he will become insane, and then they recognize in the words of the prince the fourth sign. On the advice of Puddleglum, they obey the sign, for obedience's sake, even though it means breaking a promise and they don't know what it will lead to.

In the His Dark Materials trilogy, the alethiometer guides Lyra and Will on their journey but there comes a point where it no longer works and they have to take responsibility for their own decisions. This is what growing up involves. This, by implication, is what moral maturity is about. In The Chronicles of Narnia on the other hand, maturity means recognizing reality, that is, Aslan, and following his guidance. Two factors mitigate the charge that this leads to an infantile morality. First, Aslan is not always in evidence. In fact he appears only occasionally. For most of the time the children do indeed have to struggle on their own in deciding what to do. Second, they are always left free with, sometimes, as in the example just cited, a genuine struggle to discover what is the right thing to do. That said, we cannot avoid the conclusion that there are two genu-inely competing moral perspectives at this point. From one standpoint, moral maturity means getting rid of all supernatural guidance and looking only to oneself. From the other, moral maturity involves recognizing our supreme and ultimate good in God, the ground of our being and the goal of our longing, and letting our life move to that music. A decision between the two understandings of moral maturity cannot be made on moral grounds alone because what counts as moral is shaped by different religious perspectives.

The Narnia series also conveys the idea of judgement. In *The Last Battle*, all the animals come before Aslan, with the talking animals who chose the wrong side losing their ability to talk and becoming the kinds of animals the characters in the book have no qualms about eating. The dwarfs who have been so tricked and cheated that they have become totally cynical and incapable of trusting anyone, even Aslan, go into oblivion. If all this seems too hard, though hardly less hard than many passages in the Bible, it is important to note one crucial point: salvation is not only for conscious believers in Aslan. Those who have lived faithfully by the light they had are welcomed. Emeth had served the rival god Tash all his life but Aslan says to him:

> Child, all the service thou hast done to Tash, I account as service done to me ... if any man swear by Tash and keep his oath for the oath's sake, it is by me that he has truly sworn, though he know it not, and it is I who reward him. And if any man do a cruelty in my name, then, though he says the name Aslan, it is Tash whom he serves and by Tash his deed is accepted.[23]

We can also note that two ordinary, decent non-religious people, the cabbie and his wife, are quite specifically welcomed into heaven. Also relevant is the fact that Aslan tells the children that they know only their own story. We know our own life from the inside and what we have made of our life chances. We don't know other people's stories.

Emeth tells Aslan that he has to admit honestly that he has been seeking Tash all his life. But Aslan replies, 'Beloved, unless thy desire had been for me thou wouldst not have sought so long and so truly. For all find what they truly seek.'[24]

This statement can be both threatening and encouraging. For it poses the question as to what it is that we truly seek.

One of the strongest criticisms made against Lewis, in particular by Pullman, is the fact that the Chronicles end with the children discovering that they and their parents were in fact killed in a train crash and they now find themselves in heaven. They are told by Aslan, 'The term is over: the holidays have begun. The dream is ended: this is the morning.'[25] About this Pullman has written that Lewis was 'actually dangerous because these books celebrate death. As an end-of-term treat the children are killed: that to me is disgusting.'[26]

Here we are in something of a dilemma. For there is no doubt that historic Christianity, which Lewis sought to represent, is orientated towards heaven. Furthermore in all ages previous to our own, death was all too present, particularly with high levels of infant mortality: so familiarity with death together with an all-pervasive belief that this life was a testing ground for a better life in the hereafter, gave a cultural matrix in which Lewis's view would have fitted without comment. But our own world is very different from Lewis's. The idea of heaven has been subjected to telling moral criticism by Marx, Freud and others and even when it is still believed in, it does not occupy the controlling place it once had. In the West, and I stress the West, for the first time in human history, the standard of living and advanced medical techniques make it possible for people to believe that they can enjoy this life to the full, and live long in doing so. Some people believe that there has been a falling away from traditional moral standards because of a disbelief in Christianity. However, as Alasdair MacIntyre has argued, it could be the other way round, with a more progressive morality making the Christian faith appear irrelevant or incredible.

It is changes in our social life, together with a dramatic rise in our standard of living, which have enhanced expectations about the possibilities of this life and marginalized the concept of heaven. Where Lewis fails, therefore, as an author writing for a particular audience at a particular time, is not being sensitive to this fundamental shift in perspective, with the result that his ending can come across as cruel. We ask why the children don't at least recognize the loss of the possibilities that their earthly life held and mourn those whom they have left behind. It's not Lewis's postulation of heaven as such which is the problem, for heaven remains part of Christian orthodoxy, but suggesting that a rapid transition of children to heaven by way of a train crash is seen as unproblematic. In defence, it might be said that while all priests dealing with a bereaved person know that their most important role is to be alongside the person and easy talk of heaven might be pastorally insensitive, Lewis was not being a pastor but a storyteller. Furthermore, very sadly, people do die young in accidents; and yes, Christian faith tells us that there is a better world ahead.

Pullman has also strongly criticized the way Digory, seeking a cure for his mother's illness, resists the temptation to pluck a life-giving apple for her, because of a promise he made, but is later given such an apple by Aslan. Pullman has said:

> Now that is one of the most dishonest narratives I've ever read. Just think what it means: it means that the mother's life is in the hands of her son, and

that her survival depends on how he behaves. Now transfer that to the real world, and imagine a child reading that, a child whose mother is dying of cancer. The implication of the story is that there *are* magic apples, there are miracles, and that *if we're good*, and *only if we're good*, then a miracle will happen and our mother will get better.[27]

I think this criticism, coming from an author who knows and understands children very well, in contrast to Lewis, who had none of his own and did not teach them, needs to be taken seriously. It has two aspects. First, it is central to Pullman as much as Lewis that moral obligations are primary and must override all other considerations. From that point of view, the fact that Digory resists the temptation to pluck an apple for his mother because he believes it is wrong cannot be faulted. The fault lies in the emphasis on magic. Indeed it is surprising that Lewis made so much use of the theme of magic, when the whole Christian tradition is so strongly opposed to it. In contrast to Lewis, Pullman's characters, though they avail themselves of supernatural powers, such as the ability to cut through into other worlds and be guided in life by the aletheometer, return to the real world of unalterable facts, a world without magic. Lewis was of course in a dilemma, for as a Christian he believed that in the end things would come right. He also believed in miracles in an old-fashioned sense. No doubt he saw magic as a pointer to miracles, especially the supreme miracle of Christ's resurrection. But the fact is that, for example, people who suffer from cancer are not in the normal run of events cured by miracles, however much they long and pray for this. In the world as it is, we have to face hard facts. Pullman creates a world in which we have to do this; Lewis, at least in this story does not. That, I think, is the force of the criticism. Lewis might have written it very differently after his own experience as described in *A Grief Observed*.

Different understandings of maturity

Though the His Dark Materials trilogy and The Chronicles of Narnia are written from totally different theological perspectives they have fundamental values in common, values which are central to both stories. Courage, loyalty and promise-keeping, for example, are held up for our appreciation. The weakness in Lewis is his tendency to see everything in terms of a moral obstacle course, with some consequent insensitivity to the actuality of human life. By contrast, Pullman has the capacity to enter into the minds and, more important, the feelings of children on the threshold of adolescence.

There remains also a fundamental contradiction between the two perspectives, with consequences for how moral maturity is to be understood. The great themes of Pullman's trilogy are love of this life and the necessity of getting rid of authoritarian religion as a precondition of taking full responsibility for one's actions within it. For Lewis, the supreme reality is God and therefore moral maturity means taking responsibility for our own actions before God and with his grace. This means that openness to the possibility of divine leading, responsiveness, in traditional terminology, obedience, are inseparable from living as a moral being; and this life, however much it is to be loved and relished, points beyond itself to a consummation beyond space and time. Believing all this to be the case, it was impossible for Lewis to sit light to it. Moreover such a hope necessarily throws its light over everything else. In so far as these two approaches lead to different moral universes, those moral universes cannot be evaluated on moral grounds alone, for they depend upon what is believed or disbelieved theologically.

Pullman has written that while he acknowledges the pull of George Eliot's peremptory and absolute call of duty, even in the absence of God and immortality, he feels that as human beings we need, in addition, a sense of joy and interconnectedness with all of creation. So in his trilogy he seeks to give us such enchantment, but in stories which don't pretend to be true, stories which drive us back to the real world. The moral nub of these stories is tough, almost stoical. He suggests that all human beings are ultimately alone. Will does not allow the angel Balthamos, who has lost the love of his life, Baruch, to feel sorry for himself. The children are told that gaining wisdom and passing it on is the key to life, and if

> you help everyone else in your worlds to do that, by helping them to learn and understand about themselves and each other and the way everything works, by showing them how to be kind instead of cruel, and patient instead of hasty, and cheerful instead of surly, and above all how to keep their minds open and free and curious . . . then they will renew enough to replace what is lost with one window.[28]

It has yet to be seen whether human beings, through the work of authors like Philip Pullman, can indeed re-enchant the world in such a way as will undergird and reinforce that moral vision – or whether the enchantment which Christianity gave to it, for all its flaws and failings, remains irreplaceable.

15

Marilynne Robinson
Christian contrarian

Introduction

Marilynne Robinson (1943–) is best known for four novels: *Housekeeping* (1980) and the trilogy comprising *Gilead* (2004), *Home* (2008) and *Lila* (2014). They draw on the history and culture of Iowa, where she has lived for most of her life. She taught at the Iowa Writers' Workshop from 1991 to 2016 and has delivered a number of prestigious lectures in different universities. She is also a distinguished essayist, with an interest in a wide range of subjects, which have been collected together in a number of books, most recently *The Givenness of Things* (2015) and *What Are We Doing Here?* (2018). She is the recipient of several prizes and awards, including the Pulitzer Prize for Fiction in 2005 and the Orange Prize for Fiction in 2009. President Obama, speaking about 'an open heart', said, '[w]hat a friend of mine, the writer Marilynne Robinson, calls: that reservoir of goodness, beyond, and of another kind, that we are able to do each other in the ordinary course of things'.[1] Brought up as a Presbyterian, she became a Congregationalist.

The challenge of writing about Christian themes in a largely secular culture

Novelists who want to bring Christian themes into their work today in a secular culture like that of Europe or certain cities in the USA face a fundamental challenge. This has two aspects. First, religious concepts are no longer a natural part of everyday conversation. They can therefore come across as awkward and strained. Even more serious, when such language is used there is an instinctive tendency for it to be subsumed in other forms of discourse, such as psychology or sociology. The challenge is not new or confined to the secular world. As discussed earlier, Shusaku Endo, for example, is very conscious of a similar challenge in trying to write novels from a Christian perspective in Japanese culture. Again, as discussed earlier, Flannery O'Connor solved the problem by setting her novels in the Deep South of the USA, where Christian language is still natural to the culture and was even more so in the early twentieth-century period in which she wrote, and in which Christian concepts like sin and redemption are still taken seriously.

Marilynne Robinson has also chosen to write about a culture in which it was natural for the characters to use religious language and in which belief was taken with the utmost seriousness. It is not the Deep South, but the Midwest, Iowa, where she has lived most of her life. Furthermore it is not just the present about which she writes but three generations of a family spanning a hundred years or so from the Civil War of 1861–5 until the late 1950s, just before the time when secularism first started seriously to encroach on such a society. In addition, the family about which she has chosen to write don't just happen to be religious: the main male characters are preachers, ministers of religion with Calvinist leanings. So religious themes, including the most daunting theological questions, are fundamental to the lives of the characters in a culture which also took them seriously. In Marilynne Robinson's trilogy, there is more profound theology than will be found in a thousand books ostensibly on that subject. But you do not have to share the theology to appreciate the extraordinary depth and subtlety of the writing, or the insights she offers into the USA's turbulent history.

Gilead

Gilead is in the form of a letter written by the Revd John Ames, an old man with a weak heart who is conscious that he may die at any moment, to his young son. He was born in 1880 and is writing in 1956. His theological views have been shaped by an eclectic group of writers including John Donne, George Herbert, Karl Barth and John Calvin. This widely embracing theological sympathy indicates both the richness of his reading and its main theological thrust. The purpose of the letter is to help the son when he is older, and he himself dead, to understand what kind of person his father was, and this means talking about the shaping influences on his own life and that of his father and grandfather. His preacher grandfather was a fierce abolitionist. British readers would need to be reminded that Iowa, the state in which Gilead is placed, borders on Kansas, which before the Civil War was the scene of a fierce struggle between abolitionists and their opponents. In Iowa, close to the border with Kansas, refuges were built for runaway slaves, who were hidden from the Confederate forces coming over to seek them. The grandfather had gone down there to help the struggle, during which he had lost an eye. A fierce preacher, he castigated those who were not on his side. He also sought to follow to the letter the gospel injunctions about generous giving. He tried to give away everything in his household, to the extent that his wife had to hide things from him. Even more than that he took items from members of his congregation to give to others. In the end, the old man decided to wander off back to Kansas by himself and was not heard of again.

In 1892, the young John Ames is taken by his father to look for the old man's grave in Kansas, which takes some time and involves much hardship and poverty on the way, but it gives him a chance to get to know both his father and grandfather better. His father had reacted against his father's militancy and become a Quaker, which made the old man bitter and was the reason he had left home and gone back to the scene of the great struggle.

Against the background of his father and grandfather we can see both their influence on him and the way he has reacted against them. Fundamental to all of them is their faith, but while John admires them hugely his faith while being no less intense or sincere is more balanced and humane, less judgemental and more optimistic about human beings.

John is now living quietly at home with his much younger wife Lila and young son. He had an earlier marriage many years before but both his first wife and young daughter died. For most of his life he has lived as a widower, until a surprise late second marriage. The tension in the novel begins to build up when his godson returns after many years away and starts seeing them. What helped to keep John going through his lonely years was the friendship of a fellow cleric, Boughton, and in recognition of this friendship Boughton had not only asked John Ames to be a godfather and do the baptism; he had named the child John Ames Boughton. John Ames Boughton was the darling of his family but inexplicably had a streak of meanness in him which was directed towards his godfather in particular. He was in one kind of trouble after another, including with the police, though all the time the family tried to protect and forgive him. Eventually young Boughton left home, made a girl from an impoverished family pregnant and abandoned her. This caused a huge breach and he left home for 20 years or so, to the great grief of his doting father. When he suddenly appears and starts meeting up with Lila and his young son, John Ames fears the worst, and the question on his mind is whether he should tell his wife that the man is not to be trusted. He keeps quiet, and indeed he kept quiet about all the acts of meanness done to him those years before because he did not want to upset his old friend, young Boughton's father. But in keeping quiet he comes to realize that in fact he has never really liked the young man, and his Christian forbearance was covering up a fair degree of hostility.

John Ames tries to have a frank conversation with his godson, but they keep misunderstanding one another and failing. Eventually, however, they succeed, and what emerges is not something of sinister intent at all, which John Ames feared. It was that in the years away he had come to love what in those days in the USA was called a 'coloured' girl and had a child by her. He regarded himself as married to her but her family were totally opposed to the wedding and he returned home to seek his father's understanding and help to get married properly. The novel comes to a head when young Boughton allows John Ames to bless him before he leaves and this both reveals and seals a change that has taken place in both of them.[2] The revelation that occurs in the mind of John Ames is that this man who has had love showered on him, but who in their experience has returned nothing but meanness to others, had showed that he was after all capable of love. The faith of John Ames, that we are all made in the image of God and have something lovable about us, is vindicated.

Despite the strong overall religious vision a sceptical element is present throughout. John's brother has gone to Germany, read Feuerbach and lost his faith. Young Boughton has found his father's faith unbelievable from the beginning. Lila's experience is certainly such as to make her doubt there can be a power of goodness behind life.

There is much hardship and suffering in the novel. First, the West was only opened up for settlement in the mid-nineteenth century, so the grandfather was part of a settler generation that had to struggle to survive. Then there was the Civil War, with its vast number of casualties.[3] In the twentieth century, there was the Great Depression, and a terrible drought in the Midwest caused the countryside to become a dustbowl. John Ames had lost his young wife and daughter, and Boughton too had experienced much grief. They both ministered to congregations that were harrowed in many ways. One of the ways in which this is hinted at is that Lila, whose full story waits to be told, has eyes in which there is much sadness and anger.

Yet, despite the poverty, hardship and suffering, the strongest note in the novel is a love of life in its sheer existence, as well as its beauty. The faith of John Ames is a strong one and he has an unshakeable belief in an afterlife which will be much more glorious than this one. Yet in extolling the glories of that life he affirms no less strongly the beauty of this one in all its details. He is watching his young son blow bubbles, with Lila, the boy's mother, kneeling beside him and the cat jumping up to catch the bubbles and all of them laughing. 'Ah, this life, this world,' he thinks.[4] He loves the overlooked beauty of the Midwest prairies:

> I love the prairie! So often I have seen the dawn come and the light flood over the land and everything turn radiant at once, that word 'good' so pro-foundly affirmed in my soul that I am amazed I should be allowed to witness such a thing.[5]

He looks at life with a sense of astonishment and awe, especially the human face.[6]

The theological insight of the novel is that there is redemption not just after affliction but in it. A visionary moment occurs when a church is struck by lightning and burnt down. Rain is falling and all is blackened but the congregation are still singing hymns. John's father breaks a biscuit in two and gives it to the young boy. It seemed like Holy Communion, and 'much of my life was comprehended in that moment'.[7]

The faith of John Ames is fundamental to his being, and he is a genu-inely good man, who prays much of the time and who does his best to communicate this faith to his flock. But he is acutely aware that there is a huge gap between what his faith means to him and the inadequacy of the words when they come out of his mouth. This gap is highlighted by the way, when Lila first turned up in his church, she listened with an intensity that unnerved him. She really wanted to hear something that spoke to her sadness and anger, but he knows he can never put into words anything that will really convey what he in fact believes. But her intent and honest listening helps to keep him real. And this is one of the reasons he will not engage in ordinary religious discussions and questions of whether God exists or not, all of which he regards as totally useless and harmful, for the words have no relation to the reality.[8]

This concern for serious truth, emotional as well as intellectual, also comes out in his relationship with his godson, the wayward John Ames Boughton; for both as a young man and when he returns he always has a grin on his face when talking to the pastor, as though he sees through him and knows what he is really thinking and feeling. And this is unnerving because, as eventually emerges, the Christian love and forbearance which the preacher has shown to his godson in fact hides a certain coldness and hostility. So, genuinely good man though he is, the preacher has to face the fact that some of his behaviour is a facade.

In an important review, the distinguished scholar of American litera-ture Sarah Churchwell pointed out an even more fundamental failure in

John Ames that most other critics have missed.[9] The novel ends with words from Lear's great speech 'I'll pray then I'll sleep.' This is a speech about his failure to care for the poor and homeless in his kingdom. John Ames, and indeed the whole population of Gilead, has failed to care for their black sisters and brothers. They hardly noticed when the church of a black congregation was burnt down and they moved out of the area, so there are no black people in the town now. Iowa was once a shining light of radical abolitionism, and to vote Republican was to vote for what Abraham Lincoln stood for. Now they will vote for the Republican Party of Eisenhower. So, as Churchwell writes, 'the Gilead novels can be read as an act of national and cultural recovery, resurrecting powerful ghosts to remind America of a forgotten moral lineage'.[10] Although John Ames is aware of his frailty and weakness as an individual, he, together with his flock, have failed to see the wider impact of their lack of concern for the black congregation, their social sin.

Home

The setting of *Home*[11] is the home of John Ames's close friend, the Revd Boughton, who is old and ailing. Two of his children have returned. One is Gloria, after the end of a relationship of many years on which she had set hopes. The other is Jack, who has been away for 20 years, whose story we learned from the point of view of his godfather, the Revd John Ames, in *Gilead*. The focus of the book is Jack, and what makes us turn over the pages is the mystery of his person. As a child he was wayward from the first, stealing, lying, going out of his way to torment Ames. Then he made a girl pregnant and disappeared. The strength of the novel is the developing relationship between Gloria, the young sister, still called 'pigtails', and her elder brother. All the time, the aged, loving but authoritarian father is in the background. In subtle, sophisticated dialogue, brother and sister gradually reveal a little of their past to each other and develop a bond they never had before. Gloria has to face the fact that she was duped by a man, which made her support him financially, when he had no intention of marrying her. Jack has led a destitute life as an alcoholic, in prison and on the streets. But behind this is a secretive self, given over to self-laceration and despair. He avoids any suggestion of intimacy by irony or further self-hatred. The mystery is why he has turned out like this.

A cheap psychological explanation might put it all down to the serious religious atmosphere of the house, an oppressive religion against which he reacted. But the household was not like that. It was intelligent and educated. He has grown up in a loving family all of whom love him despite everything, and he continues to be the favourite of his father who continually makes excuses for him, forgives him and has been living for his return. Jack himself cannot understand why he has turned out as he has. He even toys with the idea that he must have been one of those predestined to be perverse, and there are theological discussions with his father on the theme of predestination. Yet he also accepts responsibility for being the person he is.

There is something, however, which is understandable in his reaction against his home background. There was a certain complacency about it. It was after all religious America at the height of US power in the mid 1950s. They are blind to the situation of the black population, for example. Furthermore, in addition to this confidence, there is an unwillingness to face what people are really feeling. All the stress is on forgiving and loving, but underneath there is a fair amount of anger and hostility. Jack probably senses this. And as the relationship of Gloria and Jack develops and deepens, and their ailing father is brought into it, something of this honest anger breaks through. At this time Jack nearly commits suicide.

Jack's unwillingness to open his real self to others, and his continual self-criticism, might appear tedious in reality. But in the novel the reader, like Gloria and others, warms to him, feels desperately for his despair, and thinks of him as a fundamentally 'good man'. A sign of this goodness was displayed when he fell in love with a woman, who turned out to be black, and whom he wanted to marry. He was however prevented from doing so by her father, a minister, who regards Jack as no good. Back at his childhood home he waits for a letter from her, but the only ones he receives are his own to her marked 'return to sender'.

We never finally penetrate the mystery of Jack. There may be an element of genuine perversity in his behaviour, a reaction against the good just because it is good. Certainly that is how he feels about himself, and there is a genuine goodness in the family in which he was brought up. At the same time there is a justified reaction against the unthinking Christian confidence of that family, its desire to have him conform and its lack of emotional honesty.

There is nothing as obvious as a reference to the parable of the prodigal son in the novel;[12] nevertheless, it brings that story to mind, but with some new twists. The son does indeed go to a far country, and the father, at least in his mind, scans the horizon daily for his return. But in the novel it is partly because of the father that the son has fled home in the first place. And instead of an elder brother who resents the welcome given to the returning prodigal, there is a younger sister who offers a real love from a similar position of emotional destitution.

Lila

We first meet Lila in *Gilead* as the much younger surprise second wife to the Revd John Ames. In this novel, we hear her story. Lila, who never knew who her parents were, had been virtually pushed out of the house to die. But she is snatched up by a woman called Doll who keeps her alive and cares for her. With occasional help from strangers they somehow survive. It is the time of the Great Depression but, teaming up with a travelling group of people who live rough and get what work they can when they can, again Doll and Lila survive. They even have a good period when Lila goes to school for a year. But they have to move on and Doll, who has murdered someone, disappears. Lila is on her own and even works in a brothel for a period. Eventually in the cold and rain she seeks shelter in a church and is befriended by the minister. At the heart of the book is the strange relationship between this rough field hand, Lila, and the gentle, old widowed preacher. They agree to marry and Lila conceives his child. The book is her remembering and recounting her past life to herself wondering how at the end of it all she ended up where she did, loved and in a safe home. At the same time there is a wildness in her that hankers after that very hard but free life and she imagines herself going back to it with her son when her old husband dies, which they both know cannot be too many years away.

Lila says, 'I just been wondering lately why things happen the way they do,' to which the old preacher replies, 'I've been wondering about that more or less the whole of my life.'[13] So the book is not only about a very unusual kind of love between the two but an exploration of that question from two very different points of view: hers from the standpoint of someone with no background, who has lived a very hard life and has no illusions, his from his background of immersion in the gospel. She brings a tough honesty that questions all his answers. Among his beguiling qualities is his awareness that he doesn't have all the answers and that he needs her sense of reality to keep him truthful: 'I know I am not – adequate to the subject. You have to forgive me.'[14] What particularly bothers Lila is the assumption in the church that those who are not baptized believers will go to hell,[15] when all the people she has known until now have had a desperately hard struggle just to keep going, and are still capable of acts of kindness as well as meanness: 'What could the old man say about all those people born with more courage than they could find a way to spend, and then there was nothing to do with it but just get by?'[16]

Lila has started to read the strange and difficult parts of the Old Testament, copying down some passages; and because the minister is steeped in the world of biblical language and Calvinist theology, religious language is part of the culture and the questions about whether or not there is a point in what happens and whether there is a good God behind it all are posed with particular sharpness and honesty. Lila wonders why she, and people in general, go on living. 'I have been wondering why I even bother. There must be a reason but I don't know what it is.'[17] She thinks she can just live at peace with the sights and sounds of the natural world, which she loves, without raising any further questions:

> It was Doll taking her up in her arms that way. Live, yes, what then? She thinks.
> He said 'I'm glad you do. Bother.'[18]

Lila does know about existence, even though she learned the word itself only from him; it is about the only thing she does know about:

> The evening and the morning, sleeping and waking. Hunger and loneliness and weariness and still wanting more of it. Existence. Why do I bother? He couldn't tell her that either. But he knows, she could see it in him. Why does he want more of it, with his house so empty, his wife and child so long in the ground? The evening and the morning, the singing and the praying. The strangeness of it.[19]

Later he says to her, 'It's remarkable, whatever else.'[20]

The minister knows that the question Lila asks is much more powerful than any answer he can give, and he knows that to act on his faith as if it is true in any way is ridiculous. Yet, at the same time, 'It is ridiculous also to act as if it were not absolutely and essentially true all the same.'[21]

At one point he writes a considered sermon and lets her read it before he delivers it. It contains his fullest answer to the question that has been bugging them. It is that we don't know the meaning of why things happen now because meanings are always changing in the light of subsequent events. The final meaning comes from a future that God in his freedom offers us. 'The future always finds us changed.' We don't know the meaning now because God is unknowable. We have no way of reconciling the different elements in our existence. What we have is 'God's grace in sustaining us as creatures we can recognise as ourselves.'[22]

In the end, Lila has a kind of daydream in which she imagines an eternity in which all the people she has ever known, good and bad, find a place in God's grace.

Some themes

I found that a number of key themes in my last book, *The Beauty and the Horror*,[23] were given consummate literary expression in Marilynne Robinson's trilogy. Stating them very briefly, they are as follows. First, the sheer difficulty, if not impossibility, of putting religious conviction into words: yet the necessity of doing so. At the same time, however necessary this may be, words can only seem inadequate and hollow to the one who uses them. As John Ames says to Lila, 'I know I am not – adequate to the subject. You have to forgive me.'[24] Second, the hardship and horror of human existence, which is focused on Lila. Her face contains sorrow and anger. Third, at the same time, there is the sheer beauty of the world and of life itself. John Ames lives with a sense of astonished rapture, as shown in an earlier quotation. Fourth, the mystery of how someone surrounded by love can act perversely, as we see in Jack. Fifth, how good and evil are intertwined, so that an apparently feckless person like Jack can show courageous love and respectable good people can be blind to manifest social evils. Sixth, how much of life, particularly when people get old, is simply struggling on; behind this struggle is a love of existence as such at least in the old minister John Ames. And seventh, a firm hope in an afterlife in which God's redeeming love holds sway over all that has existed.

As mentioned in the introduction Marilynne Robinson is also a serious lecturer and essayist, whose work reveals her stance on a wide range of issues in American culture, and this in turn sets her great trilogy in relation to current concerns in American intellectual life. In her fifth collection, *The Givenness of Things*,[25] Marilynne Robinson identifies herself as a 'contrarian' and it is clear from this collection that she feels seriously out of sympathy with a great deal both of American culture in general and American religion as it is now practised. A number of themes emerge. First, a sharp criticism of all forms of reductionism; especially that put forward by some neuroscientists. For her the starting point is the unique worth and dignity of the human self or soul, a word she is not afraid to use, and what human beings have achieved in human history. It is this self which we both directly experience and which we know through the humanities. She refuses to allow this to be subsumed into any other category.[26] Second, a huge admiration for Calvin. She shows that his judgements were much more generous and widely embracing than those usually attributed to him, as was his sense of the majesty of God and his wisdom in the whole of creation. She also much admires John Wycliffe and William Tyndale and, as she points out, they as well as Calvin were deeply learned men, superb translators and stylists who helped to shape our culture in decisive ways. She traces some of their influence in the literature of the period, in Shakespeare's themes of grace and reconciliation, for example, and William Langland's stress on poor faithful servants who epitomize the God who became a servant for us. As Langland put it in *Piers Plowman*, 'Our joy and our healing, Christ Jesus of heaven, always pursues us in a poor man's apparel, and looks upon us in a poor man's likeness, searching us as we pass with looks of love.'

From the standpoint of this learned, cultured, deeply serious Reformation culture, she is highly critical of American 'born again' evangelicalism, which she regards as a trivial and superficial narrowing of what the great Reformation divines stood for. She is no less critical of the mainstream denominations, whom she regards as offering a very watered-down form of Christianity, unwilling to stand up either for the great Christian orthodoxies, or to offer a serious critique of the prevailing secular culture in American intellectual circles. Finally, the market-driven, competitive culture of Western society really exasperates her with the way it writes religion off and out of serious consideration.

Yet Marilynne Robinson remains optimistic that away from the cynicism and vulgarity which are such obvious features of US life there is a better America, drawing on its history and seen in its less strident sections including its immigrant students. Tucked away behind the flashiness of a celebrity-driven culture she still sees the sterling values which were once so much part of small-town USA. Democracy she believes requires 'a presumption of goodness in other people', which she and President Obama agreed that they shared.[27]

In her novels, Marilynne Robinson shows how the Christian faith can face the deepest questions of our time in a way which is deeply serious, which is definite in its claims while at the same time being highly aware of the great mystery of life. The perspective she offers stands in sharp contrast both to the shallowness of so much secular intellectual culture and to the inadequacy of too much Christianity on offer whether of a fundamentalist or a liberal kind.

Pervading everything she writes, both in her novels and essays, is an overwhelming sense of the astonishment before life, awe at the sheer givenness of things. Being is amazing, she says, remarkable, miraculous, cause of ceaseless wonder. One of the reasons she is a churchgoer is that from a very early age she discovered that the only place where this sense of astonishment before life found a place was in church services.[28] No less amazing is the way the human mind is able to explore this amazing world and reflect on itself and the meaning of it all. She is particularly critical of the way that so many fail to see this, treating the mind simply as an object to be studied from outside itself. This results in all the humanities and civilization itself being diminished. Finally, there is, in God, an ultimate hope. This emerged in her great trilogy, and it finds expression in what she writes about Shakespeare's late plays, in which the theme of reconciliation is so strong. She does not want to claim Shakespeare for a particular form of faith, Catholic, Calvinist or Anglican, but argues he was theologically serious. In contrast to Christopher Marlowe, for example, the characters in many of the plays are aware that they live in relation to another world beyond this one.

The key words in the late plays of Shakespeare are 'forgiveness' and 'grace'; in short, reconciliation. This present book of mine, *Haunted by Christ: Modern Writers and the Struggle for Faith*, began with a discussion of Dostoevsky and the protest of Ivan that he cannot envisage any final reconciliation and harmony. By way of contrast, in all the murder, madness and cruelty of the plays of Shakespeare it is grace that has the last word. Among the most striking sentences in the English language according to Robinson are those spoken by Prospero to his treacherous brother, Antonio, in the fifth act of *The Tempest*:

> For you, most wicked sir, whom to call brother
> Would even infect my mouth, I do forgive
> Thy rankest fault – all of them.

And as Lucio says in *Measure for Measure*, 'Grace is grace, despite of all controversy.'[29]

Marilynne Robinson clearly feels seriously out of sympathy with both the intellectual zeitgeist of our age and Christian responses to it in the form of fundamentalism and liberalism. In her essays and lectures, she has tried to rescue the high intellectual tradition of the classical Protestant reformers, showing up the shallowness of the stereotypes by which they are judged today. In her great trilogy, *Gilead, Home* and *Lila*, she shows the working out of this tradition in the life of one family before it finally faded in the 1960s. The Christian lives lived out in those novels offer no easy certainties and are mostly free of self-righteousness, but they take seriously the biblical revelation of a wise and loving God who has a purpose for humanity; and they show a faith which has to be lived out even in the midst of human sin, personal and social, ignorance and frailty.

Notes

Introduction

1 From a talk given at the Edinburgh International Book Festival on 12 August 2002, as reported in *The Guardian*.

2 T. S. Eliot, *Four Quartets*, 'Little Gidding', II, l. 127, in *The Poems of T. S. Eliot*, ed. Christopher Ricks and Jim McCue (London: Faber & Faber, 2015), vol. 1, p. 205.

3 Les Murray, 'Poetry and Religion', in *Collected Poems* (Manchester: Carcanet Press, 1998), p. 267.

4 Murray, 'Poetry and Religion', p. 267.

5 Malcolm V. Jones, 'Dostoevskii and Religion', in *The Cambridge Companion to Dostoevskii*, ed. W. J. Leatherbarrow (Cambridge: Cambridge University Press, 2002), pp. 149, 173.

6 Alec Vidler, *The Church in an Age of Revolution, 1789 to the Present Day* (Harmondsworth: Penguin Books, 1961), p. 113.

7 I explored this in *God Outside the Box: Why Spiritual People Object to Christianity* (London: SPCK, 2012).

8 Elizabeth Jennings, *Christianity and Poetry* (London: Burns & Oates, 1965), p. 91.

9 Catherine Phillips (ed.), *Gerard Manley Hopkins, Selected Letters* (Oxford: Oxford University Press, 1990), pp. 169–70.

1 Fyodor Dostoevsky: Through a furnace of doubt

1 The phrase comes from Dostoevsky's notebook, Malcolm V. Jones, 'Dostoevskii and Religion', in *The Cambridge Companion to Dostoevskii*, ed. W. J. Leatherbarrow (Cambridge: Cambridge University Press, 2002), p. 148. The reference to the notebooks, in Russian, is given there.

2 Donald Nicholl, *Triumphs of the Spirit in Russia* (London: Darton, Longman & Todd, 1997), pp. 151, 173.

3 Anna Dostoevsky, *Dostoevsky Reminiscences* (London: Wildwood House, 1975), p. 170.

4 Fyodor Dostoevsky, *The Brothers Karamazov*, trans. Richard Pevear and Larissa Volokhonsky (Harmondsworth: Penguin Books, 2004), ch. 11, in the dialogue with Smerdyakov, who implies that Ivan not only wants to murder his father but has inspired him to do the deed.

5 Fyodor Dostoevsky, *Crime and Punishment*, trans. David Magarshak (Harmondsworth: Penguin Books, 1951), p. 343. We know from the marks that Dostoevsky made with his thumb nail on his New Testament while in prison (his only reading matter) that the Gospel of John and other Johannine writings meant much to him; Jones, 'Dostoevskii and Religion', p. 162.

6 Dostoevsky, *Crime and Punishment*, p. 435.

7 See Rowan Williams, *Dostoevsky: Language, Faith and Fiction* (London: Continuum, 2008), p. 152.

8 Dostoevsky, *Crime and Punishment*, p. 536.

9 Williams, *Dostoevsky*, p. 152.

10 Dostoevsky, *Crime and Punishment*, p. 435.

11 Dostoevsky, *Crime and Punishment*, p. 537.

12 Dostoevsky, *Crime and Punishment*, pp. 358–9.

13 A vivid picture of this way of life is conveyed in Andrew Louth (ed.), *The Way of a Pilgrim* (Harmondsworth: Penguin Classics, 2017).

14 Fyodor Dostoevsky, *The Idiot*, trans. David Magarshak (Harmondsworth: Penguin Books, 1955), p. 38.

15 Letter to Apollon Maikov in January 1868, quoted by David Magarshak in the Penguin edition of *The Idiot*, p. 9; discussed in Malcolm V. Jones, 'Dostoevskii and Religion', in *The Cambridge Companion to Dostoevskii*, ed. W. J. Leatherbarrow (Cambridge: Cambridge University Press, 2002), p. 163.

16 Dostoevsky, *Idiot*, p. 28.

17 Dostoevsky, *Idiot*, p. 345.

18 Dostoevsky, *Idiot*, p. 372.

19 Dostoevsky, *Idiot*, pp. 52, 214.

20 Dostoevsky, *Idiot*, p. 376.

21 Dostoevsky, *Idiot*, p. 561.

22 In Switzerland he came to love a donkey because it was 'long suffering'; Dostoevsky, *Idiot*, pp. 83, 130, 146.

23 Jones, 'Dostoevskii and Religion', pp. 164–5.

24 Dostoevsky, *Idiot*, p. 283.

25 Dostoevsky, *Idiot*, p. 133.

26 Dostoevsky, *Idiot*, pp. 240, 474.

27 Dostoevsky, *Idiot*, p. 627.

28 Dostoevsky, *Idiot*, pp. 337, 346, 356.

29 Dostoevsky, *Idiot*, p. 343.

30 Williams, *Dostoevsky*, pp. 47–57.

31 Contrast the Jesus of Pier Paolo Passolini's film *The Gospel according to St Matthew* (1964), for example, in which Jesus is driven by a great sense of urgency.

32 Dostoevsky, *Idiot*, p. 89.

33 Dostoevsky, *Idiot*, p. 378.

34 Dostoevsky, *Idiot*, p. 495.

35 Dostoevsky, *Idiot*, pp. 253–5.

36 Fyodor Dostoevsky, *The Brothers Karamazov*, trans. Richard Pevear and Larissa Volokhonsky (Harmondsworth: Penguin Books, 2004), pp. 257, 260.

37 D. H. Lawrence, 'Preface to Dostoevsky's *The Grand Inquisitor*', in *Dostoevsky, a Collection of Critical Essays*, ed. René Wellek (Englewood Cliffs, NJ: Prentice-Hall, 1962), p. 90.

38 Letter of 1854 to Natalya Fonviniza, quoted in Williams, *Dostoevsky*, p. 245,

who gives the Russian source. A translation is given in Jones, 'Dostoevskii and Religion', pp. 155–6.

39 See Jones, 'Dostoevskii and Religion', p. 148. 'A purging flame of doubts' can also be translated 'a furnace of doubt', as in the title of this chapter.

40 Sutherland, drawing on Wittgenstein, writes about the different 'forms of life' in the novel; Stewart Sutherland, *Atheism and the Rejection of God* (Oxford: Basil Blackwell, 1977).

41 Dostoevsky, *Idiot*, p. 253.

42 Dostoevsky, *Brothers Karamazov*, vol. 1, p. 287.

43 Dostoevsky, *Brothers Karamazov*, vol. 1, p. 287.

44 Richard Harries, *The Beauty and the Horror, Searching for God in a Suffering World* (London: SPCK, 2016), chs 12, 14.

45 Dostoevsky, *Brothers Karamazov*, p. 298.

46 Williams, *Dostoevsky*, p. 171.

47 From his notebooks for *The Devils*; Jones, 'Dostoevskii and Religion', p. 166.

48 Jones, 'Dostoevskii and Religion', pp. 166–7.

49 Jones, 'Dostoevskii and Religion', p. 155.

2 Emily Dickinson: A smouldering volcano

1 The full scholarly edition of her poems with variants, is published in three volumes edited by R. W. Franklin, *The Poems of Emily Dickinson: Variorum Edition* (Cambridge, MA: Belknap Press of Harvard University, 1998). The letter F will be used for this. However, for ease of reference for the general reader a reference to the poems is also given from Thomas H. Johnson, *The Complete Poems* (London: Faber & Faber, 1970). The letter J will be used for this. It should be noted that there are sometimes textual variants and for scholarly purposes Franklin should be used.

2 These are cited from Thomas H. Johnson, *The Letters of Emily Dickinson* (Cambridge, MA: Belknap Press of Harvard University, 1958). The letter L will be used with the number of the letter in Johnson.

3 This short study does not go into the details of the publication or the poems or of Emily Dickinson's life as a whole. A life is provided by Alfred Habegger, *My Wars Are Laid Away in Books: The Life of Emily Dickinson* (New York, NY: Modern Library, 2001). A detailed study of her relationship to the Christian faith written from her own conflicted evangelical experience is provided by Kristin LeMay, *I Told My Soul to Sing: Finding God with Emily Dickinson* (Brewster, MA: Paraclete Press, 2013). My study, while not contradicting LeMay's, offers a different focus.

4 'The Soul unto itself', F 579, J 683.

5 Habegger, *My Wars*, p. 168. See also L 10 and L 11, to her school friend Abiah Root.

6 'He showed me heights I never saw', F 346. There are two variants of this poem. This is the version in the fascicle. The variant was in a letter to Susan Dickinson and begins 'I showed her heights she never saw', F 446.

7 Towards the end of her life she fell in love with Judge Otis Lord, who wanted to marry her. She wrote, 'Cupid taught Jehovah to many an untutored mind', L 562.

8 Habegger, *My Wars*, p. 408.

9 L 260.

10 L 342b. The dates and some of the details in this and the two preceding paragraphs are taken from John A. Garraty and Mark C. Carnes (eds), *American Dictionary of National Biography* (New York, NY: Oxford University Press, 1999).

11 L 350 and L 621.

12 'A letter always seemed to me like Immortality, for is it not Mind alone, without corporeal friend?', L 788.

13 'To be alive, is Power –', F 876, J 677.

14 L 342.

15 L 342a.

16 L 381.

17 'The Soul that hath a Guest', F 592, J 674. See also 'Never for Society', F 783, J 746.

18 'Conscious am I in my Chamber', F 773B, J 679.

19 L 77.

20 L 268.

21 'I heard, as if I had no Ear', F 996, J 1039.

22 'This consciousness that is aware', F 817B and A, J 822. See also 'I shall not murmur if at last', F 1429, J 1410.

23 'Soto! Explore thyself!', F 814C, J 832.

24 L 233.

25 L 405.

26 Jackson wrote, 'You are a great poet – and it is wrong to the day you live in, that you will not sing aloud', L 444a.

27 'To put this World down, like a Bundle –', F 404, J 527.
'Renunciation – is a piercing Virtue –', F 782, J 745.

28 'Publication – is the Auction', F 788, J 709.

29 'Fame of Myself, to justify', F 481, J 713.

30 'Each Life Converges to some Centre –', F 724B, J 680.

31 'Of all the Souls that stand create –', F 279, J 664.

32 'My Life had stood – a Loaded Gun –', F 764, J 754.

33 'One need not be a Chamber – to be Haunted –', F 407, J 670.

34 L 233, where the image, though not the exact phrase, is used.

35 'I have never seen "Volcanoes" –', F 165, J 175.

36 Habegger, *My Wars*, pp. 177, 285.

37 Habegger, *My Wars*, p. 514.

38 'At least – to pray – is left – is left', F 377, J 502.

39 'Life – is what we make it –', F 727, J 698.

40 'Of Paradise' existence', F 1421, J 1411.

41 '"Remember me", implored the Thief!', F 1208, J 1180.

42 'Recollect the Face of me', F 1306, J 1305.

43 'Perhaps you think me stooping', F 273B, J 833.

44 'My worthiness is all my Doubt', F 791, J 751.

45 'Saviour! I've no one else to tell –', F 295, J 217.

46 'One Crucifixion is recorded – only –', F 670, J 553.

47 'Title divine – is mine!', F 194, J 1072.

48 'I should have been too glad, I see –', F 283C, J 313.

49 'Jesus! thy Crucifix', F 197A, J 225.

50 Her treatment of Christ's resurrection is arresting and interesting: L 776 and L 767 and 'Obtaining but our own extent', F 1573, J 1543.

51 'I live with him – I see his face –', F 698, J 463.

52 L 641.

53 'To own the Art within the Soul', F 1091, J 855.

54 'Growth of Man – like Growth of Nature –', F 790, J 759.

55 'Tell all the Truth but tell it slant –', F 1263, J1129.

56 L 273.

57 L 843.

58 'I fear a Man of frugal speech –', F 663, J 543. See also 'The words the happy say', F 1767, J 1750.

59 'Embarrassment of one another', F 1057, J 662.

60 L 413.

61 'I found the words to every thought', F 436, J 581.

62 'Speech is one symptom of affection', F 1694, J 1681.

63 'My period had come for prayer –', F 525, J 564.

64 'That after Horror – that 'twas *us* –', F 243B, J 286.

65 L 280.

66 L 298.

67 'The Only News I know', F 820, J 827. It is true, though, that this was written in wartime to Higginson, L 290.

68 'The Bobolink is gone', F 1620. J 1591 is an example of her jaunty joyful confidence in relation to 'The Presbyterian birds' at their meeting.

69 L 3.

70 'These are the days when the Birds come back –', F 122, J 130.

71 L 280. See also '"Best Gains – must have the Losses" Test –', F 499, J 684.

72 L 785.

73 'While it is alive', F 287, J 491.

74 'That Such have died enable Us', F 1082, J 1030. See also L 731 for a very positive statement on immortality.

75 'The Tint I cannot take – is best –', F 696, J 627.

76 'Dare you see a Soul *at the White Heat*', F 401, J 365.

77 'Take all away from me, but leave me ecstasy'. There are six versions of this poem, F 1671B, J 1640.

78 A good example is L 731.

79 L 278.

80 L 269, 1862.

81 'To hear an Oriole sing', F 402, J 526.
82 'The first Day's Night had come –', F 423, J 410.
83 'I shall keep singing!', F 270, J 250.
84 'Better than music! For I – who heard it –', F 378, J 503.
85 'Essential Oils – are wrung –', F 772, J 675.
86 'I sometimes drop it, for a Quick –', F 784, J 708.
87 'The loneliness One dare not sound –', F 877, J 777.
88 'They say that "Time assuages" –', F 861, J 686.
89 '"*Speech*" – is a prank of *Parliament* –', F 193, J 688.
90 'Experience is the Angled Road –', F 899, J 910.
91 L 673.
92 'I bring an unaccustomed wine', F 126, J 132. See also ' Lift it – with the Feathers', F 1362, J 1348, and 'The World – feels Dusty', F 491, J 715.
93 'The Love a Life can show Below', F 285B, J 673.
94 'Sweet Mountains – ye tell Me no lie', F 745, J 722.
95 'This World is not Conclusion', F 373, J 501.
96 L 710.

3 Gerard Manley Hopkins: 'Away grief's gasping'

1 From an unpublished lecture quoted in Valerie Eliot and John Haffenden (eds), *The Letters of T. S. Eliot*, vol. 5: *1930–1931* (London: Faber & Faber, 2014), p. 251.
2 Robert Bernard Martin, *Gerard Manley Hopkins: A Very Private Life* (London: HarperCollins, 1991).
3 Catherine Phillips (ed.), *Gerard Manley Hopkins, Selected Letters* (Oxford: Oxford University Press 1990), p. 212.
4 Martin, *Gerard Manley Hopkins*, pp. 368ff.
5 Martin, *Gerard Manley Hopkins*, p. 368.
6 Phillips, *Selected Letters*, p. 276.
7 Martin, *Gerard Manley Hopkins*, p. 376.
8 Martin, *Gerard Manley Hopkins*, p. 377.
9 Martin, *Gerard Manley Hopkins*, p. 376.
10 W. H. Gardner and N. H. MacKenzie (eds), *The Poems of Gerard Manley Hopkins*, 4th edn (Oxford: Oxford University Press, 1970), p. 101.
11 Phillips, *Selected Letters*, p. 289.
12 Martin, *Gerard Manley Hopkins*, p. 414.
13 Phillips, *Selected Letters*, p. 12.
14 Phillips, *Selected Letters*, p. 214.
15 Gardner and MacKenzie, *Poems*, p. 99.
16 Paul Tillich, *The Courage to Be* (London: Fontana, 1965), p. 171.
17 Phillips, *Selected Letters*, p. 207.
18 Gardner and MacKenzie, *Poems*, p. 106.
19 Gardner and MacKenzie, *Poems*, p. 100.
20 Martin, *Gerard Manley Hopkins*, p. 386.

21 Gardner and MacKenzie, *Poems*, p. 101.

22 Martin, *Gerard Manley Hopkins*, p. 385.

23 Phillips, *Selected Letters*, p. 237. Phillips notes that the manuscript originally reads 'necessary' rather than 'true'.

24 Phillips, *Selected Letters*, p. 237.

25 Gardner and MacKenzie, *Poems*, p. 101.

26 Gardner and MacKenzie, *Poems*, p. 90.

27 'Comments on the Spiritual Exercises of St Ignatius Loyola', *Gerard Manley Hopkins, Poems and Prose* (Harmondsworth: Penguin Books, 1988), p. 145.

28 Gardner and MacKenzie, *Poems*, p. 102.

29 'Rules for the Discernment of Spirits', vol. 8, Father Morris's edn, 1887, quoted in Norman H. MacKenzie, *A Reader's Guide to Gerard Manley Hopkins* (London: Thames & Hudson, 1981), p. 185.

30 Phillips, *Selected Letters*, p. 232.

31 Martin, *Gerard Manley Hopkins*, p. 396.

32 Phillips, *Selected Letters*, p. 232.

33 Gardner and MacKenzie, *Poems*, p. 102.

34 Gardner and MacKenzie, *Poems*, p. 106.

35 Gardner and MacKenzie, *Poems*, pp. 106–7.

36 Phillips, *Selected Letters*, p. 215.

37 Martin, *Gerard Manley Hopkins*, pp. 110, 395, 410.

38 Joseph Phelan, Review in *Times Literary Supplement*, 13 April 2018, p. 8.

39 Gardner and MacKenzie, *Poems*, p. 31.

40 Gardner and MacKenzie, *Poems*, p. 105.

41 Gardner and MacKenzie, *Poems*, p. 194.

42 Martin, *Gerard Manley Hopkins*, p. 413. However, he does not include the words 'I loved my life': they were included by an earlier biographer.

43 *Times Literary Supplement*, 12 April 1991. Other recent writing on Hopkins is open to the same criticism. As P. N. Furbank puts it in a review of Norman White's biography, 'As against Norman White and Robert Martin, then, I am inclined to respect Hopkins's decision in matters of religion', *Times Literary Supplement*, 27 March 1992.

4 Edward Thomas: The elusive call

1 Matthew Hollis, *All Roads Lead to France* (London: Faber & Faber, 2011).

2 John Powell Ward, in *Branch-lines: Edward Thomas and Contemporary Poetry*, ed. Guy Cuthbertson and Lucy Newlyn (London: Enitharmon, 2008), p. 229.

3 Dannie Abse, in Cuthbertson and Newlyn, *Branch-lines*, p. 85.

4 David Constantine, in Cuthbertson and Newlyn, *Branch-lines*, p. 97.

5 Kevin Crossley-Holland, in Cuthbertson and Newlyn, *Branch-lines*, p. 102.

6 Helen Farish, in Cuthbertson and Newlyn, *Branch-lines*, p. 116.

7 Grevel Lindop, in Cuthbertson and Newlyn, *Branch-lines*, p. 148.

8 James Nash, in Cuthbertson and Newlyn, *Branch-lines*, 182.

9 Edna Longley (ed.), *Edward Thomas, The Annotated Collected Poems* (Hexham, UK: Bloodaxe Books, 2008), p. 87.

10 We are also reminded of Thomas Hardy's leaning on a stile and hearing a bird sing, expressing 'Some blessed hope whereof he knew, and I was unaware.'

11 Longley, *Annotated Collected Poems*, p. 55.

12 In his war diary, printed at the back of Edward Thomas, *The Childhood of Edward Thomas* (London: Faber & Faber, 1983), amid the descriptions of shells landing and being fired, there are evocative descriptions of the countryside and the weather, but above all of the birds he hears in the midst of all the noise.

13 Adrian Hastings, *A History of English Christianity, 1920–2000*, 4th edn (London: SCM Press, 2001), p. 54.

14 Catherine Phillips (ed.), *Gerard Manley Hopkins, Selected Letters* (Oxford: Oxford University Press, 1990), p. 207.

15 Helen Thomas, *As It Was and World Without End* (London: Faber & Faber, 1981), p. 39.

16 Thomas, *As It Was and World*, p. 47.

17 Longley, *Annotated Collected Poems*, p. 37.

18 Longley, *Annotated Collected Poems*, p. 41.

19 Helen Thomas, *Under Storm's Wing* (Manchester, UK: Carcanet Press 1988), esp. pp. 188, 191 and 200, for Helen's account expressed in letters to friends of how she felt about their relationship.

20 Longley, *Annotated Collected Poems*, p. 110.

21 Longley, *Annotated Collected Poems*, p. 73.

22 Longley, *Annotated Collected Poems*, p. 113.

23 Longley, *Annotated Collected Poems*, p. 64.

24 Longley, *Annotated Collected Poems*, p. 117. Other poems that relate to the relationship of Edward and Helen include 'After You Speak' (p. 124); 'When We Two Walked' (p. 44); 'It Rains' (p. 50); 'Some Eyes Condemn' (p. 61); and 'Those Things That Poets Said' (p. 155).

25 Longley, *Annotated Collected Poems*, p. 83. See also 'May 23', p. 62.

26 Longley, 'Early One Morning', in *Annotated Collected Poems*, p. 126. See also two poems, each called 'An Old Song', pp. 46, 47.

27 Longley, 'The Lofty Sky', in *Annotated Collected Poems*, p. 53.

28 Longley, 'The Sign Post', in *Annotated Collected Poems*, p. 37.

29 Longley, 'Rain', in *Annotated Collected Poems*, p. 105.

30 Longley, 'No One Cares Less Than I', in *Annotated Collected Poems*, p. 123.

31 Andrew McNeillie, in Cuthbertson and Newlyn, *Branch-lines*, pp. 171, 174.

32 Lachlan Mackinnon, in Cuthbertson and Newlyn, *Branch-lines*, p. 151.

33 John Keats, 'Ode to a Nightingale'.

34 His war diary for January to April 1917 reveals an extraordinarily calm state of mind and he writes disparagingly of some fellow officers who 'have the wind up because of the shells'. There is also the strange entry of HAMLET in capital letters with no explanation. The diary is printed at the end of Thomas, *Childhood*, pp. 168, 175.

35 Longley, *Annotated Collected Poems*, p. 135.

36 D. H. Lawrence, *Complete Poems* (London: William Heinemann, 1972), vol. 2, p. 726.

37 Longley, 'Roads', in *Annotated Collected Poems*, p. 106.

38 Longley, 'The Child on the Cliffs', in *Annotated Collected Poems*, p. 65.

39 Longley, 'Out in the Dark', in *Annotated Collected Poems*, p. 138.

40 Longley, *Annotated Collected Poems*, p. 36.

41 T. E. Hulme, *Romanticism and Classicism*.

42 Eleanor Farjeon, *Edward Thomas: The Last Four Years* (Stroud: Sutton Publishing, 1997), p. 6.

43 Edna Longley, in Cuthbertson and Newlyn, *Branch-lines*, p. 39.

44 Edward Thomas, *Wales* (Oxford: Oxford University Press, 1983), pp. 10–15.

45 R. S. Thomas, *Selected Poems of Edward Thomas* (London: Faber & Faber, 1964), p. 11.

46 Longley, *Annotated Collected Poems*, p. 123.

47 Longley, *Annotated Collected Poems*, p. 31.

48 Longley, 'Fifty Faggots', in *Annotated Collected Poems*, p. 90.

49 Longley, *Annotated Collected Poems*, p. 45.

50 Longley, *Annotated Collected Poems*, p. 52.

51 Patrick McGuiness, in Cuthbertson and Newlyn, *Branch-lines*, p. 164.

52 John Wain, *Professing Poetry* (London: Macmillan, 1977), p. 353, quoted by Cuthbertson and Newlyn, *Branch-lines*, p. 21.

53 Thomas, *Childhood*, pp. 31–3.

54 Thomas, *Childhood*, p. 33.

55 Thomas, *Childhood*, p. 172.

56 R. George Thomas (ed.), *Edward Thomas: Letters to Gordon Bottomley*, Letter 62, 26 December 1906 (Oxford: Oxford University Press, 1968), p. 129.

57 'February Afternoon', in Longley, *Annotated Collected Poems*, p. 109.

58 For a discussion of this see Richard Harries, *C. S. Lewis: The Man and His God* (London: Collins, 1987), chs 2, 9.

59 C. S. Lewis, *Surprised by Joy* (London: Fontana, 1959).

60 C. S. Lewis, 'The Weight of Glory', in *Transposition and Other Addresses* (London: Geoffrey Bles, 1949), p. 31.

61 Simone Weil, *Waiting on God* (London: Fontana, 1959), p. 121.

62 T. S. Eliot, *Four Quartets* (London: Faber & Faber, 1959), p. 51.

63 Eliot, *Four Quartets*, p. 59.

64 R. S. Thomas, 'Abercauwg', in *Collected Poems* (London: J. M. Dent, 1993), p. 340.

65 R. S. Thomas, *Selected Prose, Poetry* (Bridgend: Poetry Wales Press, 1983), p. 164.

66 Longley, *Annotated Collected Poems*, p. 70.

67 R. George Thomas, *Edward Thomas: A Portrait* (Oxford: Oxford University Press, 1987), p. 55.

68 Thomas, *Edward Thomas*, p. 93.

69 Part of the last page in his diary in April 1917, in Thomas, *Childhood*.

70 Longley, *Annotated Collected poems*, p. 85.

5 T. S. Eliot: Out of hell

1 Valerie Eliot and John Haffenden (eds), *The Letters of T. S. Eliot*, vol. 3: *1926–1927* (London: Faber & Faber, 2012), pp. 404, 572.

2 Eliot and Haffenden, *Letters*, vol. 3, p. 412.

3 Robert Crawford, *Young Eliot: From St Louis to The Waste Land* (London: Jonathan Cape, 2015), pp. 168–71.

4 Crawford, *Young Eliot*, p. 220.

5 Lyndall Gordon, *Eliot's Early Years* (Oxford: Oxford University Press, 1977).

6 Christopher Ricks and Jim McCue (eds), *The Poems of T. S. Eliot*, vol. 1: *Collected and Uncollected Poems* (London: Faber & Faber, 2015), p. 243.

7 Gordon, *Eliot's Early Years*, p. 39.

8 Eliot and Haffenden, *Letters*, vol. 3, p. 24.

9 Eliot and Haffenden, *Letters*, vol. 3, p. 192.

10 Eliot and Haffenden, *Letters*, vol. 3, p. 257.

11 Eliot and Haffenden, *Letters*, vol. 3, p. 336.

12 Eliot and Haffenden, *Letters*, vol. 3, p. 177.

13 Eliot and Haffenden, *Letters*, vol. 3, p. 221.

14 Valerie Eliot and John Haffenden (eds), *The Letters of T. S. Eliot*, vol. 7: *1934–1935* (London: Faber & Faber, 2017), p. 751.

15 Eliot and Haffenden, *Letters*, vol. 3, p. 41.

16 Gordon, *Eliot's Early Years*, p. 71.

17 Valerie Eliot and John Haffenden (eds), *The Letters of T. S. Eliot*, vol. 4: *1928–1929* (London: Faber & Faber, 2012), p. 96.

18 William Shakespeare, *Troilus and Cressida*, I, iii.

19 Eliot and Haffenden, *Letters*, vol. 3, pp. 572–3, n. 1.

20 Eliot and Haffenden, *Letters*, vol. 3, p. 424.

21 Eliot and Haffenden, *Letters*, vol. 3, p. 739. See also p. 568, where he writes to ask Russell, 'Why don't you stick to mathematics?'

22 Eliot and Haffenden, *Letters*, vol. 3, pp. 711–13.

23 Valerie Eliot and John Haffenden (eds), *The Letters of T. S. Eliot*, vol. 6: *1932–1933* (London: Faber & Faber, 2016), pp. 156–71 and notes there.

24 Eliot and Haffenden, *Letters*, vol. 6, p. 290.

25 Eliot and Haffenden, *Letters*, vol. 6, p. 125.

26 Eliot and Haffenden, *Letters*, vol. 4, p. 128.

27 Eliot and Haffenden, *Letters*, vol. 4, pp. 432–3.

28 Eliot and Haffenden, *Letters*, vol. 4, p. 572. See also p. 567.

29 Eliot and Haffenden, *Letters*, vol. 4, pp. 267–8, n. 1.

30 Eliot and Haffenden, *Letters*, vol. 3, pp. 572–3, n. 1.

31 Valerie Eliot and John Haffenden (eds), *The Letters of T. S. Eliot*, vol. 5: *1930–1931* (London: Faber & Faber, 2014), pp. 209–10, 292–3.

32 Eliot and Haffenden, *Letters*, vol. 5.

33 Eliot and Haffenden, *Letters*, vol. 5.

34 T. S. Eliot, 'The Pensées of Pascal', in *Selected Essays* (London: Faber & Faber), p. 411.

35 Eliot, 'Pensées', p. 411.

36 T. S. Eliot, *Notes Towards the Definition of Culture: Selected Prose of T. S. Eliot*, ed. Frank Kermode (London: Faber & Faber), p. 292.

37 Eliot and Haffenden, *Letters*, vol. 5, pp. 209–10, 292–3.

38 Ricks and McCue, *Poems*, vol. 1, p. 762.

39 Ricks and McCue, *Poems*, vol. 1, p. 765.

40 Ricks and McCue, *Poems*, vol. 1, p. 730.

41 Ricks and McCue, *Poems*, vol. 1, p. 750.

42 Lyndall Gordon, *Eliot's New Life* (Oxford: Oxford University Press, 1988), p. 12.

43 Ricks and McCue, *Poems*, vol. 1, p. 743.

44 Ricks and McCue, *Poems*, vol. 1, pp. 96–7.

45 Ricks and McCue, *Poems*, vol. 1, pp. 107–8.

46 'Marina', in Ricks and McCue, *Poems*, vol. 1, *Poems*, p. 107.

47 Ricks and McCue, *Poems*, vol. 1, p. 775.

48 Gordon, *Eliot's New Life*, p. 14.

6 Stevie Smith: A jaunty desperation

1 'Away, Melancholy', in Stevie Smith, *Collected Poems* (London: Allen Lane, 1975), p. 328.

2 Smith, 'Not Waving but Drowning', in *Collected Poems*, p. 303.

3 Interview with John Horder, *Guardian*, 7 June 1965, quoted by Frances Spalding, *Stevie Smith, a Biography* (New York, NY: Norton, 1989), p. 17.

4 Smith, 'A House of Mercy', in *Collected Poems*, p. 410.

5 'Some Impediments to Christian Commitment', in Jack Barbera and William McBrien (eds), *Me Again, the Uncollected Writings of Stevie Smith* (London: Virago, 1981), p. 154.

6 Smith, *Collected Poems*, p. 388.

7 Jack Barbera and William McBrien (eds), *Stevie, A Biography of Stevie Smith* (London: Macmillan, 1986), pp. 236–7.

8 Stevie Smith, 'The Necessity of Not Believing', *Gemini* 2(1), spring 1958, quoted in Spalding, *Stevie Smith*, p. 241.

9 'Some Impediments to Christian Commitment', in Barbera and McBrien, *Me Again*, p. 153.

10 Spalding, *Stevie Smith*, pp. 236–7.

11 Valerie Eliot and John Haffenden (eds), *The Letters of T. S. Eliot*, vol. 5: *1930–1931* (London: Faber & Faber, 2014), pp. 209–10, 292–3.

12 Eliot and Haffenden, *Letters*, vol. 5, pp. 209–10, 292–3.

13 Smith, 'The Airy Christ', in *Collected Poems*, p. 345.

14 Barbera and McBrien, *Me Again*, p. 157.

15 Smith, 'Thoughts about the Christian Doctrine of Eternal Hell', in *Collected Poems*, p. 387.

16 Spalding, *Stevie Smith*, p. 240.

17 Smith, 'An Agnostic' and 'A Religious Man', in *Collected Poems*, p. 347.

18 Spalding, *Stevie Smith*, p. 219.

19 Spalding, *Stevie Smith*, p. 227.

20 Smith, *Collected Poems*, p. 516.

21 Quoted in Spalding, *Stevie Smith*, p. 216.

22 Smith, 'So to Fatness Come', in *Collected Poems*, p. 538.

23 Quoted by Spalding, *Stevie Smith*, p. 229.

24 Barbera and McBrien, *Me Again*, p. 153.

7 Samuel Beckett: Secular mystic

1 James Knowlson, *Damned to Fame: The Life of Samuel Beckett* (London: Bloomsbury, 1996), pp. 16, 24.

2 Knowlson, *Damned to Fame*, pp. 67–8.

3 Samuel Beckett, *Breath and Other Shorts* (London: Faber & Faber, 1971).

4 Ruby Cohn, *Just Play: Beckett's Theatre* (Princeton, NJ: Princeton University Press, 1980), p. 4.

5 Samuel Beckett, *Waiting for Godot* (London: Faber & Faber, 1965), p. 89.

6 Beckett, *Waiting for Godot*, p. 91.

7 Samuel Beckett, *Endgame* (London: Faber & Faber, 1964), p. 12.

8 Beckett, *Endgame*, p. 26.

9 Beckett, *Waiting for Godot*, pp. 63–5.

10 Samuel Beckett, *Happy Days* (London: Faber & Faber, 1966), p. 20.

11 Beckett, *Happy Days*, p. 12.

12 Beckett, *Happy Days*, p. 42.

13 Beckett, *Happy Days*, p. 44.

14 Beckett, *Endgame*, p. 22.

15 Beckett, *Waiting for Godot*, p. 12.

16 Beckett, *Waiting for Godot*, p. 52.

17 George Craig, Martha Dow Fehsenfield, Dan Gunn and Lois More Overbeck (eds), *The Letters of Samuel Beckett*, vol. 2: *1941–1956* (Cambridge: Cambridge University Press, 2011), pp. 319, 391, 506, 507, 594.

18 Samuel Beckett, *Not I* (London: Faber & Faber, 1973).

19 Samuel Beckett, *Play* (London: Faber & Faber, 1968), p. 16.

20 Beckett, *Play*, p. 22.

21 Beckett, *Play*, p. 10.

22 Craig et al., *Letters*, vol. 2, p. 522.

23 *The Unnamable, The Beckett Trilogy* (London: Picador, 1979).

24 Beckett, *Endgame*, p. 23.

25 Beckett, *Waiting for Godot*, p. 58.

26 Beckett, *Happy Days*, p. 26.

27 Beckett, *Not I* (London: Faber & Faber, 1973), p. 1.

28 Deirdre Bair, *Samuel Beckett* (London: Jonathan Cape, 1978), p. 640.

29 Samuel Beckett, *Krapp's Last Tape* (London: Faber & Faber, 1965), p. 16.

30 Craig et al., *Letters*, vol. 2, pp. 84, 102, 166, 170, 343.

31 Craig et al., *Letters*, vol. 2, p. 596.

32 Samuel Beckett, *Worstward Ho*, in *Company/Ill Seen Ill Said/Worstward Ho/Stirrings Still* (London: Faber & Faber, 2009), p. 81.

33 See especially George Craig, Martha Dow Fehsenfeld, Dan Gunn and Lois More Overbeck (eds), *The Letters of Samuel Beckett*, vol. 4: *1968–1989* (Cambridge: Cambridge University Press, 2016).

34 George Craig, Martha Dow Fehsenfeld, Dan Gunn and Lois More Overbeck (eds), *The Letters of Samuel Beckett*, vol. 3: *1957–1967* (Cambridge: Cambridge University Press, 2014), p. 119.

35 Bair, *Samuel Beckett*, p. 405.

36 Beckett, *Endgame*, p. l 9.

37 Beckett, *Krapp's Last Tape*, p. 13.

38 Cohn, *Just Play*, p. 199.

39 Knowlson, *Damned to Fame*, p. 237.

40 John Calder (ed.), *Beckett at Sixty: A Festschrift* (London: Calder & Boyars, 1967), p. 99.

41 Knowlson, *Damned to Fame*, p. 279.

42 Beckett, *Happy Days*, p. 40.

43 Beckett, *Endgame*, p. 18.

44 Beckett, *Unnamable*, p. 382.

45 Bair, *Samuel Beckett*, p. 528.

46 Samuel Beckett, 'Dante … Bruno. Vico … Joyce', an essay in *Our Exagmination Round His Factification for Incamination of Work in Progress* (London: Faber & Faber, 1972), p. 14.

47 Quoted by Cohn, *Just Play*, p. 131.

48 This has never been found in the works of St Augustine and it appears that Beckett made a mistake here.

49 Craig et al., *Letters*, vol. 2, p. 605.

50 Craig et al., *Letters*, vol. 3, p. 83.

51 Craig et al., *Letters*, vol. 3, p. 668; Knowlson, *Damned to Fame*, pp. 269–71.

52 Knowlson, *Damned to Fame*, pp. 429, 669.

53 John Gray, *Seven Types of Atheism* (London: Allen Lane, 2018), p. 146.

8 W. H. Auden: 'Bless what there is for being'

1 W. H. Auden, 'Twelve Songs', in *Collected Poems*, ed. Edward Mendelson (London: Faber & Faber, 1976), p. 120.

2 Arthur Kirsch, *Auden and Christianity* (New Haven, CT: Yale University Press, 2005). The book is the result of a lifetime's study of Auden and is both scholarly and judicious, with no religious axe to grind, either for or against.

3 An example was a major BBC2 documentary on 30 September 2017 that made no mention of his faith.

4 'T. S. Eliot, So Far', in *W. H. Auden: Prose*, vol. 3, ed. Edward Mendelson (London: Faber & Faber, 2007), p. 353.

5 Contribution to *Modern Canterbury Pilgrims*, Auden's contribution to a book of that name, in Mendelson, *Prose*, vol. 3, p. 574.

6 Auden came to dislike some of his earlier poetry and did not include this in his *Collected Poems*.

7 *Forewords and Afterwords*, selected by Edward Mendelson (New York, NY: Random House, 1973), pp. 69–70.

8 Interview with Roy Perrott, *Observer Review*, 28 June 1970.

9 Perrott, *Observer Review*, 28 June 1970.

10 Auden, 'The More Loving One', in *Collected Poems*, p. 445.

11 Mendelson, *Prose*, vol. 3, p. 579.

12 According to Harold Norse, who was Auden's part-time secretary from 1939 to 1945, it was a 'marriage made in hell', and Auden was 'a complete door mat' emotionally, *The Advocate*, the national gay American journal.

13 Edward Mendelson, 'Auden and God', *New York Review of Books*, 6 December 2007.

14 Auden, 'Precious Five', in *Collected Poems*, p. 447.

15 Auden, 'A Lullaby', in *Collected Poems*, p. 672.

16 Auden, 'As I Walked out One Evening', in *Collected Poems*, p. 114.

17 Auden, 'Epistle to a Godson', in *Collected Poems*, p. 624.

18 Auden, 'In Praise of Limestone', in *Collected Poems*, p. 414.

19 *Listener*, 22 December 1937.

20 Arthur Kirsch, *Auden and Christianity* (New Haven, CT: Yale University Press, 2005), pp. 169–70.

21 T. S. Eliot, *Four Quartets*, in *The Complete Poems and Plays of T. S. Eliot* (London: Faber & Faber, 1969), p. 180.

22 Auden, 'Tonight at Seven-Thirty', in *Collected Poems*, p. 533. 'Olam' comes from the Hebrew, and combines that which is hidden with a vast period of time; so perhaps 'everlasting'.

23 Auden, 'Anthem', in *Collected Poems*, p. 257.

24 Mendelson, 'Bile and Brotherhood', in *Prose*, vol. 3, p. 589.

25 Mendelson, 'The Things Which Are Caesar's', in *Prose*, vol. 3, p. 203.

26 Mendelson, 'The Things Which Are Caesar's', in *Prose*, vol. 3, p. 207.

27 Mendelson, 'The Things Which Are Caesar's', in *Prose*, vol. 3, p.199

28 Mendelson, 'The Things Which Are Caesar's', in *Prose*, vol. 3, p. 209

29 Auden, 'The Truest Poetry Is the Most Feigning', in *Collected Poems*, p. 470.

30 John Fuller, *W. H. Auden: A Commentary* (London: Faber & Faber, 2007), p. 453.

31 Emily Dickinson, *The Complete Poems*, ed. Thomas H. Johnson (London: Faber & Faber, 1970), p. 506.

32 Auden, 'Epistle to a Godson', *Collected Poems*, p. 624.

33 Auden, 'Epithalamium', in *Collected Poems*, p. 571. See especially the last verse.

34 Auden, 'Horae Canonicae', in *Collected Poems*, p. 475.

35 Auden, 'In Memory of W. B. Yeats', in *Collected Poems*, p. 197.

9 William Golding: Universal pessimist, cosmic optimist

1 John Carey, *William Golding: The Man Who Wrote Lord of the Flies* (London:

Faber & Faber, 2009), p. 160, drawing on a lecture, 'Fable', published in *The Hot Gates* (London: Faber & Faber, 2009), pp. 85ff.

2 Carey, *Golding*, p. 82.

3 Carey, *Golding*, p. 261.

4 Carey, Golding, p. 82.

5 William Golding, *Pincher Martin* (London: Faber & Faber, 1962), p. 184.

6 Carey, *Golding*, p. 192.

7 Carey, *Golding*, p. 194.

8 Carey, *Golding*, p. 196.

9 William Golding, *Free Fall* (Harmondsworth: Penguin Books, 1963), p. 140.

10 Carey, *Golding*, p. 266.

11 Lionel Blue, *My Affair with Christianity* (London: Hodder & Stoughton, 1998), ch. 5, entitled 'Help!'.

12 Francis Thompson, 'The Kingdom of God', in *The New Oxford Book of Christian Verse*, ed. Donald Davie (Oxford: Oxford University Press, 1981), p. 256.

13 Carey, *Golding*, p. 285.

14 The first major, and still valuable, study of Golding's novels to this point is Mark Kinkead-Weekes and Ian Gregor, *William Golding, a Critical Study* (London: Faber & Faber, 1967).

15 Carey, *Golding*, p. 367.

16 William Golding, *Darkness Visible* (London: Faber & Faber, 1979), p. 264.

17 Carey, *Golding*, p. 367.

18 Carey, *Golding*, p. 373.

19 William Golding, *The Double Tongue* (London: Faber & Faber, 1993).

20 Carey, *Golding*, p. 45.

21 Carey, *Golding*, p. 125.

22 Carey, *Golding*, p. 122.

23 Carey, *Golding*, pp. 349–50.

24 Carey, *Golding*, p. 217.

25 Carey, *Golding*, p. 357.

26 Carey, *Golding*, pp. 291, 490.

27 Carey, *Golding*, p. 520.

28 Carey, Golding, p. 490.

29 Carey, *Golding*, p. 194.

30 Carey, *Golding*, p. 301. See also p. 517, where he describes himself as a monster.

31 Carey, *Golding*, p. 166.

32 'Belief and Creativity', in William Golding, *A Moving Target* (London: Faber & Faber, 1982), pp. 185ff.

33 Golding, 'Belief and Creativity', pp. 198–9.

34 Golding, 'Belief and Creativity', p. 201.

10 R. S. Thomas: Presence in absence

1 R. S. Thomas, *Song at the Year's Turning* (London: Rupert Hart-Davis, 1955), p. 14.

2 R. S. Thomas, 'Salt', in *Collected Poems* (London: J. M. Dent, 1993), p. 394. See also R. S. Thomas, 'Album', in *Collected Poems*, p. 350.

3 Later he seems to have come to terms with his parents and writes about 'a bitter affection' for them and their influence on him. See R. S. Thomas, 'In Memory', in *Collected Poems*, p. 310.

4 Interview with Naim Attallah in *The Oldie*, issue 79, October 1995, p. 12. His mother had been brought up by a relation who was a cleric, so she had acquired an admiration and fondness for the priesthood.

5 Thomas, 'A Peasant', in *Collected Poems*, p. 4.

6 Thomas, 'Funeral', in *Collected Poems*, p. 125.

7 From a particularly harsh poem indicting the hypocrisy of Welsh chapel religion, R. S. Thomas, 'The Minister', *Collected Poems*, p. 42.

8 *Guardian*, 27 September 2000, p. 8.

9 Thomas, 'The Dark Well', in *Collected Poems*, p. 96.

10 Byron Rogers, *The Man Who Went into the West: The Life of R. S. Thomas* (London: Aurum, 2006).

11 Sandra Anstey (ed.), *R. S. Thomas: Selected Prose* (Bridgend: Poetry Wales Press, 1983), pp. 177ff.

12 Rogers, *Man*, p. 283.

13 Interview with Attallah in *Oldie*, p. 12.

14 Thomas, 'Welsh Landscape', in *Collected Poems*, p. 37.

15 Mario Basini, *Welsh Mail*, 26 September 2000.

16 Thomas, 'A Marriage', in *Collected Poems*, p. 533.

17 Thomas, 'The Way of It', *Collected Poems*, p. 323.

18 R. S. Thomas, 'Self-Portrait', in *Laboratories of the Spirit* (London: Macmillan, 1975), p. 27. This was not included in his *Collected Poems*.

19 R. S. Thomas, 'Former Paths', in *Autobiographies*, translated from the Welsh by Jason Walford Davies (London: J. M. Dent, 1997).

20 R. S. Thomas, 'The Qualities of Christmas', in *R. S. Thomas: Selected Prose*, ed. Sandra Anstey (Bridgend: Poetry Wales Press, 1983), p. 55.

21 Interview on Radio 4, 31 July 1981.

22 Thomas, 'The Moor', in *Collected Poems*, p. 166.

23 Thomas, 'The Bright Field', in *Collected Poems*, p. 302; Thomas, 'The Mountains', in *Selected Prose*, p. 95.

24 Thomas, 'Two Chapels', in *Selected Prose*, p. 41.

25 Sometimes the realism of his view of nature is startling and shocking, but still true. See Rogers, *Man*, p. 11.

26 Thomas, 'Pisces', in *Collected Poems*, p. 63.

27 Thomas, 'The Fair', in *Collected Poems*, p. 236.

28 Thomas, 'H'm', in *Collected Poems*, p. 232.

29 Interview on Radio 4, 31 July 1981.

30 Thomas, 'The Coming', in *Collected Poems*, p. 234.

31 Thomas, 'The Island', in *Collected Poems*, p. 223.

32 Grevel Lindop, *Times Literary Supplement*, 16 December 1983.

33 Talk at Great St Mary's Church, Cambridge, 17 October 1982.

34 Thomas, 'Via Negativa', in *Collected Poems*, p. 220.

35 Interview on Radio 4, 31 July 1981.

36 Thomas, 'The Absence', in *Collected Poems*, p. 361.

37 Simone Weil, *Gravity and Grace* (London: Routledge & Kegan Paul, 1952), p. 99.

38 Thomas, 'Abercauwg', in *Collected Poems*, p. 340.

39 Anstey, *Selected Prose*, p. 164.

40 Ronald Blythe, Obituary, *Church Times*, 6 October 2000.

41 See note 4.

42 Barry Morgan, *Strangely Orthodox: R. S. Thomas and His Poetry of Faith* (Llandysul: Gomer, 2006), p. 56.

43 Catherine Phillips (ed.), *Gerard Manley Hopkins, Selected Letters* (Oxford: Oxford University Press, 1990), pp. 169–70, 194.

44 Thomas, 'Kneeling', in *Collected Poems*, p. 199.

45 Thomas, 'Sea-watching', in *Collected Poems*, p. 306.

46 Thomas, 'Suddenly', in *Collected Poems*, p. 426.

47 Thomas, 'Arrival', in *Collected Poems*, p. 427.

48 R. S. Thomas, 'But the Silence in the Mind', in *Collected Later Poems, 1988–2000* (Tarset: Bloodaxe Books, 2004), p. 118.

49 It was pointed out to me by Piers Plowright that despite this distrust of Yeats, the 'hare' image discussed on page 133 is a clear echo of a line of his.

50 Thomas, 'Waiting', in *Collected Poems*, p. 376.

11 Edwin Muir and George Mackay Brown: Light from the Orkneys

1 Edwin Muir, *An Autobiography* (London: Hogarth Press, 1987), p. 14.

2 Muir, *Autobiography*, p. 52.

3 Edwin Muir, 'The Annunciation', in *Collected Poems* (London: Faber & Faber, 1960), p. 117.

4 Maggie Fergusson, *George Mackay Brown: The Life* (London: John Murray, 2006), p. 109.

5 Fergusson, *Life*, p. 110.

6 Fergusson, *Life*, p. 111.

7 Muir, *Autobiography*, p. 170.

8 Muir, *Autobiography*, p. 54.

9 Muir, 'The Annunciation', in *Collected Poems*, p. 223.

10 Muir, *Autobiography*, pp. 277–8.

11 Muir, *Autobiography*, p. 278.

12 Muir, 'The Horses', in *Collected Poems*, p. 246.

13 Muir, 'One Foot in Eden', in *Collected Poems*, p. 227.

14 Muir, *Autobiography*, p. 280.

15 Fergusson, *Life*, p. 11.

16 Fergusson, *Life*, p. 57. See also p. 91.

17 Fergusson, *Life*, p. 57.

18 Fergusson, *Life*, p. 84.

19 Fergusson, *Life*, p. 89.

20 Fergusson, *Life*, p. 130.

21 Fergusson, *Life*, p. 137.

22 George Mackay Brown, 'Thorfinn', in *The Collected Poems of George Mackay Brown*, ed. Archie Bevan and Brian Murray (London: John Murray, 2005), p. 20.

23 Fergusson, *Life*, p. 155.

24 Brown, *Collected Poems*, p. 45.

25 George Mackay Brown, 'Celia', in *A Time to Keep* (Edinburgh: Polygon, 2006), p. 16.

26 Brown, 'Mhairi', in *Collected Poems*, p. 443, v. 5.

27 Fergusson, *Life*, p. 193.

28 Fergusson, *Life*, p. 193.

29 Fergusson, *Life*, p. 246.

30 Brown, 'Prologue', in Fergusson, *Life*, p. 1.

31 Brown, 'A Work for Poets', in *Collected Poems*, p. 378.

12 Elizabeth Jennings: Poet of pain and praise

1 Elizabeth Jennings, *New Collected Poems* (Manchester, UK: Carcanet Press, 2002), p. xix. If a poem does not appear in this collection, the original collection in which it appeared is cited.

2 Elizabeth Jennings, *Christianity and Poetry* (London: Burns & Oates, 1965), p. 11.

3 Elizabeth Jennings, 'Boston', in *New Collected Poems*, p. 317.

4 Jennings, 'Wisdom of the Fields', in *New Collected Poems*, p. 289.

5 Elizabeth Jennings, 'The Liberation', in *In the Meantime* (Manchester, UK: Carcanet Press, 1996), p. 14.

6 Jennings, 'Prawning', in *New Collected Poems*, p. 288.

7 Jennings, 'One Flesh', in *New Collected Poems*, p. 81.

8 Lawrence Goldman (ed.), *Oxford Dictionary of National Biography, 2001–4* (Oxford: Oxford University Press, 2007), p. 572.

9 Jennings, 'Reasons for Not Returning', in *New Collected Poems*, p. 320.

10 Jennings, 'Sequence in Hospital', in *New Collected Poems*, p. 62.

11 Jennings, 'Night Sister', in *New Collected Poems*, p. 74.

12 Jennings, 'On a Friend's Relapse and Return to a Mental Clinic', *New Collected Poems*, p. 76.

13 Jennings, 'Never Such Peace', in *New Collected Poems*, p. 137.

14 Elizabeth Jennings, 'An Answer to Odd Advice', in *Moments of Grace* (Manchester, UK: Carcanet Press, 1979), p. 8.

15 Jennings, 'Walking in the Dark', in *New Collected Poems*, p. 312.

16 Jennings, 'The Right Givers', in *New Collected Poems*, p. 287.

17 Jennings, 'Friendship', in *New Collected Poems*, p. 89.

18 Jennings, 'Sonnets to Narcissus, I, II and III', in *New Collected Poems*, p. 299.

19 Jennings, 'Oxford, Heatwave, Tourists', in *Meantime*, p. 22.

20 Jennings, 'Story Tellers', in *New Collected Poems*, p. 296.

21 Jennings, 'An Act of the Imagination', in *New Collected Poems*, p. 297.

22 Jennings, 'A Meditation in March 1979', in *Moments of Grace*, p. 9.

23 Jennings, 'I Count the Moments', in *New Collected Poems*, p. 138.

24 Jennings, 'Mid-May Meditation', in *New Collected Poems*, p. 321.

25 Jennings, 'Praises', in *New Collected Poems*, p. 319.

26 Elizabeth Jennings, *Every Changing Shape: Mystical Experience and the Making of Poetry* (London: André Deutsch, 1961), pp. 17–18. See also Jennings, 'A Metaphysical Point About Poetry', in *New Collected Poems*, p. 322.

27 Jennings, 'A Unique Gift', in *New Collected Poems*, p. 313.

28 Austin Farrer, 'Epstein's Lazarus', in *The End of Man* (London: Hodder & Stoughton, 1973), p. 37.

29 Jennings, 'Lazarus', in *New Collected Poems*, p. 48.

30 Jennings, 'Lazarus Again', in *New Collected Poems*, p. 309.

31 Jennings, 'A View of Lazarus', in *New Collected Poems*, p. 311.

13 Grace in failure: Four Catholic novelists – Graham Greene, Flannery O'Connor, Shusaku Endo and Evelyn Waugh

1 Rowan Williams, *Dostoevsky: Language, Faith and Fiction* (London: Continuum, 2008), p. 5.

2 Robert Browning, 'Bishop Bloughram's Apology', lines 395ff.; Henry J. Donaghy, *Conversations with Graham Greene* (Jackson: University Press of Mississippi, 1992), p. 48.

3 Graham Greene, *A Sort of Life* (Harmondsworth: Penguin Books, 1974), p. 122.

4 Marie-Françoise Allain, *The Other Man: Conversations with Graham Greene* (Harmondsworth: Penguin Books, 1984), p. 184.

5 A full discussion with relevant interviews is given in Norman Sherry, *The Life of Graham Greene*, 3 vols (London: Jonathan Cape, 2004), vol. 3, ch. 48.

6 Allain, *Other Man*, p. 173.

7 'Across the Bridge', in *Twenty-One Stories* (Harmondsworth: Penguin Books, 1938), p. 74.

8 Allain, *Other Man*, p. 156.

9 Allain, *Other Man*, p. 163.

10 Allain, *Other Man*, p. 155.

11 Graham Greene, *Ways of Escape* (Harmondsworth: Penguin Books, 1981), p. 66.

12 Greene, *Ways of Escape*, p. 66.

13 There is a full discussion in Sherry, *Graham Greene*, vol. 1, pt 8.

14 See Sherry, *Life*, vol. 3, ch. 47.

15 Allain, *Other Man*, p. 156.

16 Graham Greene, *Monsignor Quixote* (London: Vintage, 2006), p. 185.

17 Roger Sharrock, *Saints, Sinners, Comedians: The Novels of Graham Greene* (London: Burns & Oates, 1984), p. 274.

18 Sally Fitzgerald (ed.), *The Habit of Being, Letters of Flannery O'Connor* (New York, NY: Vintage, 1979), p. 163.

19 See Angela Alaimo O'Donnell, *The Province of Joy: Praying with Flannery O'Connor* (Brewster, MA: Paraclete Press, 2012).

20 Flannery O'Connor, *Mystery and Manners: Occasional Prose* (London: Faber & Faber, 1972), p. 33.

21 O'Connor, *Mystery and Manners*, p. 167.

22 O'Connor, *Mystery and Manners*, p. 108.

23 Flannery O'Connor, *Parker's Back*, in *Everything That Rises Must Converge* (London: Faber & Faber, 1985), p. 219.

24 Sally Fitzgerald (ed.), *Habit of Being*, pp. 559–60.

25 O'Donnell, *The Province of Joy*, p. 92.

26 Shusaku Endo, *The Samurai* (Harmondsworth: Penguin Books, 2017), p. 121.

27 Endo, *Samurai*, p. 242.

28 Endo, *Samurai*, p. 245.

29 Endo, *Samurai*, p. 262.

30 It can be argued that Jesus himself was a satirist, and there is a line of Christian satire from Jonathan Swift and Sydney Smith through to Waugh and our own time. It is no accident that Richard Ingrams and Ian Hislop, the main figures in the satire boom from the 1960s onwards, have strong church connections.

31 Evelyn Waugh, *Brideshead Revisited* (Harmondsworth: Penguin Books, 1951), p. 331.

32 Waugh, *Brideshead Revisited*, p. 288.

33 Evelyn Waugh, *Helena* (Harmondsworth: Penguin Books, 1950), p. 156.

34 Waugh, *Brideshead Revisited*, p. 213.

35 Waugh was to write, 'What we can learn from Helena is something about the workings of God; that he wants a different thing from each one of us, laborious or easy, conspicuous or quite private, but something which only we can do and for which we were each created', Evelyn Waugh, 'St Helena Empress', in *The Essays, Articles and Reviews of Evelyn Waugh*, ed. Donat Gallagher (London: Methuen, 1983), p. 410.

36 Waugh, *Helena*, p. 239.

14 C. S. Lewis and Philip Pullman: Competing myths

1 I respond to a key moment in that book in *The Beauty and the Horror: Searching for God in a Suffering World* (London: SPCK, 2016), p. 34.

2 The relationship between authors' views and the views of their characters is a highly contentious one. In this chapter I am writing about the views of the characters in the books and the moral and spiritual thrust of the books as a whole. Both Lewis and Pullman make it clear that a particular view of the world is being conveyed, and it is these which are being compared.

3 A talk at St Andrew's Church, Linton Road, Oxford.

4 C. S. Lewis, *The Lion, the Witch and the Wardrobe* (London: HarperCollins, 2001), p. 51.

5 Philip Pullman, *The Amber Spyglass* (London: Scholastic Press, 2001), p. 206.

6 Rose Macaulay, *The Towers of Trebizond* (London: Collins, 1956), p. 161.

7 Philip Pullman, *The Subtle Knife* (London: Scholastic Press, 2001), p. 100.

8 C. S. Lewis, *The Silver Chair* (London: HarperCollins, 2001), p. 194.

9 It was interesting to receive at least one letter from America in effect asking how I, a mere mortal, dared to criticize Lewis. And I always wondered about the relationship between that criticism and the rather speedy withdrawal of my book from the American market.

10 Lewis, *Silver Chair*, p. 194.

11 Austin Farrer, 'The Christian Apologist', in *Light on C S Lewis*, ed. Jocelyn Gibb (London: Geoffrey Bles, 1965), p. 40.

12 C. S. Lewis, *The Horse and His Boy* (London: HarperCollins, 2001), p. 216.

13 Pullman, *Amber Spyglass*, p. 382.

14 Pullman, *Amber Spyglass*, p. 520.

15 Heinrich von Kleist, 'On the Marionette Theatre', trans. with a commentary by Idris Parry, *Times Literary Supplement*, 20 October 1978.

16 Pullman, *Amber Spyglass*, p. 519.

17 'Pullman's Purpose' by Mark Greene, London Institute for Contemporary Christianity.

18 I once did a study day with Philip Pullman in which I subjected his trilogy to a critique and he examined my book *God Outside the Box: Why Spiritual People Object to Christianity*. Interestingly Philip Pullman refused to define himself as a spiritual person. On the other hand, he did say that while God, that is the God in whom Christians claim to believe, was not part of the circle of his experience, he acknowledged that there might be a reality outside his awareness. In short, a genuinely agnostic position – though it includes strongly rejecting what he is clearly aware of and morally disapproves of: the Church and its beliefs as he has encountered them.

19 Rowan Williams, *Guardian*, 10 March 2004, G2, p. 11.

20 C. S. Lewis, *Prayer: Letters to Malcolm* (London: Fount, 1977), p. 91.

21 C. S. Lewis, *The Last Battle* (London: HarperCollins, 2001), p. 168.

22 Philip Pullman, 'The Republic of Heaven', in *Horn Book Magazine*, November–December 2001, p. 659.

23 Lewis, *Last Battle*, pp. 201–2.

24 Lewis, *Last Battle*, p. 202.

25 Lewis, *Last Battle*, p. 224.

26 *Sunday Telegraph*, January 2002.

27 A talk at St Andrew's Church, Linton Road, Oxford.

28 Pullman, *Amber Spyglass*, p. 520.

15 Marilynne Robinson: Christian contrarian

1 'President Obama and Marilynne Robinson: A Conversation', *New York Review of Books*, 11 and 19 October 2015.

2 Marilynne Robinson, *Gilead* (London: Virago, 2005), p. 276.

3 Roughly 1,264,000 American soldiers have died in the nation's wars – 620,000 in the Civil War and 644,000 in all other conflicts. It was only as recently as the Vietnam War that the number of American deaths in foreign wars eclipsed the number who had died in the Civil War.

4 Robinson, *Gilead*, p. 10.

5 Robinson, *Gilead*, p. 281.

6 Robinson, *Gilead*, pp. 64–5, 75–6.

7 Robinson, *Gilead*, pp. 109, 117.

8 Robinson, *Gilead*, pp. 22, 24, 77, 156.

9 Sarah Churchwell, *Observer*, 8 November 2014.

10 Sarah Churchwell, *Observer*, 8 November 2014.

11 Marilynne Robinson, *Home* (London: Virago, 2008).

12 Luke 15.11–52.

13 Marilynne Robinson, *Lila* (London: Virago, 2014), p. 29.

14 Robinson, *Lila*, p. 31.

15 Robinson, *Lila*, pp. 98–9.

16 Robinson, *Lila*, pp. 39, 225.

17 Robinson, *Lila*, p. 59.

18 Robinson, *Lila*, p. 59. See also p. 112.

19 Robinson, *Lila*, p. 75.

20 Robinson, *Lila*, p. 113.

21 Robinson, *Lila*, p. 77.

22 Robinson, *Lila*, pp. 222–3.

23 Richard Harries, *The Beauty and the Horror: Searching for God in a Suffering World* (London: SPCK, 2016).

24 Robinson, *Lila*, p. 31.

25 Marilynne Robinson, *The Givenness of Things: Essays* (London: Virago, 2015).

26 This was a major theme of a lecture at Westminister Abbey on 7 March 2017. See <http://www.westminster-abbey.org/institute/charles-gore/past-lectures/2017/march/the-charles-gore-lecture-2017-integrity-and-the-modern-intellectual-tradition>, accessed 21 May 2018.

27 'President Obama and Marilynne Robinson', 11 and 19 October 2015.

28 Marilynne Robinson, 'Psalm Eight', in *The Death of Adam* (New York, NY: Picador 1998), pp. 228–9.

29 Robinson, 'Grace', in *Givenness*, pp. 31–49.

Acknowledgements

The chapters on Gerard Manley Hopkins and Samuel Beckett are based on chapters that first appeared in Richard Harries, *Questioning Belief* (London: SPCK, 1995).

The chapter on Edward Thomas is based on a lecture delivered to the Edward Thomas Society in 2008.

The chapters on W. H. Auden, R. S. Thomas, George Mackay Brown, Edwin Muir and T. S. Eliot are based on lectures given at Gresham College, the first three when I was Gresham Professor of Divinity.

The chapter on C. S. Lewis and Philip Pullman is based on a lecture given in Edinburgh on moral education.

I am grateful to Piers Plowright for reading an early draft of this book and for his comments.

I am also grateful for permission to quote extracts from the following:

On pp. 20, 21, 22, 23, 24, 25, 26, 27, 29 and 30, 'Fame of Myself, to justify', F 481, J 713; 'I have never seen "Volcanoes" –', F 165, J 175; 'Recollect the Face of me', F 1306, J 1305; 'Jesus! thy Crucifix', F 197A, J 225; 'Embarrassment of one another', F 1057, J 662; 'That after Horror – that 'twas *us* –', F 243B, J 286; 'The Only News I know', F 820, J 827; 'Take all away from me', F 1671B, J 1640; 'The Love a Life can show Below', F 285B, J 673; 'This World is not Conclusion', F 373, J 501 by Emily Dickinson, in *The Poems of Emily Dickinson: Variorum Edition*, edited by Ralph W. Franklin, Cambridge, Mass.: The Belknap Press of Harvard University Press, copyright © 1998 by the President and Fellows of Harvard College. Copyright © 1951, 1955 by the President and Fellows of Harvard College. Copyright © renewed 1979, 1983 by the President and Fellows of Harvard College. Copyright © 1914, 1918, 1919, 1924, 1929, 1930, 1932, 1935, 1937, 1942 by Martha Dickinson Bianchi. Copyright © 1952, 1957, 1958, 1963, 1965 by Mary L. Hampson.

On pp. 63, 73 and 74, 'Burnt Norton', from *Four Quartets*, *Ash Wednesday* and 'Marina', copyright © Estate of T. S. Eliot, in *The Poems of T. S. Eliot*, vol. 1: *Collected and Uncollected Poems*, ed. Christopher Ricks and Jim McCue (London: Faber & Faber, 2015). Reproduced by permission of

Faber & Faber Ltd. Also from *Collected Poems 1909–1962* by T. S. Eliot. Copyright © 1936 by Houghton Mifflin Harcourt Publishing Company, renewed 1964 by Thomas Stearns Eliot. Reprinted by permission of Houghton Mifflin Harcourt Publishing Company. All rights reserved.

On pp. 80 and 81–2, 'An Agnostic', 'A Religious Man' and 'So to Fatness Come', copyright © Estate of Stevie Smith, in *Collected Poems* by Stevie Smith (London: Allen Lane, 1975). Reproduced by permission of Faber & Faber Ltd in the UK and by kind permission of New Directions in the USA.

On pp. 84, 85, 87, 90, 94, *Waiting for Godot* by Samuel Beckett (London: Faber & Faber, 1965), copyright © Estate of Samuel Beckett. Reproduced by permission of Faber & Faber Ltd. Also copyright © 1954 by Grove Press, Inc.; copyright © renewed 1982 by Samuel Beckett. Used by permission of Grove/Atlantic, Inc. Any third party use of this material, outside of this publication, is prohibited.

On pp. 142, 144, 146 and 147, 'The Annunciation' and 'One Foot in Eden', copyright © Estate of Edwin Muir, in *Collected Poems* by Edwin Muir (London: Faber& Faber). Reproduced by permission of Faber & Faber Ltd.

On pp. 150 and 153, 'Thorfinn', in *The Collected Poems of George Mackay Brown*, ed. Archie Bevan and Brian Murray (London: John Murray, 2005), and 'Prologue', in Maggie Fergusson, *George Mackay Brown: The Life* (London: John Murray, 2006).

On pp. 156, 157, 158, 159, 160, 161 and 162–3, 'Prawning', 'One Flesh', 'Sequence in Hospital', 'Night Sister', 'On a Friend's Relapse and Return to a Mental Clinic', 'Walking in the Dark', 'The Right Givers', 'Friendship', 'Sonnets to Narcissus, I, II and III', 'Oxford, Heatwave, Tourists', 'Story Tellers', 'An Act of the Imagination', 'A Meditation in March 1979', 'I Count the Moments', 'Mid-May Meditation', 'Praises', 'A Unique Gift', 'Lazarus', 'Lazarus Again' and 'A View of Lazarus', in *New Collected Poems* by Elizabeth Jennings (Manchester: Carcanet Press, 2002). Reproduced by permission of David Higham Associates.

Every effort has been made to seek permission to use copyright material reproduced in this book. The publisher apologizes for those cases in which permission might not have been sought and, if notified, will formally seek permission at the earliest opportunity.

Index

Tyler's Story

A little story about learning to read in prison

It's probably my drinking that got me into prison. That and not having a proper job.

I wasn't bothered about school, but in prison I had a chance to join a reading group. The books are interesting but not too hard to read.

In one book, *Forty-six Quid and a Bag of Dirty Washing*, we read about Barry, a guy who got mixed up with a drug dealer, but has now just left prison. I saw how he had to make good choices every day – and fill in lots of forms – to stay out of prison. I don't want to end up back inside again, so I've decided that I'm not going to drink on my way home. I won't get home drunk before the evening's even started – that just makes me drink more. And I'm going to get better at reading so I can fill in forms when I get out.

Inspired by a true story. Names have been changed.

Help us to tell more stories like Tyler's. Support the Diffusion Fiction Project. Just £4.99 puts an easy-to-read book in prisoners' hands, to help them to improve their reading confidence while encouraging them to think about life's big questions. Visit www.spck.org.uk to make a donation or, to volunteer to run a reading group in a prison, please contact prisonfiction@spck.org.uk.